My Journey to Zen

(an Iranian Zen Monk)
Dotetsu

London | New York

Published by Clink Street Publishing 2020

Copyright © 2020

First edition.

The author asserts the moral right under the Copyright, Designs and Patents Act 1988 to be identified as the author of this work.

All rights reserved. No part of this publication may be reproduced, stored in a retrieval system or transmitted, in any form or by any means without the prior consent of the author, nor be otherwise circulated in any form of binding or cover other than that with which it is published and without a similar condition being imposed on the subsequent purchaser.

ISBN:
978-1-913568-00-9 - paperback
978-1-913568-01-6 - ebook

This book is dedicated to all my family and also the spirits of my parents whose kindness has always been a lamp on our way.

Introduction to my Autobiography (My Journey to Zen)

A motive is an impulse that causes a person to act. Motivation is an internal process that makes a person move towards something or a goal. Motivation, like intelligence, cannot be directly observed. Instead, motivation can only be inferred by noting a person's behaviour.

When I started narrating my observations and experiences to my co-religionists and my close friends, almost all of them – both English and Iranian – encouraged me to collect the incidents and stories and put them into a book. At first, it was difficult but, when I started to do so, all the memories, which had been hidden in my subconscious mind for years, started erupting in such great abundance that I was surprised as to where all this information had been hiding during all those lean years.

Being in India for eight years and also travelling to different parts of the world, meeting different teachers, training in different ashram and temples, I felt obliged and was also enthusiastic to narrate my experiences to my own people. I wanted to tell them my story in the hope that it might serve them as a source of inspiration. The tenor of my observations (biography) was mostly spiritual, rather than political or material. Sadly, I failed to realise my dreams in Iran due to misunderstanding by those who have the audacity idea to call themselves the messengers of God or selected by God. This forced me to move elsewhere.

It is much to be regretted than Iran, which is counted as a one of the most ancient civilisations going back 6000 years with highly-educated people, with a wonderful cultural and historical background, is now in the hands of some medieval rulers whose reactionary thought have changed the real face of Persia. Their medieval way of thinking has been hanging like a sinister shadow over the land of Persia, bringing nothing of benefit or value. For this reason, I decided to express myself and to reveal the reality of what life is like in Iran. I am aware of many other Iranians who are speaking out. We have all had to leave our country in order to do this because of the lack of freedom of speech in our country.

Frankly speaking, my command of the English language is not so good because English is my second language, but I was asked to write something in English to be read by people in an English-speaking country. Therefore, I wrote this book at first in broken English with a hope to find someone to correct and edit it.

I wrote it in English because

1. I had written and translated books in Iran but they were banned from publication by the Islamic Guidance Organisation on the grounds that divergent books can mislead the minds of the youth away from the officially approved ways of thinking.

2. Being a Zen teacher in London, I had to write my book in English for both English readers and Iranians alike in the UK who are (were) familiar with English language in order to encourage them to adopt certain cultural practices and Zazen practice.

3. To make it clear that the brain drain of most Iranians in the early 1990s was not because of poverty, nor to seek a better job or position in other countries or for any other purpose, but to save themselves first and then to express themselves freely in democratic countries.

4. To speak out concerning the violation of human rights and repression not only affecting me, but also many other innocent religious minorities and educated people as well.

5. Prior to this book, I had also written a book in 2006 under the title *Zen-Mind, Arya-Mind* and it was welcomed by the students and others. The same book was translated into Persian under the title *The Dialectic of Zen*. However, distribution in Iran was prohibited because it became stuck in the Islamic Guidance Organisation which refused to issue a permit. This biography book is based on facts. All the stories and incidents are authentic, and even the places and the persons are genuine. I have censored some parts of my stories lest the readers may count them as exaggerated. This book, in narrating the gist of my biography both inside and outside Iran, is enough for the intelligent reader to comprehend the things about which they know little.

Another point which is necessary to mention is that this is not an attempt to propagate a particular way of thinking, nor to suggest its priority over other ways of thinking. I have no intention to gather more followers like a Spartan army. There is no aim to convert others to a new religion, nor to disparage other schools of thought or belief. The purpose is merely to introduce myself to my readers, to explain how I passed through hardship in Iran and how I succeeded outside Iran in achieving my ambitions.

I have studied and practised with different, famous spiritual teachers and also experienced different schools of thought. Finally, with no attachment to any particular technique or particular teacher, I could follow my own interests during the course of my research.

Although my research is mainly cultural and therapeutic, in some parts of the book I have mentioned Zen Buddhism as a new way of thinking, based on my experience and my true observation. However, this does not mean I have restricted my research to only one field or school of thought. On the contrary I have preferred to give a full description of my research to my readers. The word Zen is the equivalent of the Chinese Cha'an which is derived from Sanskrit Dhyana,[1] Pali Jhana (deep Samadhi) and Persian Moraghebeh, all of which are translated in English as 'meditation'. Therefore, Zen is not in a monopoly of Japan, or China, or the ancient teaching of Persia's Zoroaster. For example, we use aeroplanes but nobody can claim that aeroplanes belong to a particular country or persons. The invention of flight goes back even to 400 BCE and was developed by many people in the process of time. Everybody can use it without the necessity of knowing about the inventors. In fact, the history of flight is a process of evolution. So also, the history of meditation goes back to years unknown. In fact, there is no beginning and no end to any process of evolution. Similarly, any spiritual training can be an evolutionary process. Zen is not an exception. Zen is, in fact, a practice, Zen is a therapy (treatment), and nothing else. I have always advised my students "Don't walk (follow) in the footsteps of others, understand yourself or in other words develop your own understanding." This is the golden principle which I followed myself.

As constructive criticism is always helpful and creative, I would be glad to know of any deficiencies in this book so that I may improve or correct it for the next edition.

---

[1] Dhyana is the Sanskrit name, in Pali Jhana, in Chinese Cha'an, in Japanese Zen, in Persian Moraghebeh, in English Meditation.

A note of thanks must go to the London Buddhist Vihara who encouraged me to write the book, especially to Ven. Seelawimala, the head abbot of the London Buddhist Vihara, whose suggestions helped to bring about corrections. My sincere thanks and appreciation must go to Mr Richard Jones, a member of the London Buddhist Vihara, whose patience and accurate attention to each chapter made this book complete and available to you. If it were not for him, you would not have this book in your hands.

This is a green leaf[2] presented by a mendicant in order to find more friends who are interested in the subject.

May all of us have extraordinary energy to serve all the peoples of the world to help them to get rid of their sufferings.

Khosrow Haidari 'Dotetsuzenji' (Iranian Zen Monk)
London 2020

---

2   The expression 'green leaf' is a metaphor used in the Persian language. A mendicant or monk lives a life of material poverty, therefore he has nothing to offer to other people in terms of something material. However, he can offer a green leaf which is taken to symbolise freshness and something which comes from a pure and compassionate heart. He is rich in spirit, but poor in material things.

Preface

We are all human. We may come from different backgrounds, follow specific religion, have disagreements on certain topics, have different beliefs and different colours, but we are all human. All human beings are born free and equal in prestige and proper rights. We are endowed with reason and conscience and should act towards one another in a spirit of brotherhood. We all dream for a better future, a sane society where to live peacefully, harmoniously and solidarity with the rest of the world. We should be treated all equally and everyday is another day closer to realizing this dream.
We must respect everyone and do not slander others, defame them, lie about them. Similarly we should not be behaved in a wrong way. During my researches I have travelled around and have encountered many different people with different mentalities, different cultures and traditions. This includes people of strict religious views, as well as those who would follow the religious precepts as a way of salvation. I've understood that, others would use practical ways to develop the human characteristics innate in us such as, loving-kindness, compassion and desire to help others. According to Confucius," It is man who makes truth great, not truth which makes man great." For this reason "humanness" or human heartedness was always felt to be superior to "righteousness", since man himself is greater than any idea which he may invent. These are times when men's passions and humanistic behaviours are much more trustworthy than their principles. Supreme virtue can be attained only from within, the human nature.

I believe that creating enmity or any kind of malice or rumour is not moral, especially if that is coming from leaders, group of people, a religion or any other sources. A true human being should analysis matters thoughtfully with no sense of malicious or vengeful.

Moral conscience teaches us that the information given to people should be based on facts and not on guesswork or conjecture, plausible reasoning and rumour. For the same reason I've implemented genuine information in my book with no exaggerations, no embellishments. However, in some tyrannical government, we are sometimes like slaves to be exploited by the way of their thinking and it is our rights to revolt against it by writing, speech etc… and to reflect the inhumane behaviours truthfully worldwide as it is (was). It is not always easy but there is always an opportunity for us to express our opinions as we wish to be and not to be mislead by damaging indoctrinations.

The series of events that had unjustly happened to me in my own country, after years of research, were not only unjust but also inhuman, especially by some of the government fanatic groups both "Reformists" and the "Radicals" of the same Islamic system.

In this book I want to share with the readers the events happened to me during my presence in my own country, enthusiastic to establish a small non-profit Zen center based on my thirty years of research and experience to apply it in the framework of Islamic government for the benefit of one and all. It is interesting to know that how a mock government react to a simple demand of a caring, committed citizen.

It is indeed unfortunate to be unnecessarily involved in unexpected circumstances and end up facing injustice and inequality. It is indeed worse if those circumstances are in your home country and those individuals are your countrymen. But again as respected Dr Martin Luther King JR states, "Injustice anywhere is a threat to justice everywhere". We therefore need to eliminate injustice and ignorance with rationalism not only in word but in action. Knowledge and wisdom are the tools which can help us eradicate it forever even if this may takes us a little longer.

I want to be clear that I've written this book not out of hatred or enmity, but as my personal experience as it has been triggered the events explained in the book in details.

I do feel a sense of sadness when I reflect on how those prejudiced Islamic groups treated me and also the misbehavior and coercion I faced during my sincere services to my people as a government teacher. The fact is, the fundamentalists possibly are unaware of their outrageous behaviours which are inhumane, unjustly, oppressive, uncivilized, as in their mind there's only one specific ideology with the intention that to globalize it at any rate.

I do hope I get to see everyone has the freedom of choosing what to feed their minds so that instead of brutality, we have understanding and instead enmity we have solidarity, instead of war we have peace.

I have been working hard for more than twenty years to establish a small wholesome centre for the benefit of my people and many others to teach them as how to develop more positive thoughts and also mind development.

It is indeed sad to see Iran, which is counted as a one of the most ancient civilisations with antecedent of nearly 6,000 years of glory with highly-educated people, with a wonderful cultural and historical background, with their eminent philosophers, writers, poets ...is now in the hands of some totalitarians whose reactionary thoughts have changed the real face of Persia and the Persians. I believe that the Iranians will come to the realisation of the fact that they deserve better living among all other nations and need to work together to rebuild a sane society after 40 years of political isolation and enmity with the world.

My dream has always been to build a first Zen Temple in my home country and teach people mediation. Up till now, I keep this dream very close to my heart as I am hopeful this will soon become a reality.

My people, like many other peoples of the world have talents and creativities to come back to their previous majesty and credibility to pace with the other civilized progressive nations all over the world if they have normal ideal circumstances like other democratic countries. But, this requires unanimity among the enlightened people to reach their ambition in order to rebuild a sane society with no obstacles on their way. I'm sure my people can easily withstand against these crisis happened to them during 40 years of the government incompetence such as, corruption, poverty, dishonesty, wretchedness, lying,... and more importantly the migration of millions of Iranians' elites to other countries.

Honestly speaking, the aim of this book is not for profit, nor to expect to be a best seller book. It is a revelation in a simple language about some Islamist fundamentalists who by hook or by crook high jacked the uprising of the Iranians who struggled for a better life. From the beginning, the people were deceived by the the so called Islamic revolutionaries with, their spurious promises and indoctrination in order to consolidate their power over a civilized nation with their newfangled Islam. Their promises to people never came true. Another political instability of the the regime was their incompatibility with their own people, animosity with their neighbours and their stubbornly opposition with the western world. The result of these hostility is increasing political and economic isolation both from the West and East led the Iranians in to the most difficult conditions they have ever faced.

Someone may hesitate that such objections against the Islamic rulers explained in the book are somehow exaggeration, but those who are aware of political situation of the present Iran and those who have been involved in such circumstances have no doubts about it. This fact, for example, has been proven by the Human Rights Activists - Amnesty International reports, that religious minorities (or, we better call them Iranian ethnics) who are following their own simple precepts and observing their religious ceremonies, or other opponents who think differently are not safe in their own land of Iran. According to the Islamic authorities, Buddhists are atheists, Baha'is are spies, Marxists are infidels, Dervishes, (who are part of Shiite Islam), are regarded as having deviated from the Quran, Christianity is a plot of the West, Jews are untouchable, Sunnis are not pure Muslims, and those who are not in conformity with their way of their thinking are enemies to Islam. They called all of these people non-believers and according to their Fatwa (Islamic law) they are doomed to persecution and prosecution and even executions. To prove my claim, the Islamic regime has executed many opposition activists only because they were thinking differently (see the Human Rights' articles about Iran

Those who have actively observed the present situation of Iran and have compared it with the previous government, they'd fully realize the considerable differences between our past growing tendency and our present circumstances which is disastrous. For the same reason I've written this monograph in unprofessional English language mostly for the English language readers who are curious to know more about untold.

I'd like to sign off with a big thank to the readers who are reading this monograph. Thank you for reading this monograph for helping me grow as a writer. And also my sincere thanks for being a part of my journey.

May wisdom removes the shadow
of ignorance in life

"May all beings be happy"

Dotetsuzenji
(Khosrow Dehdasht Heidari) – 2020

Chapter 1

Autobiography

"The meaning of Life is whatever we choose. The meaning of life is not simply to exist, to survive, but to move ahead, to go up, to achieve, to conquer. We get to choose the meaning for our lives. Our lives mean exactly what we say they do – no more, no less." – an author.

The Meaning of my Life [Nature of life-nature of man]

Zen and ordination

I have written this book in the hope that it will tell any interested reader the story of my life and how I came, via many vicissitudes and obstacles, to be ordained in Japan as a Zen Buddhist[1] monk by persistence, perseverance, and a motivation to reach a spiritual growth.

Ordination in Zen is not as easy as some other spiritual schools. The would-be ordinand has to undergo a long period of training under a Roshi[2] who has been closely observing his disciple for months or even years, observing his behaviour, his faith, intelligence, receptivity and his commitment to the practice. This is a long process which ultimately ends with the recognition by the Roshi that his pupil has reached the required standard after the comprehensive approbation. The Roshi then makes the decision that the pupil can be ordained. I do not want to go into all the details, but I can say that ordination is even more serious than accepting an offer of employment because it requires a deep level of

---

1 Zen Buddhism: A Chinese and Japanese school of Mahayana which has been described as the revolt of Chinese mind against the intellectual Buddhism of India. Buddhism was developed in China as 'Ch'an' by the Parthian monk and the first and the most translator of the Buddhist texts and Sutras the Ven, An Shigao in AD 148 during the Han dynasty. (See the formation of Ch'an by the same author.)

2 Roshi (old teacher): It is a name given to the Zen master of a monastery who takes the pupil-monks and laymen in San-Zen and gives them Zen instruction. He may be at the same time the Abbot.

sincere commitment. Most of the Rinzai Zen[3] temples in Japan at first prefer to reject the applicants and say they cannot be ordained. Their purpose is see whether the novice will withdraw at the first rejection, or eare they really ready to accommodate themselves to the rigorous practice of Zen? In fact they put a big obstacle in the way to disappoint them and deter them from joining in the temple's practice. But those who succeed in this test will find a peaceful and friendly atmosphere during the practice. This test shows that there is not an immediate warm welcome extended to new applicants. Whilst there is certainly no cruelty or indifference, it does mean that the initial steps are deliberately made tough in order to test the novice's determination and dedication. (This kind of notion is quite different with other religions who are attempting to attract people to their way of their thinking and their ideology by hook or crook.)

This helps to ensure that the temples select only those who want to practise seriously and sincerely. Sometimes it takes one to five years before the Roshi and the Sangha[4] (community) decide that the pupil is sufficiently qualified to become a Zen monk. This tradition has been passed to the present Zen temples and monasteries since past centuries with no discrimination. Throughout this time there is much hard practice, affecting both body and mind. Those who have been to the Rinzai Zen temples in Japan are very aware of this fact. I do not know whether the rules have been changed subsequently, but at the time of my own ordination (1985), I saw lay devotees waiting during this period of uncertainty, hoping to become a member of the Rinzai Zen family.[5] I also have my own story to tell and this will be explained in the next chapters unfolding for me as a natural process. I strongly believe that the teachings which I found there during my years of practice under the instruction of a contemporary Zen master and the system of training found throughout all the Rinzai Zen temples in Japan can be of benefit to all mankind. I do not want to press people into this, as ordination is not for everyone, but I want to describe a peaceful way of life and a way of reaching a perfect understanding of both the outer and the inner world. It works for me, but each of us must decide for him/herself what path to follow in life. It is not my intention to persuade anyone to follow any particular religion or faith because I myself did not come to Zen merely by listening to

---

3 Rinzai Zen: A school of sudden awakening. Koan and Mondo are used in Rinzai Zen. Koan is a kind of riddle, a word or phrase of nonsensical language which cannot be solved by the intellect. Mondo is a short pithy dialogue between Zen masters and their disciples to find the answer to the Koan.

4 Sangha: An assembly. The monastic order founded by the Buddha. The members are called Bhikkhus (monks) or Bhikkhunis (nuns).

5 I visited Sogenji Zen temple for more training in 2000–2001, and also twice in 2017. The rules of ordination have changed to some extent and, a little softer than the time of my ordination in 1985.

words, advice, logic, preaching or other kinds of suggestion. Zen, like other martial arts, needs extreme enthusiasm, faith, persistence and perseverance. Only a few people possess these qualities and are prepared to commit themselves to a lengthy period of hard practice. Therefore to propagate Zen is not an easy matter because it does not have universal appeal. Besides, Zen does not seek merely to increase the number of its devotees, regardless of their quality or level of understanding. One faithful devotee is far more important than dozens of blind followers. Zen masters are clever enough to test his disciples anyhow. Those who are willing to enter in to the world of Zen, they must pass initial tests suggested by the Roshi for further practice or to show their capabilities to go on. There are some tricks known as the games of Zen master to find out the abilities of the novices if they are able to continue the path.

Here's a Zen story which proves the approval of the novice by the Roshi:

> [Tosui was a well-known Zen teacher of his time. He had lived in several temples and taught in various provinces.
>
> The last temple he visited accumulated so many adherents that Tosui told them he was going to quit the lecture business entirely.
>
> He advised them to disperse and to go wherever they desired. After that no one could find any trace of him.
>
> Three years later one of his disciples discovered him living with some beggars under a bridge in Kyoto. He at once implored Tosui to teach him.
>
> "If you can do as I do for even a couple of days, I might," Tosui replied.
>
> So the former disciple dressed as a beggar and spent a day with Tosui. The following day one of the beggars died.
>
> Tosui and his pupil carried the body off at midnight and buried it on a mountainside. After that they returned to their shelter under the bridge.

Tosui slept soundly the remainder of the night, but the disciple could not sleep. When morning came Tosui said: "We do not have to beg food today. Our dead friend has left some over there." But the disciple was unable to eat a single bite of it.

"I have said you could not do as I," concluded Tosui. "Get out of here and do not bother me again."[6]]

There are many such Zen stories which illustrate the hard practice of Rinzai Zen since the time of Hakuin Zenji.[7]

Since this book is merely an autobiography, and at the same time my awakening in the teaching of Buddhism, I have not tried to give an interpretation of any particular religion or school of thought. Of course, in my other books I have introduced the Buddha's teaching in the form of Zen in a practical way.[8] It is my sincere wish that people all over the world, and especially in my home country of Iran, will hear about these teachings and put them into practice in their own lives as the practice plays an important part in Zen. According to Zen, recognition starts with practice. They should do this for their own benefit in order to promote their mental faculties and not to try to please some external power or authority. In Iran there is already a well-established following for martial arts. Many practitioners may be surprised and interested to learn that their disciplines are rooted in Buddhism as practised in the form of Ch'an in Chinese temples, the temples of Japan and some other Far East countries. So I hope they will come to understand the context in which these practices have grown up, and will therefore be attracted to learn about the philosophy behind these martial arts. An understanding of the background will help them to practise with deeper appreciation.

---

6   *101 Zen Stories*: 'Zen in a Beggar's Life'.

7   Hakuin Ekaku, the Zen master (1685–1768), was the father of purely Japanese Rinzai Zen Buddhism as distinct from Chinese Ch'an Buddhism. He believed in fierce direct methods in order to train the unsteady mind. He also remoulded the entire system of Koan.

8   *Zen-mind, Arya-mind*. 2006.

Encouragement from my friends

My story is long and convoluted, but at the same time interesting and instructive. It is interesting because the reader will come to know about the strange and unbelievable ideas which influence the minds and behaviour of the present rulers of the vast country known as Iran. Some of their statesmen can be seen to be paranoid with no sensible purpose and no reasonable policies for the betterment of the nation, but who serve only to steer the minds of the people in a direction which will suit their own ignorant purposes. The new generation will learn what kind of attitudes the present leaders of Iran have in their minds, which are completely divorced from reality and contrary to and in conflict with the ideals of our civilisation. There is a reactionary ideology which will be judged and narrated by future generations.

It is instructive because it reveals secret of a person or persons who patiently and persistently succeed when they have success consciousness. It is true that, when a man really desires a thing deeply that he is enthusiastically willing to stake his entire future on a single turn of the wheel in order to get it, he is sure to win. A lesson which can be informative and decisive.

To me, 'success' does not happen at random, it needs hard work, perseverance, studying, sacrifice and above all a burning desire to reach the final destination. And as Napoleon Hill says, "Whatever the mind of man can conceive and believe it can achieve."[9]

I was partially encouraged to tell l my autobiography (a small part of my autobiography) on the suggestion of my good friends both within Iran and outside, who were close to me and knew something of my life story. They suggested that I should bring together many different stories from different places in a book which might be of interest to other people. I do not want to exaggerate for my autobiography to receive more appreciation and approbation from others. There are (or were) of course opponents of the present Iranian government whose stories have been much more tragic and disastrous when compared with my own. However, I want to set down the facts concerning what happened to me, and is still happening to many other intellectuals who aimed to build their country and help their people to revolutionise their minds with thoughts such as peace, love, friendship, solidarity, creativity and other pure human endeavours. This is a true story which may shock wise men but which may make them aware of what is going on in another part of the world about which they know little.

---

9 Napoleon Hill, *Think and Grow Rich*.

In search of 'Self'

I went down many different and wrong paths, often at considerable cost to myself and my family, before I found the goal for which I had been searching for so many years. My journey started from a wish to know more about myself – more important to me than anything else was to know myself, surpassing all other forms of knowledge.

This may happen to most of us directly or indirectly. Some give importance to it and others ignore it depending on the importance of it based on their mental background. Self-knowledge is crucial not only to writing, but to doing almost anything really well. It allows us to work through from a deep place – from the deep, dark corners of our subconscious mind hidden for centuries. My brother was the Sigmund Freud's adherent and I more or less learned something from him. I was young but because of my interest to the subject I listened to my brother and he explained the theory to me clearly and in a simple way. The notion of self-knowing was induced to me by my brother and this was a push to start. I became interested in knowing the human mind and that part of it which was hidden to me. My brother was indeed helpful to me in order familiarise me with it in a simple way. As a matter of fact a motivation or an impulse especially at young age is enough to push a person to activate his/her curiosity towards something valuable. The mystery of the subconscious mind and its relation with self-knowledge led me to wonder, and wonder to curiosity and investigation. This knowledge encouraged me to start knowing myself, and its reflection to people. According to the Chinese philosopher, Lao Tze: "Knowing others is intelligence; knowing yourself is true wisdom. Mastering others is strength; mastering yourself is true power."

I wanted to know my real self, my own character, powers, and limitations, partly with the guidance of others but also by employing nonstop persistence and perseverance on my own part. Because of our curiosity about things and events around us, it is natural that we should wonder about the meaning of life and chase around to try and discover it. If life has a meaningful purpose we want to try and reach it. The gap between our ignorance and our wisdom should be filled up with our burning desire to understand and to find a way out of our darkness. But first, we must acknowledge that we are not so perfect beings and need to improve. We have to lessen the distance between what we are and what we want to be and keep on marching towards our goal. We have not been born without any purpose. There must be a meaning and a purpose to life. It is up to each of us to give our life a meaning. Different people will give different meanings to their lives. But the reality of life and the reality about ourselves is something which goes beyond imagination and hallucination. To reach an understanding requires persistent effort and careful scrutinising of our experiences. We have to consider what is important to us and what our priorities are. These are the matters to which we should pay attention in order to find our way in life. Like every normal, purposeful human being I was also searching to understand 'who' or 'what' occupied my mind. Fyodor Dostoyevsky says: "The mystery of human existence lies not in just staying alive, but in finding something to live for." It does not matter how long we spend on the earth, how much money we have gathered or how much respect we have received. It is the amount of positive vibration we have radiated in life that matters.

To know the purpose of life, we have first to study our experiences and develop insight. Insight cannot be gained in words and letters but direct observation of the reality as it is. Then we will discover for ourselves the true meaning of life. Guidelines can be given, but we must create conditions in which we can learn for ourselves.

Most of us are wrapped in ignorance regarding our true nature. We lack self-knowledge. We do not know who we are and where we are going, but these questions play a fundamental part in our life. The meaning of life in general is a very wide subject with many different interpretations. These have been handed down for countless generations. My knowledge is not based on my own original ideas, but has been influenced by my understanding and experience. Our ancestors instructed us in different ways and they advised us to ask ourselves: What unique gifts, talents and skills do we bring to this world? What specific issues represent our life challenges? How much of our life is controlled by our personality? How much can we be inspired by our spirit? What gives our lives meaning and purpose? Do we have a personal development plan? What drives the ups and downs of our existence, and who or what is controlling the rudder to steer our ship? What are our priorities?

If we cannot give definite answers to the questions above, then the ship of our life may not reach the destination according to our desire. In fact we have no compass for our wandering ship. There are thousands of people who have been able to follow a path which gives them the tools to empower themselves, together with the skills and confidence to discover their authentic or true

'Self'.[10] As we investigate these matters, we constantly look for answers and we make efforts to find something real, authentic, and genuine, something beneficial to us and to others.

To know about our inner self is indeed amazing and essential, as how to find it and not fight with the world. If we know what makes us, our personality, interests and capabilities, just use them, and everything else flows beautifully.

But one may want to know the difference between the two selves. Modern psychology has divided the self in to two. One is real self and another is ideal self.

Real self (or intact self), is what we really are from inside whereas ideal self is where we see ourselves. In other words, our real self is the person we are in reality, at present. Our real self is what we are doing or behaving. Our ideal self is the self who it should be according to our wish or desire. It comprises our image of ourselves – both in terms of our physical (body image) as well as psychological traits. For example, a guy has always been a timid person and he'd like to be brave, or an unsuccessful man and his ideal is a successful. Our real self can be changed the real to ideal if we desire to change, what we want to become. We all have specific goals and ideal self set for ourselves and thus we try to work consciously to become a better person and shorten the distance between our real self and ideal self.

What is important?

There are several prerequisites if we wish to discover the purpose of life. First, we must try to understand the true nature of man and also the nature of life. Secondly, we must keep our mind calm, peaceful and open to whatever we may discover. Then we can investigate, understand and evaluate things for ourselves. When the right conditions are established, then our questions can be solved more easily. To begin with, we do not know who we really are or what is expected of us. We know very little about ourselves. Most likely our understanding is limited to our physiology and not the depths of our mind. But we need to understand something more than the physical body and the movement of our limbs. This means we have to penetrate to our body and

---

10 True face, true nature, original self, real face are terms described as a sense of 'Self' based on spontaneous authentic experience used in Mahayana Buddhism and usually used as Koan in Rinzai-Zen to find the real, original face or non-duality. Dr Donald Woods Winnicott the English paediatrician and psychoanalyst is best known for his idea of 'true self and false self' and also the transitional object. Before Winnicott, were Helene Deutsch the Austrian-American psychoanalyst and colleague of Dr Sigmund Freud and also Dr Joan Riviere, the British psychoanalyst (Freud's earliest translator who produced the theory of ego). Later Dr Erich Fromm explained the distinction between real face (original self), and pseudo 'Self'.

our mind and come to know them at the subtlest level.[11] It is our mind which matters most. It plays an important role in moulding our character and our destiny. Mind is superior because it is an organ which refers to an individual's capacity for self-examination, self-observation, introspection and personal insight. It also includes an ability to recognise and see the links between current problems within oneself and with others, and the ability to investigate one's past, particularly for its impact on our present attitudes and functioning.

Our interpretation of things external to us may be logical and right, but in penetrating inside our own mind we are still immature and weak. Unfortunately, our entire way of life and the way of life of other people has been built on this lack of understanding. This is the cause of much unhappiness and uncertainty. We need to know what is of primary importance and what is secondary. Knowingly or unknowingly we are students of life, but the findings of each one of us are different and they may vary according to our needs. A true student must come closer to his or her true self. He/she needs to investigate their own mind and their own body, to discover how they function and how they interact with each other. Aren't these important to us? Surely these are important and interesting endeavours.

Science of mind

Most psychologists and philosophers are agreed that the most important matter in this world is the science of the human mind focusing on 'self-realisation', and then understanding other people and helping them in the right direction. According to Ernest Holmes: "The road to freedom lies, not through mysteries or occult performances, but through the intelligent use of Nature's forces and laws. The Law of Mind is a natural law in the spiritual world." We came into this world with a blank slate. Our minds were clear, yet open to receive even the most subtle impressions. As time passed, we unknowingly let these impressions shape our perceptions of who we think we are today. We have let others – parents, government, spouse, boss, teachers – define who we are. But we must remember that no one can show us our true face, our true nature, unless it is discovered by ourselves, with our own effort and perseverance which we undertake voluntarily and not at the dictation of outside influences. If we let people decide who we are, what we are, then we are not living on our own. We won't be able to shape our mind. We cannot

---

11 Penetrating deep in to our mind and our body is called 'introspection'. It is introspection, pure observation of what is happening inside. It is the 'Mind–Body' analysis. Observing every movement of complex machinery of our mind–body.

become what we want to be. Changing mind intelligently means changing the world skilfully. A sharp and quiet mind works as a powerful torch to go through the dark angles of our life in order to find the 'way' easily.

We must realise that life will not last forever, we must ask ourselves: who am I? Why am I here? Where am I going? Am I living life on my own terms? Or am I living my life as I believe others expect me to? Or am I living my life based on unquestioned assumptions, a prisoner of blind beliefs imposed on myself from outside?

We will never resolve our problems or serious life issues if we do not understand the real purpose of our life. The real purpose of life to some people is to have a luxurious house, a lot of money, fame, name and so on. They think these are of primary importance in life. It is true that having a comfortable house and good life is better than being wretched and living in poverty, but to me this kind of life will not accomplish much because it is only a part of the whole process of life. There is another, missing part which is more important but which is often overlooked, forgotten and given less importance. 'Self-realisation' or 'Self-knowledge' is all about knowing one's own self. However, this can never be known in any of the normal ways through which we gain knowledge of worldly subjects.

Science of mind is a way of life targeted on liberation from the bondages and fetters encompassing us – freedom from fear, from hallucination and superstitions; justified by results. We point to universal spiritual principles, which are presented in a simple and direct ways. Therefore, we may each learn to live now, in the present, with the knowledge and trust that the beauty of the world is for us and not against us. All these are directed by our tamed mind.

The search

Knowingly or unknowingly, we are all in search of answers, trying to learn the lessons of life. We grapple with fear and guilt. We search for meaning, emancipation, love and power. We try to understand fear, loss, and time. We seek to discover who we are and how we can become truly happy.

To find and realise the truth in the midst of all our diverse and ever-changing experiences, one must have intense inner longing and perseverance to know and realise it. To qualify in any field of knowledge, we require the guidance of an experienced person who is already qualified in that particular field. This kind of guidance is necessary up to a point, but it is not enough. In pursuit of truth we need something more than mere guidance and that is the pursuit and verification of facts. One has to obtain indisputable truth or non-dual truth on his own by knowing what is untruth. Non-dual truth cannot be contradicted, because there is nothing exists beyond non-duality.[12] Thus, conscious and absolute awareness alone is real and all else is mere mirage. Self-awareness gives us the capacity to learn from our mistakes as well as our successes. It enables us to keep growing, understanding things as they are. People need to know that they have all the tools within themselves. Self-awareness means awareness of our body, awareness of our mental space, awareness of our relationships – not only with each other, but with life and the environment. Self-awareness is the ability to take a sincere look at our life without any attachment to it being right or wrong, good or bad, as a silent observer.

Those who are in search of their true 'Self' have first to free themselves from the prison of orthodoxy, if they are really seeking truth. Only by perfect understanding of what 'IS' (that is, the present moment and eternal NOW) can one easily reach the destination of non-duality. When ignorance has been eliminated, the real self is free from bondage and the burden of waking experience. Therefore seeking wealth, friends, sensual pleasure, scriptural studies or any sort of knowledge becomes of secondary importance.

A saying by Carl Gustav Jung: "Your vision become clear when you can look in to your own heart. Who looks outside, dreams: who looks inside, awake."

Self-inquiry

Franklin who says; "There are three things extremely hard: steel, a diamond, and to know one's self."

We have learnt that when we know nothing about ourselves, the knowledge about things external world is useless. Man, who has now become more of stranger to himself than ever before, is trying hard to reconcile with himself by any means to this spiritual values, knowing well 'self-knowing' can give benefit to him and the others as well.

Certainly this question of 'who we are' or 'what we are' is important and necessary, priority to other things.

We need to ask ourselves this question many times: "Who am I?" hoping that we will eventually find the answer we need, the answer that will make us feel complete and allow us just to be. So who am I? Am I my age, my mind, my nationality, my education, my religion, my friends, my clothes, my looks,

---

12 The non-dual truth represents no self (emptiness of self). There is no real self as a master (emptiness of all phenomena).

my transient body & mind? Who? It is even more important to ask what is this 'I', this 'me', or what is this complex machinery of man? Is it not necessary to know about this psychic phenomenon and physical phenomenon? Of course it is, it is a must for all of us. Maullana Jalal ad- Din Rumi, the Persian poet, says; "Why do you stay in prison, when the door is wide open?"

Moulding the destiny

Destiny or fate is often regarded as the 'course that life takes' and 'action' or karma (in Indian philosophy) is one of the factors that influence this course.[13]

People often believe that fate is predestined and nothing can be changed. Sometimes we hear that our destiny or fate is predetermined by some supernatural powers or gods and we should obedient to it indisputably, whereas this does not in conformity with common sense. Our destiny is shaped according to the combination of conditions predetermined at birth and other factors that we are able to change through our own efforts. Therefore, destiny is not something prearranged by celestial beings to determine our future, but it is determined by us, by our will, with our own hands, with persistence, perseverance, and a fixed goal to reach, changeable here and now.

There are factors which mould our destiny. Amongst them is our action, our karma. Karma (Pali: kamma) is 'action', that is, wholesome and unwholesome volition and their mental factors, shaping the destiny of beings. Karma is a law in itself, operating in its own field without the intervention of any external, independent ruling agency. Karma means that everything that happens to us, without exception, we ourselves, directly or indirectly, partly or entirely, set into motion at some time in the past. According to ancient wisdom; "If you want to know the past (cause), look at your present (effect). If you want to know the future (effect), look at your present (cause). When the cause gets changed, the effect will be changed accordingly. The natural reward or retribution for a deed, brought about by the law of karma." However, karma is simply a set of habits of the soul (mind)– our tendency to come up with certain thoughts or take certain actions in a certain set of circumstances. Karma does not lead to fatalistic thoughts and it is simply a factor in forming our fate or destiny.

Like every human being I was personally curious about such matters and this so occupied my mind that it became almost an obsession. I do not

---

13 Good thoughts, good words, good deeds; a phrase that represents the three pillars of Zoroastrian Faith, more than 1000 BCE.

know how and where this curiosity came from. I was very young and had no background of such curiosity and had no knowledge about its reason either. I sometimes looked at mirrors and talked to myself, and I used to ask myself about my identity. The mirror could reflect my body. I could see my physical form, but I wanted something more than that. Was there a mirror to reflect my mind also? I had many such questions but no reliable source to respond to them. At school no one was willing or able to look into the questions I was curious about. Although my parents spent time on my education, they used to answer my inquisitive questions according to their own interpretations, in order to convince me. Curiosity means wanting to ask, to learn, and find proper answers. Those who are curious are called 'inquisitive', meaning that they inquire, or ask questions, and are likely to search, explore and experiment to find an answer. In the long term they may shape their destiny. Our destiny is in our hands without the intervention of other unknown powers.

Earnest Holmes says; "The individual who can learn how to consciously change their thinking processes, can remould their destiny."

From ignorance to knowledge

To understand the real purpose of life, it is advisable for a person to choose and follow an ethical system that restrains him from doing evil deeds, encourages him to do well and enables him to purify his mind. Man may be clever enough to land on the moon and discover wondrous things in the universe. He has discovered and harnessed more of nature's forces during the past 50 years than in the entire history of the human race previous to that time. We have conquered the air so completely that the birds cannot match our flight. We have harnessed the ether, and made it serve as a means of instantaneous communication with any part of the world. We have analysed and weighed the sun at a distance of millions of miles and we have developed many ways of changing the outer world. No doubt such discoveries have helped man to feel more comfortable and relaxed. They are important but they are not enough. Man has yet to delve into the inner workings of his own mind. He has yet to learn how his mind can be developed to its fullest potential so that its true nature can be realised.

Some people still wrapped in ignorance. They do not know who they really are or how to change the course of their lives in accordance with the nature. As a result, they misinterpret everything and act on that misinterpretation. Is it not conceivable that our entire civilisation is built on this misinterpretation?

Failure to understand his own existence leads man to assume a false identity, that of a bloated, self-seeking egoist, and to pretend to be what he cannot be. Man must make an effort to overcome ignorance in order to arrive at self-realisation and enlightenment. All of the greats were born human, but they worked their way up to greatness and some became saints. Realisation and enlightenment cannot be poured into the human heart in a haphazard way. It needs hard work and pure faith. Even the most enlightened persons had to cultivate their minds to realise their real nature.

Man can be enlightened – awakened – if he breaks from the dream that is created by his own ignorant mind and becomes fully awakened. He must understand that what he is today is the result of an untold number of thoughts and actions performed in the past.[14] He is not pre-formed: He is continually involved in the process of becoming, always changing. And it is in this process of change that his future lies, because it means that it is possible for him to mould his character and destiny through the actions he chooses to perform. When a person comprehends the nature of man, then some important realisations arise. He comes to understand that, unlike a rock or a stone, a human being possesses the innate potential to grow in wisdom, compassion, pure love, and awareness – and to be transformed by this self-development and growth. He also learns that it is not easy to be born as a human being, especially one who has the chance to listen to ancient, mature wisdom which can lead him along the path of enlightenment.

This unusual story of mine which will be explained in the next chapters includes the painful memories of many of my fellow citizens who have suffered and are now suffering much worse than me under rulers who call themselves celestial beings elected by God. They have dominated the land of Persia, imposing their putrid and decayed ideology into the minds of innocent people with the help of force and hypocrisy. Such pressures and persecution have been employed with many thousands of Iranians intellectuals, philosophers, writers, journalists, artists, liberals and other members of the educated classes, whose stories are as painful as mine and this process it is still going on much worse than before. I am not going into detail concerning everything I know in order to give readers a complete picture. I know that curious people are now in direct contact with different media and also have access to advanced

---

14 Consciousness is a flux: Vinnana Sota is a Pali word which means the stream of consciousness. This notion was declared in 2500 BCE by the Sakya Sage. It is said that all the component things are nothing but flow of consciousness, the view has been recently reiterated by William James (the father of American psychology).

information technology, thereby knowing what is going on in present Iran. By using the power of my own mind to conduct an investigation into reality in great detail, I think I have gained a clearer understanding of the truth, rather than relying on the second-hand information disseminated by a minority of fanatics who have manipulated things merely to benefit themselves. These gangs of fanatics are notorious for their reactionary behaviour, acting like Middle Age rulers in the 21st century. I am writing this story out of humanitarian feelings and sympathetic appreciation of the facts. Our great poet Saadi Shirazi has a wonderful poem which has been translated in many languages. It is translated as follows:

> *Human beings are members of a whole,*
> *In creation of one essence and soul.*
> *If one member is afflicted with pain,*
> *Other members uneasy will remain.*
> *If you have no sympathy for human pain,*
> *The name of human you cannot retain.*[15]

This poem teaches us the unity of all people. It encourages our coming together not for a particular group of persons, not for the people of one nation, but out of widespread sympathy and mutual understanding towards all. It is a wish to share our true feelings and emotions with one and all. To support the development of wisdom and to fight against the forces of fundamentalism and superstition demands total unity. But in spite of all these difficulties I could break through and to find my way to where I dreamed of.

Psychologists have correctly said that "when one is truly ready for a thing, it puts in its appearance."

Some points from this chapter

- Ordination in Zen-Buddhism is different from some other spiritual discipline.

- The training of Zen is so hard that it is not surprising that only a few people are drawn to it.

---

15 Translated by the author.

- Ch'an or Zen was born from the Buddha's thoughts.

- A trained mind is the seed of shaping our destiny.

- The story of our life is tied with our destiny.

- Life is constantly being hungry. The meaning of life is not simply to exist, to survive, but to move ahead, to go up, to achieve, to conquer.

- My knowledge is not based on my own, original ideas, but has been influenced by my understanding and experience.

- Our aim in this world is to know ourselves, preferably in a way which is practical and beneficial in our daily lives.

- When we cannot control our mind, we are controlled by it.

- We must realise that life will not last forever, we must ask ourselves: who am I? Why am I here?

- Changing mind intelligently means changing the world skilfully.

- When a person comprehends the nature of man, then some important realisations arise.

- Because we are persistence in our tracking of our deepest destiny, we will continue to grow. We cannot choose the day or time as it is spontaneous and it happens in its own time.

- We determine our destiny by changing the habit pattern of our mind.

- Man can be enlightened – awakened – if he breaks from the dream that is created by his own ignorant mind and becomes fully awakened.

- When one is truly ready for a thing, it puts in its appearance.

- The individual who can learn how to consciously change their thinking processes, can remould their destiny.

- When we know nothing about ourselves, it is useless to ponder on things outside us.

- Self-knowledge is in fact a basic need for the mind's stability, not in word but in practice.

- Our interpretation of things external to us may be logical and right, but in penetrating inside our own mind, we are still immature and weak.

- Curiosity means wanting to ask, to learn, and to find proper answers.

Chapter 2

My Background in Islam – My First Experience

> *"Character cannot be developed in ease and quiet. Only through experience of trial and suffering can the soul be strengthened, ambition inspired, and success achieved."*
> HELEN KELLER.

My childhood was safe and sane brought up in a labour environment, labour region of Abadan. My father was a farmer and then moved to Abadan city and was employed as a worker in the oil refinery established by Anglo-Persian Oil Company (later BP).

Abadan is (was) one of the biggest and more important cities of the Khuzestan province. It is an island in southwest of Iran which is bordered with Iraq.

Abadan is very close to the Persian Gulf, quite near the Iraq–Iran border. The population has now reached nearly 300,000 people.

Abadan was (is) important not only because of its strategic position in the Persian Gulf but being an important industrial city. A huge oil refinery (the largest in the Middle East) was established with the help of the Iranians experts and the British Petroleum who had strong and effective presence in the Abadan city at that time.

Education also was remarkable in this city compared to other cities of Iran except Tehran the capital. In such an environment and condition I was born, brought up and educated. This is a brief version on Abadan before the Islamists undertake the whole power.[16]

---
16 – More about the Abadan city in Chapter 11.

No abuse and no traumas in my childhood in the framework of my family. We were three brothers and three sisters. I was surrounded by a large and loving family. My parents used to teach us the importance of hard work and the importance of education. Among my sisters and brothers I was more curious than them and this curiosity encouraged me to penetrate things around me and about the world I was living in. Although my parents were following moderate religious precepts, the rest of the family were not much interested in it, but I was more curious in this field.

My visual memory is good to some extent about my childhood and more about my adolescence. I can speak less what happened before the age of ten but more about my adolescence.

Our parents although were religious but they were open minded and they permitted us to make our own decisions for life, encouraging us by their good suggestions.

The memory of my adolescence starts at high school at the age of 12–13 years old. My subject of study was experimental science. In those early days, I developed the skills that gave me a certain degree of success in the course of my high school. At high schools, the textbook was limited to subjects related to our scholastic studies allocated by the education office. Most of the high schools had a small library of their own, but not much enough to promote our variety of knowledge. I was enthusiastically willing to learn more than the textbooks designated to us at high schools. To have my favorite books I had to go a long way to a bookshop in the middle of the city to borrow books. There was a big bookshop far from my house. I used to go there sometimes on foot and sometimes with my bicycle. There was competition between me and two of my cousins in finishing the books as quickly as possible so as not to pay much money for the lend. There was a rule by the manager of the bookshop. If we could return the books within two days then we would pay less amount and could borrow more books. The quicker we finished the book the less the payment for us. We tried to finish the books of nearly 200 pages book or more in two days to pay less. This casual reading did not disturb our high schools' textbooks. Besides, psychologically, we were more energetic for other subjects at schools.

My favourite books

I was interested in some mysterious and detective books by Sir Arthur Conan Doyle (the detective stories of Sherlock Holmes) and Agatha Christie and some books by Jules Verne all in Persian translations. I was curious to follow unknown to known and enjoyed it. In this way I involuntarily increased the power of my imagination.

I remember that I used to reiterate the exciting stories to my classmates who were very interested in the stories. In the classroom I also used the same stories as the subject of my composition. In this way I not only amused the students out of the class but I got good marks from the teacher of presenting such good scientific stories.

System of education

The system of education in those days in Abadan (before the so called Islamic Revolution) was excellent. It was indeed typical among other cities and could only be compared with Tehran city (the capital) in many ways. Not only that we had many ideal facilities in this industrial city such as a golf club and international airport (second to Tehran), Big advanced clubs for entertainment, different sports clubs, horse racing, local TV and radio stations and other good facilities. Besides, we had Jewish virtual library, a Christian church just beside the mosque (called Behbani's Mosque) with only one wall in between them. Both Muslims and Christians jointly celebrated Easter Eve each year. The best schools and high schools with the best educated teachers from different cities were employed by the Abadan Education Office and many other facilities. Abadan was one the most important industrial city with special educational system in Iran. In such an environment I grew up, studied and I was educated.

Family and religion

In the structure of family, I was born into a middle-class religious family. My parents were Muslims, observing the traditional Islamic precepts. My grandfather and grandmother were Muslims too, and my parents were happy for their children to follow the same precepts and maintain this religious tradition which had been preserved and followed by our ancestors for centuries. In other words, we were traditionally bound to pass on the religion from our ancestors to the future generation. This kind of religious tradition has been the prevailing custom for centuries in many religions, especially Islam.

My brothers and sisters were all well-educated. However, we were living in a city which was not regarded as a place of religious importance, nor are its people renowned for their piety and interest in participating in religious activities particularly if these activities are based on commandments using the terms 'must' or 'must not'. In such a commercially oriented environment it is not so easy to introduce religious ideas, especially into the minds of the youth who are reluctant to learn about religious beliefs, or to listen to sermons. Such people as these want to live their lives free from boundaries and restrictions, not wishing to be dependent on and obligated to an ideology taught by a conservative clergy advancing doctrines which have been around for centuries. By contrast, I was always curious about religious practices, spiritual training and so forth. This is not because I was looking for a religion to stick to with blind fanaticism or because I wanted to identify myself with it through unquestioning dedication. Rather, I wanted to find a spiritual practice which could lead me to a relaxed and peaceful state of mind and which could answer my questions concerning the unknown and thereby satisfy by natural curiosity.

I was 13 years old and looking for something to answer my questions about the nature of the mind, its functioning and also its relation to the world. I wanted to learn about my destiny and finally to discover my position in this world and my duty to serve people if I'm eligible to. I wanted to know what I could gain from this world while I was alive and what duties and obligations I had to the world. Perhaps, for many people such questions do not matter, but being inspired by my father, I had a burning desire to learn and I tried my best to know more at every stage in my experience.

Purpose, ambition and curiosity

To me, a true religion or any school of thought should answer most of the important questions of its enquirers and not leave any space for doubts regarding the happiness and salvation of mankind. This sense of curiosity made me investigate in a rational scientific way the deepest and most profound answers concerning physical reality and the nature of man. In general, curiosity and an enquiring mind are most valuable traits. I do not think you can find an intellectual giant who is not a curious person. Most of the inventors, discoverers, artists, and successful men and women were filled with curiosity to achieve their desires. Curiosity is so important because it makes our mind active instead of passive and leads it to investigate causes and their effects. Persons with curiosity always ask questions or direct their minds in search of meaning. Their minds are always active and ready to face the unknown. Since the mind is like a muscle which becomes stronger through continual exercise, the mental exercise caused by curiosity makes our mind stronger and stronger. Besides, it makes our minds observe new ideas, see new worlds and discover possibilities which are normally invisible. These things are hidden under the surface of normal life. It takes a curious mind to look beneath the surface and discover these new worlds and possibilities. In fact, you are not going to lose anything if you are looking for something valuable persistently with perseverance.

Brainwashing

I was neither a genius, nor extraordinary but just an ordinary individual, filled with curiosity, searching for the meaning of life. My father used to tell me to read books, listen to the old stories of great men and women, and watch movies to learn something new. He never tried to transmit his idea to me unless I was ready for it, but on the contrary my Islamic advisers and clergymen always used to tell me confidently that "Islam can give you whatever you want from life." We were told the same things at schools, mosques, and Islamic communities. Now I know, this kind of teaching from different sources was a kind of brainwashing which is knowingly or unknowingly used by some authorities. Here, I would like to underline two simple definitions of brainwashing:

1. Intensive, forcible indoctrination, usually political or religious, aimed at destroying a person's basic convictions and attitudes and replacing them with a fixed ideology.
2. The use of some effective means (tools) of persuasion, such as repeated suggestion in order to make a motivation.

In psychology, the study of brainwashing, often referred to as thought-reform, falls into the sphere of 'social influence'. Social influence happens every minute of every day. It is the collection of ways in which people can change other people's attitudes, beliefs and behaviours, or the imposition of a belief on the mind of a new visitor. For instance, the compliance method aims to produce a change in a person's behaviour and is not concerned with his attitudes or beliefs. It is the 'Just do it'. Persuasion, on the other hand, aims for a change in attitude, or "Do it because it'll make you feel good and successful." The education method (which is also called the 'propaganda method' when you do not believe in what is being taught) goes for the social-influence goal, trying to affect a change in the person's beliefs, along the lines of "Do it because you know it's the right thing to do." Brainwashing is a severe form of social influence that combines all of these approaches to cause changes in someone's way of thinking without that person's consent and often against his or her will. Through the ages the history, this kind of brainwashing has always been exerted by some tyrannical government whether religious or non-religious and millions of people were converted by it. In developing countries, especially my country, where there is no freedom of selection but the acceptance of only one ideology, brainwashing becomes a solution to prevent citizens from investigating the outside world, especially when a government needs long-term stability in order to consolidate their power over a nation or country. These fanatical, prejudiced rulers go further. They establish the compliance method as a parliamentary law in order to ensure their selfish, long-term survival. The raw material of people's minds can be shaped easily by their rulers by imposing an ideology on the present and future generations.

The above-mentioned explanation is a fact that how a totalitarian system in the name of religion try their best to attract the youth and convince them to accept their putrid ideology in the form of washing their brains.

Experiencing Islam

I had to believe the authorities because at that time the only source I had to trust was Islam and its messengers. I gave myself to it wholeheartedly without any doubts. Besides, I was constantly practising at home the form of Islam inherited by my ancestors and passed down obediently according to tradition. The type of Islam which I was imitating at home and which prevailed in society at large was moderate at that time as my parents were a calm and peaceful couple. But in the stories of the Islamic leaders (the prophets) I heard some rather different things. I was fortunate that in the Islam introduced to me by my parents, I could find a moral code like many other religions, but at the same time I did not want to accept the violent part of Islam which I heard in the sermons and saw in the deeds of the clergy. Revenge, enmity and killing were all included in the teachings found in the treatises of the so-called Islamic religious leaders. They were widely accepted, especially in some sects which placed emphasis on the use of violence. Whether one accepts these customs or not, the precepts handed down from the past centuries remain intact. I became very interested in Mystic Islam or Sufism which had developed in Iran and spread all over the world. Sometimes my father used to tell me the stories of some Islamic Gnostics such as Attar Neishaboori,

Mansoor-ebn-e Halladj, Aboosaeed Abulkheir and Shahaboddin Sohrevardi and many other Iranian mystics. I found their true stories very interesting and quite different from fundamentalist Islam. Unfortunately, I could not access this kind of teaching more deeply for two important reasons:

1. This knowledge was (and is) mystical and rarely shown to everyone.
2. The fundamental Islam or traditional Islam has little to do with Mystical Islam, either in thought or practice.

The religious extremists want to increase the number of their devotees, especially using their tools for brainwashing. Such clergy are more concerned with the quantity of their followers rather than the quality of their behaviour. To them, absolute obedience from their followers is (was) more crucial for them. They never leave decisions to be made by the people. Throughout the ages, history shows us that religious leaders of this kind always impose their rules on their followers.

It is believed that Sufism is the science by which one knows the method of travelling towards the king of kings. It is also the means to the purification of the internal from defeat and its adornment with all virtues. The believers say, "Sufism is the method by which the creation is obliterated, lost in the vision called 'SHOHOOD' or intuition of the truth." From its birthplace in Iran, Sufism spread to many countries including parts of Africa, India and other eastern countries. As a matter of fact the Iranians gave shape to the superstitious Islam and changed it to a genuine doctrine.

Sufism or the way of 'Dervish' known as 'TASAVWOF' or the so-called 'Iranian mystics' indicates the spirituality of Islam or in other words the truth to be discovered within us. Sufism has been described in many different ways by scholars writing in English, but they all consider it to be an inner, esoteric, mystical or purely spiritual dimension to the religion of Islam. Sufism is the spiritual path, 'Tarighat', of Islam which has been called 'Islamic Mysticism' by Western scholars. The directness of this path has some similarities with Buddhism. We can find mystics in many religions, including Christianity and Hinduism. Nowadays, however, many Muslims and non-Muslims think that Sufism is outside the sphere of Islam, even though, according to Iranian mysticism the core and the essence of Islam has been discovered by the mystics. Most of the great Persian poets, philosophers, writers, artists and thinkers such as Hafez, Saadi, Sanaii, Avicenna (Abualisina) and Molana Jalaldin known as

'Rumi', and many others studied Islamic mysticism. Attar of Neishabouri, the great Persian poet and mystical philosopher regarding pure Islam says; "We removed the brain from Quran, we threw the skin over the desert."

Manipulated Islam

The knowledge about Islam which I got from my society and my local mosques was limited to precepts concerning what to do and what not to do. What is to be obeyed and what to be denied. I learned these precepts from my family, the local mosque, schools, society and the cultural environment. They were given to me as absolute truth, with no room for analysis, investigation, personal experience or criticism. Over time, I joined various religious groups performing different kinds of religious ceremonies, all of them in the Islamic tradition. Sometimes I used to sit by the pulpits of the clergy for hours to hear the story of the prophets, with interpretations differing from one speaker to another. Then we had some outdoor ceremonies. These were too violent for me to follow. They involved breast-beating, beating oneself with daggers and axes, or harming oneself in painful ways to prove one's loyalty to Imam Hussain, the third Imam, a prophet who was killed in a battle in nearly AD 680. These practices usually took place in the annual ceremonies held to mark the death of prophets or saints who had been killed or martyred. Practice for rituals of this kind was usually done inside the mosques, according to the ideas of the Islamic clergy, and the actual performance was done outdoors.

In accordance with my inner nature, I would not get involved in such violent activities, chiefly because my own temperament could not respond to them positively. I saw some fanatics who opened their skulls with daggers or axes in the trance state of mind as instructed by the religious leaders during these ceremonies. These violent scenes cannot be agreeable to anyone with a reasonable or sensitive turn of mind. On one occasion, I fainted and became unconscious on seeing such bloody scenes performed by these so-called devotees. These activities were in fact part of the Islamic tradition according to the narrow interpretation of some Islamic clergy, but they did not suit my own disposition and I did not want to pretend to be a fanatical Muslim. However, for years I followed most of these same precepts, reading treatises, reciting Islamic verses as dictated to me by our community, the mosques and the wider society in which we lived. I was too young and my mind was not retentive enough to record the incidents in detail, whether good or bad. However, when an innocent mind encounters violence it reacts against it.

Negative psychological effects

I am not going to condemn any stream or school of thought, nor am I going to comment in detail on any ideology. I am not a student of comparative religion, but the fact is I could not find a solution to my questions in this kind of Islam; it could not meet what I thought were my reasonable expectations. I expected something more than mere obedience or submission. I was looking for something positively helpful, for something more than dull or negative acceptance. Although I participated for years in all the usual Islamic activities, I could not find what I wanted. Surely a mark of any valid religion or school of thought is that it can attract newcomers. If its ideas are reasonable and accord with observable facts, then the followers can accept it and apply it in their daily life. Yet, the kind of Islam which I encountered did not seem capable of changing my personality for the better or bringing me any peace of mind, which is what I expected from a religious practice. Day by day I felt a growing conflict within myself. Phobia and paranoia started growing within me based on the clergy's teaching. Naturally these wrong practices can generate emotions which can negatively affect the mind and cause feelings to be suppressed in our subconscious for years. If these negativities are not eradicated, they can certainly create different kinds of psychological problems in the long run. Emotional suppression sometimes serves a useful, even essential, purpose but sometimes it damages the personality for years, depending on how deeply and effectively the events were hidden in our minds. When suffering a severe traumatic injury the body automatically passes into the physiological state of shock, blocking all feeling and sensation and numbing consciousness, so that the injured person can better begin recovery from the experience. Similarly, when children or young boys experience physical, emotional, or other shocking events, they commonly report feeling numb, losing consciousness, and sometimes even leaving their bodies (they may remember objectively observing the event from above). Here, I am not going to go into the details of such psychological affects but to say that bad experiences in the past can affect the present circumstances especially when deep rooted in our subconscious mind.

During my youth I was not fortunate to have a variety of good or positive experiences, but rather some bad or negative ones.

I found myself being drawn towards ideas of enmity and revenge. We were being taught that it was our duty to support with fanatical determination the ideology of Islam against all other religions, and if necessary to be prepared to fight in its defence. I was sorry to see that in my community the faces of people were always sorrowful, afflicted and mournful, rather than cheerful, hopeful and happy especially in the mourning ceremonies which was performed time to time. We used to perform death rituals instead of enjoying life by being happy and high-spirited. Perhaps what I expected from Islam was unrealistic or maybe I was not fitted to the particular 'Way' which I had been following for years. Perhaps the Islamic clergy were not wise enough to convey the real teaching of the original religious leaders. Every religion, philosophical system and school of thought has come into existence for some purpose and reason. Nobody can deny them or condemn them without investigation, but the adoption of these diverse ideologies depends on the understanding of the persons concerned. We human beings are limited in our powers of understanding, but we can push back the borders of our ignorance. An understanding of our own need to grow enables us to search out suitable principles and ideas, knowing that the more we learn, the more clearly we can focus on reality and see it clearly. The principles do not change, but our understanding of them does.

We cannot adhere to firm principles without first being aware of established patterns of thinking, and then understanding how to shift them to align them with a correct path. We cannot become centred on certain principles without having a vision of and a focus on the unique contribution that these principles will make.

Like every ordinary person, my mind was eager to receive knowledge and ideas which were in agreement with my nature and not opposed to it.

In fact I gave my whole being to a system to learn, to guide me to a peaceful and harmonious life, but I was misguided by their teaching. The road which was shown to me was dark and full of ambiguity. Even my basic needs to lead me to a philanthropic doctrine was failed and I got disappointed when I encountered a wrong way.

My expectations

Curiosity made me open my eyes to things unknown to me, revealing facts previously foreign to my experience and helping to change my path through life. I was intelligent enough to open my eyes to things analytically in order that they could lead me to what I actually wanted. To choose is easy, but the application of the chosen ideas can seem difficult and sometimes they can be completely rejected by the mind if they are not in sympathy with our natural behaviour and our temperament. To gaze at only one dimension of a thing means we know nothing about other dimensions. To see or to believe in one dimension of a thing, risks getting involved in prejudices – sometimes with fatal consequences. Fanaticism, enmity, hatred, revenge, conceit, etc. are states of mind which come from the same seed. Some sects in the name of religion support this kind of unwholesome actions.

Therefore, in the process of time I realised that the gap between what I was following and my real nature was getting wider and wider. I started asking myself questions and I expected to find the answers from an external source. Sometimes, I stood in front of a big mirror and asked myself questions. An inner conflict started demonstrating its presence in me. I studied and practised Islam as it came to me from different sources – from my parents, society and the Islamic communities around me. From an early age I tried to follow the teachings of Islam according to my understanding and my faith, but I made no progress in the field of mind development and behavioural changes, which is what I hoped for.

Adherence to precepts

Some religions have their own rules and regulations and their followers are bound to obey the precepts by mere submission. These laws are strictly followed by fundamentalists in all religions, be it Islam, Christianity, Hinduism, Jainism, Judaism, Buddhism and by all those who believe in the blind, unquestioning acceptance of long-established precepts and form. In fact, most of the religions of the world have been misunderstood by deluded or ignorant so-called clergy, who seek to impose their interpretations on their followers and who expect unquestioning devotion and respect. Although some doctrines seem logical and rational, their scope may be limited merely to precepts and speculative advice. The leaders give no guidance on how to achieve individual awakening or self-mastery. They do not teach a path to the development of wisdom or how to apply it in order to support their beliefs. True wisdom is misunderstood by them and their teaching is instead concentrated on killing, enmity, revenge, sacrifice, suicide and extreme acts of self-mortification to mark the anniversary of the death of a saint. Precepts, tradition, customs, inference, deduction, conjecture, logic, plausible reasoning, are the tools used by some religious followers to defend their way of thinking. There is little emphasis on looking into our inner self. In other words, they do not want their followers to become more curious about what goes on inside them and to tread a path of self-realisation. Unbiased observation, which helps all of us to feel the reality of life as it is, has been totally ignored by some religious teachers who merely emphasise precepts, tradition and the like.

A true religion

Yet self-investigation is a matter which can help us come closer to ourselves, rather than to escape from ourselves. Self-knowledge is in fact a basic need for the mind's stability, not in word but in practice. Some religious preachers want to show people the way of salvation and the path of deliverance, but their teaching works with only a few faithful devotees who respond with blind obedience to their teacher. These preachers think the quantity of their followers is more important than the quality of their teaching. But suffering people strive for years to be released from the bondage in which they are entangled. Any religion which brings freedom and deliverance to people in order to enable them to solve their own problems by themselves is a true religion and it can be 'holy' to follow it. But absolute submission or obedience to a religion, or the mere following of precepts without direct experience, is nothing but blind faith and is far from the development of true wisdom. It leads to futile wandering in a circle with no end. For the same reason some religions teach a system of mere belief, rather than seeking to make a fundamental change in man by transforming his behaviour from weakness to strength and from bad to good. True religion must have the power, based on deep psychology, to transform a man in thought, word and deed to realise his full potential as a human being. Without this, spiritual growth is impossible.

Religion against science and human right

A human being is a thoughtful and creative being. He has to have a sense of curiosity about what he is and where he is going. His eyes should be open to see what is before him, and to scrutinise everything in order to discover its nature. He should study ideas and different ways of thinking in order to choose the one that seems best for himself. Intelligent human beings should not limit themselves to blindly following their ancestors' path without questioning it. They should understand that the world is changing rapidly and we have to move in harmony with this changing world. Now let's see what is the religionists' impact on science?

Some religionists deliberately ignore scientific findings, or trivialise them, because they think that they are either in deep conflict with science, or they fear that the tales weaved in to the minds of their followers over the years may, one day, be revealed as false attitudes. Therefore, they insist on their dogmas with the threats of damnation or excommunication, no matter how much harm they may bring to mankind. Their response to scientific research is neither rational nor practical.

An obvious and vivid example is the evolutionary theory of Charles Darwin. Some religionists believe that God created man. Darwin postulated that man is the result of the gradual evolution of the ape. This theory undermines the doctrine of creation. While most scientific thinkers have accepted Darwin's theory, opposition groups have no rational response or practical tools to support their ideas. Instead, they cling to their old interpretations of man, God, the soul, the world and creation. The fact is, the religionists need not fear these scientific investigations. They may simply counter them with the very same scientific tools and convincing reasoning if they have.

Man is not like an animal to follow something without thinking and without analysing. Thinking, choosing, analysing, recognising and understanding are qualities which differentiate man from animals. He needs to express himself according to what he sees and not be led by mere belief. Curiosity and creativity are behind man's greatest achievements and successes. We should not follow unquestioningly ideas which go back to the Middle Ages. A man has to choose his own way. A Christian should know about Islam and a Muslim too and build it together, and also they add more knowledge to the sum total of our experience. The doors of the temples, churches, mosques and synagogues must be open to all. Every normal man needs to know about other religions if he wants to be able to express opinions or views which will be accepted by everyone. The truth has to be able to withstand examination and investigation from every possible direction.

A polygon, for example, has many surfaces. It cannot be described from one side only. The hidden faces of the polygon should be considered as part of a total unity. There are many schools of thought and there are different religions with different interpretations, but there is no hierarchy with one religion superior to the others. Yet, from childhood, we are taught to accept one ideology and to stick to it in the bigoted belief that it is superior, without acknowledging that we know nothing about other systems of belief. If we follow that notion, then we think that paradise has already been reserved for us and, if not, we have to suffer burning in the fire of hell forever. When people seriously try to identify what matters most to them in their lives, and what they really want to be and to do, they become very reverential. They start to think in terms of a larger perspective than just today and tomorrow.

Although the Islamic principles did not change me or help me to grow as I expected them to do, I do not want to criticise them in a negative way. Maybe my logic was too weak to understand the precepts or I was not made for it. Maybe, I studied and practised only that part of Islam which was related to tradition and ceremonies and which did not go beyond that. I was not lucky enough to study Mystic Islam, or what might be called the 'true Islam'. Instead I encountered an Islam which was dogmatic and led me nowhere. I was looking for a wise teaching which would give me a more in-depth analysis of my mind and how it worked. Sad to say, the present Islam which is dominating the whole county now is the continuation of the same Islam I experienced in my childhood and the same Islam which was brought to Persia centuries ago and no change in conformity with the modern scientific age in seeing and observing that the world changing unceasingly in every respect.

For example, centuries ago the Islamic law for punishment was to cut hands or fingers, or stoning to death for the so called the sinners, or throwing the guilty down from the top of mountains as punishment. These inhuman rules are still executing in this age without a bit change. Punishment for insulting or criticising the prophets of God is heavy and sometimes this conviction will be enforced by ordinary prejudiced followers of Islam known as 'zealots' on the streets and in public views.

Paradise with the help of Mullahs

There was a local mosque near our house and my father used to take me there to listen to the clergy who knew well about the traditional Islam. My father was happy that he was showing a path of piety and the truth with the help of the messengers of God, that is, the Muslim clerics. The abstract precepts were repeatedly whispered in to my ears as a form of indoctrination. I still observe the same precepts and rules in some Muslim countries, especially in the Islamic Republic of Iran, by those who have occupied our country with having high culture and the precedence of more than 2500 years of civilisation.

There were also some so called religious Mullahs who went from house to house trying to convert other people or other ideas in to their faith and promising them the heaven with luxurious life. They claim that they are able to send us to heaven if we listen to them and to perform their religious precepts. They say they are the only authorities selected by God almighty. Many innocent people who lack of knowledge of their own ideas and beliefs, became victims of these paradise sellers. These paradise sellers were (are) also trying to mislead the people by saying that this world which is created by God is going to end very soon. Those who want to have a wonderful everlasting life in heaven must accept their particular ideology before the end of the world comes, otherwise people will miss this golden opportunity and will have to suffer in eternal hell. Some people get converted after hearing such deceptive preaching, without using their common sense. History tell us about these imposed ideology during the ages of Islam in connection with the Iranian people since centuries ago and in this way the ideology, gradually well established in the mind of million Iranians.

The opinion which claims that our own ideas are superior and other ideas are doubtful is neither reasonable nor fair. It is based on enmity and anger rather than objective analysis. Rejecting or denying ideas by mere criticising is not the way to enlightenment. It is easy to criticise others based on some emotion, but it is indeed hard to judge wisely, based on our experience or scientific study. To judge a matter to be genuine we need to analyse it in different respects starting from the assumption that other people are as wise as we are. We shall be good teachers if we teach them to choose the best from a field of variety and diversity. According to the ancient wisdom, if we think people are wise, we are wise to some extent. However, if we treat people as fools, we are indeed fools.

How to proceed?

When a person is confident in his teaching, it means he has fully understood the teaching throughout the ups and downs of his experience. This means he has benefited from it and is now willing to offer it out of compassion to his fellow creatures so that they may taste it for themselves. To know about a fact, one has to put it into practice and taste it for oneself. It is absolutely wrong to force others to accept things blindly. Nature has given us visible and invisible tools to go into all aspects of reality. Progress up the spiral requires us to learn, commit, and act on increasingly higher planes. We deceive ourselves if we think that any one of these is sufficient. To keep progressing, we must learn, commit and do. Therefore, learning, committing and doing is necessary to achieving a goal.

I personally needed something more than what I learnt from Islam. I did not want to stand still for the rest of my life just to make my ancestors happy. I wanted to find something which felt true and real to both my body and my mind. The point to remember is that some principles change in the process of time when they encounter the reality of life in a modern age. Once upon a time some people thought the earth was the centre of the universe and all the other planets went around it. However, time passed and new discoveries and new inventions ruled out this idea. When for the first time the Americans conquered the moon, some prejudiced persons committed suicide because they said man had interfered with the law of God.

Paradise and hell, for Muslims and non-Muslims

Let me speak to you frankly and openly. I express my thoughts about Islam not to insult, or to humiliate or to criticise any person or groups with bad intentions.

I am not acting out of hatred against anyone. My intention is merely an attempt to break the foundations of extremist theories and the imposition of ideas propounded by a school of thought based on the unwise interpretation of some clergy. There is a school of thought which claims that only Muslims believing in the Quran, Mohammad, etc. will go to heaven, and that all other people, regardless of how much virtue they exhibit, will go to burn in hell forever. What could be a more despicable and hatred-filled ideology? All the noble men of humanity – who sacrificed everything to plant the trees whose fruits we eat so comfortably – will go to Hell! It means all those freedom fighters, scientists, social workers, doctors, philanthropists, philosophers, religious men and women and even common men who helped us or our forefathers unselfishly are cursed to burn in hell forever simply because they do not believe in the clergy's brand of Islam! Those who gave their life for their nation and the protection of the dignity and life of common men and women, the soldiers who died fighting against invaders – they all will go to Hell. And, the likes of some terrorists, killers, evil-doers, etc. will go to Heaven because they, to their best knowledge, did everything with a belief in the Quran, Rasul, etc. Some unbiased Muslims may say, "Everyone receives results according to his/her deeds and will therefore go to either paradise or hell." If these kinds of Muslims believe in deeds, this is no doubt in agreement with the doctrine of karma which was spoken of as long ago as 600 BC, and also to the Zoroastrian principles of more than 1000 BCE.[17] This describes heaven and hell as being in this very world where beings go according to their karma. There is a Japanese story which clarifies the idea of paradise and hell. It takes the form of a conversation between Nobushige, a Samurai soldier and his Zen master.

A soldier who was curious to know about hell and paradise was advised to see a master by the name of Hakuin living in a hut in the mountains. Having gone

---

[17] Zoroastrian morality is to be summed up in the simple phrase, "good thoughts, good words, good deeds" (Humata, Hukhta, Hvarshta in Avestan). This is somehow similar to karma in Hindu beliefs.

a long way, he finally reached there. The master was making tea for himself in a small kettle hanging over burning branches in a hole in the earth. The soldier came near to the master and selfishly said: "Is there a paradise and hell?"

"Who are you?" inquired the master without paying attention to his presence (usually these are the games of a Zen master to evoke feeling and emotion in the questioners).

"I am a Samurai, from a big dynasty," the warrior replied.

"You, a Samurai soldier?" exclaimed the master. "What kind of ruler would have you as his guard? Your face looks more like that of a beggar than a samurai."

Nobushige became so angry that he began to draw his sword, but the master continued: "So, you have a sword! Your weapon is probably much too dull to cut off my head."

This time Nobushige became more furious with a red face and drew his sword seriously. The master immediately replied: "Here open the gates of hell.[18]"

At these words the Samurai perceived the master's discipline and instruction, sheathed his sword and bowed calmly with deep respect.

"Here open the gates of paradise," said the master.

In this story the master is not supposed to explain hell and paradise by way of a sermon or logic. He shows it on the spot, telling the soldier not to seek them beyond this very world. If you are calm and relaxed you are already in paradise, and if you are always agitated with anger, enmity, paranoia, etc. you are indeed in hell. According to Omar Khyyam Nishapuri Persian mathematician, astronomer and poet:

I sent my Soul through the Invisible,
Some letter of that After-life to spell:
And by and by my Soul return'd to me,
And answer'd: 'I Myself am Heav'n and Hell'

How to differentiate?

It is this version of Islam which I have denounced in my writings. I questioned the very foundations of this fanaticism. The mind should not be limited to old, dry principles. The creative mind reacts by throwing away the shell of ignorance which has dominated human beings for ages. It is a mistake to assume that

---

18 Zen Bones- Zen Flesh, by Paul reps

the way which has been imposed on us, or the way by which we have been traditionally influenced, must be followed with absolute submission. It is not a tradition we are doomed to obey forever. To me, submission or forcing people to accept a particular ideology is in fact nothing but humiliating man's dignity and creativity. And naturally our attitude and behaviours grow out of these imagined and predetermined principles which are out of sympathy with our will and what we want. It is therefore our duty to inspect the glasses through which we see the differences, the world, other people and ourselves as well, and to understand that the glasses themselves shape how we interpret the world and how we see our true nature. Established patterns of thought are powerful because they create the glasses. To my mind, the essential truth-seeker is consciously or unconsciously looking for something different. The characteristic of this searching is that it is not predetermined, nor has any ill intent behind it. At some moment, my inner being would search again for something new, and I pursued some other field of the unknown led by my curiosity, not by lengthy premeditation, but spontaneously. This perception has always made me experience things and keep on marching.

I failed on my first attempt in searching the truth but this does not mean it ends here. Dr A.P.J. Abdul Kalam has a beautiful quote. He says:

" If you fail, never give up because F.A.I.L. means "first Attempt In Learning"
- End is not the end, in fact E.N.D. means "Effort Never Dies"
- If you get No as an answer, remember, N.O, means "Next Opportunity."
So, let's be positive."

Some points from this chapter

- I was born in an educated, religious family.

- Traditionally we are bound to pass on to future generations our traditional view of Islam which we received from our ancestors.

- I was always curious to know more about those things I did not know, to know more about myself, and about how the world related to me.

- Self-knowledge was my main aim.

- Sufism emphasises self-knowing in a practical way to realise God.

- Traditional Islam concentrates on reading sutras, preaching, and obeying the precepts.

- A true religion should answer most of the questions of a seeker and not leave any empty space behind.

- Fanaticism in supporting one's own ideology at the risk of sacrificing others is nothing but religious monopoly.

- A retentive, young mind can understand what actions are good and what are bad, but we should fertilise the bed of our mind with wholesome actions.

- Following precepts, reading treatises and reciting long sutras are not going to give us practical help to know the essence of the mind.

- The adoption of philosophical ideas, religions, and different streams of thinking depend on the degree of understanding of the persons concerned.

- Islamic Sufism first developed in Iran with the understanding that knowing God is knowing oneself.

- The Islam which I learnt was based on 'form' rather than 'content'.

- Self-mortification, self-chastisement and self-harming to commemorate the death of a saint were the characteristics of the fundamental Islam I learnt.

- In the sweet days of my youth I got attracted to Islam and practised it wholeheartedly, but I did not get what I expected.

- To choose an idea is easy, but the application of the chosen idea seems difficult and it gets completely rejected by the mind if it is not in conformity with our behaviour and temperament.

- Fanaticism, enmity, hatred, revenge, conceit, etc. can plant their seeds in our mind.

- Absolute submission is a rule in some religions especially fundamental Islam.

- A wonderful power in every religion is its ability to convert a wicked man into a pure, religious one.

- To see or to believe in only one dimension of a thing risks getting enmeshed in prejudices, which we are then expected to defend to the death.

- 'Submission' is a rule in traditional Islam, but man needs perception and analysis to reach the 'truth'.

- Tradition, customs, inference, deduction, conjecture, logic and plausible reasoning are the tools by which some religious people defend their ideology.

- In some religions, salvation requires absolute obedience to a way of thinking which has been handed down by unquestioning tradition from the past up to the present.

- Purification of the mind cannot be got by sermons and commandments about what we must or must not do.

- My attitude towards Islam is to criticise positively and creatively.

- Paradise and hell can be experienced in this very world.

- Unbiased observation, which helps all of us to feel the reality of life as it is

- Self-investigation can help us come closer to ourselves, rather than to escape from ourselves.

- Some religious preachers think the quantity of their followers is more important than the quality of their teaching

- I failed in my first attempt, but a long journey starts with the first step

Chapter 3

Stepping into the World of Marxism

I would like to begin with a reference to Karl Marx's illustration of how two small creatures of nature engineer their worlds by direct action from a genetic blueprint:

> *"A spider conducts operations that resemble those of a weaver, and a bee puts to shame many an architect in the construction of her cells. But what distinguishes the worst architect from the best of bees is this, that the architect raises his structure in imagination before he erects it in reality."*
> KARL MARX, *CAPITAL*

I was young, active, enthusiastic and full of energy to pursue my natural curiosity and understand the meaning of life. In fact I failed in my first experience of investigating a new doctrine despite practicing it for years. Unfortunately I was still unsatisfied with what I achieved so far and I wanted to know more. I wanted something different, a different idea or prospect, to make me see things vividly and to stimulate my feelings. I had no inner excitement for my previous experience. Some impatient people would probably get disappointed with their first experience and consider themselves as a failure or they may consider it as their final search. They do not want to make much effort in order to take advantage of circumstances which would give them more opportunities. They think their first experiment is the beginning and the end of the whole process. They do not know that they may gain more knowledge and experience by working through their failures. Great ambitions need great patience, and continuous effort to pursue them. When desire focuses toward our victory we do not need to get disappointed, victory is certain if we do not give up. Winston Churchill said: "It is not enough that we do our best; sometimes we must do what is required." I did not regret having experienced those events; however, I was disappointed with my first experience. I was always thirsty to learn more things from different people and different sources to solve the puzzle within.

The great French sculptor Auguste Rodin once said, "Nothing is a waste of time if you use the experience wisely." Such words of wisdom result from experience.

In 1963 I started a new phase of experience.

Marxism in my family

My brother-in-law was a dedicated follower of Karl Marx, especially the Marxist–Leninist field. I witnessed him listening to the radio of the Soviet Union in the Persian language. The station was known as Radio Peik or Tude Party Radio, broadcast by the Communist Party from the Soviet Union of that time.

During the reign of Mohammad Reza Shah, listening to Peik Radio was strictly forbidden. It is true that if you prevent people by force from trying something they like, or make threats to stop them approaching something, they will certainly become more curious and greedy to investigate the forbidden things. At least that is what I believe. We question the reasons for not having the freedom to do research in other areas. Knowledge is powerful and those who obtain it, will question existing rules more as ignorance becomes a sin.

I was curious and very interested to listen to the communists' radio in secret. My brother-in-law and his friends – they were called 'comrades' – used to hold meetings at home from time to time, very cautiously and furtively. They discussed the communists' activities and talked about the philosophy of Karl Marx and Lenin's theory of revolution, all of which was new and exciting to me. I was young and curious to know what they were talking about and why they were so secretive about it. In the beginning, I could not follow their way of thinking as I was young and could get everyone in trouble if I spoke about it anywhere. However, I did not get disappointed and I did not give up. Since I was so curious, there was nothing that could stop me from knowing what their ideology is all about. I tried to come closer to them to learn what they were doing and what their ideology represented. What was the goal, and how is that so effective if put into action? I was about 15 years old. I was getting more and more interested in the most powerful ideology of that time. I was fortunate that my brother-in-law could explain Marxist–Leninist theory to me privately in simple language, breaking it down in a way that I could digest, obviously not giving me the whole prospect considering my age.

Karl Marx without a doubt and regardless of any bigotry was a good social scientist, a philosopher and the father of modern socialism and communism. What I came to learn about Marx was fascinating and I wanted to know even more. Although he was one of the greatest social thinkers during the 1800s, most of his ideas and his intellect were not recognised until after his death. He became a communist when he moved to Paris in 1843. This was when he wrote *The Economic and Philosophic Manuscripts*. These writings outlined communism which was published later. While Marx was in Paris he met the man who would become his lifelong friend and partner, Friedrich Engels. It was with Engels that he wrote *The Communist Manifesto* in 1848. Engels was a rich man and Marx from a middle-class family. Engels helped Marx survive by being one of his major sources of income during the 1850s when Marx was not able to support himself only from his writings. Marx believed that social change is what was needed for a better society, and to get social change there must be class conflict. Marx's major concern of social change was economic change. Marx's most well-known work dealt with class conflict, the opposition between the capitalists and the working class. The capitalists are also known as the bourgeoisie. Marx believed that they are the ones who are responsible for controlling the land, factories, etc. The working classes, which is also known as the proletariat, are the workers that are being exploited by the bourgeoisie.

Karl Marx was also motivated by compassion for the oppressed and the masses. We were told that Marx was a deep humanitarian; that he was possessed by the idea of helping the oppressed masses. He believed that the reason behind oppression is capitalism. As soon as this putrid system is destroyed after a time of the proletarian's rule, a new society will appear in which everyone will work and receive according to their needs. According to Marxist theory, there will be neither a state that represses individuality, nor war nor revolution, but a worldwide brotherhood of nations lasting forever. Because of these characteristics and some more scientific subjects which he proclaimed, I was deeply influenced by Marxist ideology.[19] I was happy that what I was presented with was so exciting and different from my previous

---

19 The readers can find much more knowledge about this great philosopher, his social theory and class theory in details in different books if they wish to. I've preferred to mention a brief version about him in connection with my activities in Marxism in both theory and practice. These references are enough, as I believe: "A word is enough for the wise."

experiences. I was keen to learn the methods and theories behind it, in secret of course, and try and become a comrade and joining the group. I was therefore enthusiastic to learn about the theories to be ready for joining the group.

Learning about Marxist theories- the books

My brother-in-law was happy to see my interest in Marxist philosophy and he knew I could be relied upon to keep their secrets and to be an active element in their activities as a young devotee. In order to learn about the basic teaching of Marxism, some books were given to me to read and I was given some explanations to make it easy for me to understand what I read. In this way I underwent training in the field of Marxism. I first studied these books translated in Persian language. These books were strictly forbidden at that time and the possessor of such illicit books would receive strict punishment by the government. The books were:

1. *How the Steel Was Tempered* by Nikolai Ostrovsky, a very simple and comprehensible novel which can stimulate the minds of young people to understand the struggles of the poor. Ostrovsky gave a most beautiful and attractive description of Marxist ideology, which made it easy for me to accept at my young and impressionable age.
2. *The Iron Heel* by Jack London. Jack London's novel is set in an imaginary future society in which the United States has a plan to control all financial affairs and the entire world community in order to provide and pay for their supremacy. However, this does not lead to the ending of war and elimination of crime. This novel made a deep impression on me and encouraged me to embrace the philosophy of Marxism.

London's socialist and social ideas about opposition to rule by an oligarchy[20] took hold of my mind and made me think about the suffering of the masses more deeply and our responsibility for this. Authors like George Orwell and Sinclair Lewis were influenced by this book, also Leon Trotsky and Anatole France.

3. *The Basic Principles of Marxist Philosophy* by George Politzer. This simple and concise book opened my mind to the philosophy of Marx, Hegel, Engels, and the Greek philosophers to some extent. It was interesting

---

20 Oligarchy: government by a small group of people.

and enjoyable to debate. This philosophy was explained to me in a simple way by my brother-in-law who enthusiastically took responsibility as our family teacher.

4. *Gadfly* by Ethel Lilian Voynich. She was an Irish novelist, musician and a supporter of several revolutionary causes. This novel is about the struggle of an international revolutionary in Italy. The book was very popular in the former Soviet Union and China.

This collection of books encouraged my interest in Marxist literature.

All these books were in Persian translation but could hardly found in public libraries or common bookshops. I gained a lot of knowledge by reading the books and the comrades were indeed helpful in simplify them for me. I was extremely thankful to my brother-in-law and his comrades who helped me gain a different prospective to the realities of the real world of that time, introducing valuable and informative books by famous writers to me whom I knew nothing about before. This knowledge was not diversionary but constructive.

Marxism's characteristics

Gradually my brother-in-law introduced the fundamental theories of Karl Marx into my mind. He also explained Charles Darwin's theory of evolution in a simple way so that it penetrated my mind and mesmerised me. Marxism seemed to me to be logical, as indeed were the theories of Charles Darwin, together with the interpretation of dialectical materialism which was rational and open to sensible discussion. I was indeed attracted to Marxism and I developed my knowledge by reading books and pamphlets, and also participating in the groups arranged in secret by my brother-in-law and his friends. As a matter of fact, I was educated in both the theory and the practice of the ideology. It was so exciting and precise that I was persuaded to learn more about it. At that time very few people were attracted to Marxist philosophy. I was fortunate that I found myself among the intellectuals of that time who were older than me but I could follow them because of my enthusiastic interest to the idea. Although my mother was a Muslim, she used to cooperate with the Iranian Marxist elements in some fields. For instance, she actively saved a group of Marxists and supported them in court by giving evidence which helped to release them from jail and eventually saved them from execution. I was happy that my mother had sympathy with the Marxist revolutionary doctrines. The main justification for helping and supporting the Iranian Marxists was the goal of liberating the poor from their bondage. This motivated my mother to support them.

The point which attracted me the most to the Marxism was the Marxist objective of benefiting the 'masses' and their efforts to create a classless society which was idealistic and popular at that time. In addition, I thought it is rational interpretation of the world and man were the characteristics that Marxist philosophy possessed, and they could dominate the minds of most intellectuals, leading them to show their sympathy for the suffering masses. This deep affection for people strengthened my belief in the common humanity which we all share. At that time Marxist ideology attracted me for three important reasons:

1. The rational teaching of Marxism covered the outstanding Greek philosophers, the philosophy of Hegel and Engels, and the philosophy of dialectical materialism which were rational and constructive.
2. The powerful idea of liberating the farmers and the workers from their bondage and to lead them to a happy, peaceful life.
3. Establishing a sane society where everyone has their rights and privileges.

The triple aims of liberating the working and farming classes and establishing a proletarian government to emancipate the poor from injustice, inequality and oppression were the main factors in influencing the intellectuals to develop a strong faith in Marxism, and I supported these ideas too.

Consequently my brother-in-law played an important role in building up the Marxist–Leninist ideology in my mind and in shaping a new dimension in my life. This opened up my mind to new horizons, and I found myself developing a genuine feeling of philanthropy together with a real appreciation of the depressed condition of much of humanity. It is true that our vision is limited, but we can push back the borders of our limitations. Adlai E. Stevenson Jr. said: "If we value the pursuit of knowledge, we must be free to follow wherever that search may lead us. The free mind is not a barking dog, to be tethered on a ten-foot chain."

Our knowledge may be limited to some particular idea or thought, but we can expand the boundaries of our knowledge. Based on the proverb that 'Knowledge is Power' I now found myself, at least to some extent, among intellectuals who were able to understand and argue about the world's problems in the light of Marxist philosophy. In order to show my loyalty to this group of Iranian Marxists, I voluntarily became a messenger between the comrades in the city and the masses (people) at work, especially the workers in the huge oil refinery of Abadan city to help them struggle for their rights. I was cautious neither to create any trouble for the comrades, nor to fall into the traps set by government police. I did my best to carry out my duties for the organisation. I owed this training to some of the comrades of the organisation which I was indirectly belonged to. In this way I was trained, educated, and committed to the Marxist–Leninist system in my own city, Abadan.

At high school, my subject of study was Experimental Science which was a good match with the precise and logical theories in Marxist literature. At school my knowledge was far more advanced compared to other students in my class because I was studying a wider range of scientific subjects than the limited coverage found in the school's textbooks. In the field of ecology, which was a part of my subject at high school, I gave a talk on evolution based on Darwin's theory. The students used to take notes because my interpretation went beyond our textbooks and it appeared to interest them. My teacher was also excited by my talk and encouraged other students to study more than just their textbooks. Gradually some students approached me and I arranged meetings to tell them more about the science I learnt about that went beyond science textbooks. I made good friends at school whom I studied with. I wanted to introduce them to Marxist Ideology; however, it was risky to tell them openly about Marxism, because that could put them in danger. After two and half years of studying of Marxism, I found myself more knowledgeable and confident. I was now a Marxist and now a comrade.

We carried out many different tasks depending on what was arranged by senior comrades for us to do. It was all in secret and, being a devotee, I felt responsible for carrying out messages and help more Iranians in joining the revolutionary movements.

I remained a comrade for a long time and this will continue in the next chapters.

Some points from this chapter

- The idea of Marxism came to my mind through my family.

- My inclination towards Marxism was spontaneous.

- I was attracted to Marxism because of its scientific impact on the world and humanity, leading to the liberation of the masses.

- The figures who shaped and developed Marxist ideology were great philosophers.

- Before getting involved in Marxism I was encouraged to read books on the theory of Marxism.

- Nothing is a waste of time if we use the experience wisely.

- In the realm of Marxism, I found myself mentally mature, realistic, and sympathetic to people.

- My brother-in-law was happy to see my interest in Marxist philosophy.

- I was reliable enough to keep their secrets and to be an active element in their activities as a young devotee.

- A man that has been stretched by a new experience can never go back to his old dimensions.

- At the age of 15 I stepped into the world of Marxism.

- The first experiment is neither the beginning nor the end of each process.

- According to learned men, "experience is a direct personal participation or observation, actual knowledge or contact."

- "Experience is the faculty by which a person acquires knowledge of contingent facts about the world, about ourselves and the people whom we deal with, as contrasted with reason."

- In the beginning, the Marxist ideology had a good effect on me.

- I got attracted to Marxism because it was rational and had popular appeal.

- The main thing which attracted me to Marxism was the Marxist goal of benefiting the 'masses' and the efforts to create a society without class.

- Reading some revolutionary books put me more deeply on the path of Marxism.

- I went beyond the limits of my narrow horizons, and I found myself developing a more realistic and true sense of philanthropy.

- It is true that our vision is limited, but we can push back the borders of our limitations.

- I was happy and very satisfied to find this new experience.

- At school, my subjects of study were in accord with my extracurricular studies. They both had a scientific approach and appeal.

- The Islam I practised was not powerful enough to answer all my questions concerning the reality of life.

- There were no teachers, no guidance, no sympathetic friends to show me the path I was looking for. I had to strive myself.

Chapter 4

My Military Service – The Training Where Steels are Tempered

Military service in Iran is compulsory, not voluntary. Youths who reach the age of 18 are required to spend the next two years in the armed forces. This service takes two years of the life of all young men, although most of them do not want to undergo this period of military discipline which is generally regarded as a waste of their time. There is no escape from this requirement, unless one can obtain total exemption from all forms of military duty, but this is not easy to gain. Before one can start looking for a job, plan to get married and settle down, get a passport, driving license, or other things, this military service is compulsory. The wages (salary) are so low that a young boy is hardly to maintain himself even for one day. However, I was fortunate that I did not serve my period of military duty as an ordinary soldier.

In 1967 I finished my high school education and got my diploma in the field of Experimental Science. Then I had to do my military service. The two years of military service were divided into:

1. Six months in garrisons with rigorous military training.
2. Eighteen months in villages as a teacher.

Military education and training is a process which intends to establish and improve the capabilities of military personnel in their respective roles and also to act as reserve forces in case of a new war breaking out. The hard training is common to all with no exception to any ranks or positions.

In some countries military education can be a voluntary or compulsory duty, but in Iran it was (is) compulsory. Before any person gets authorisation to operate technical equipment or be on the battlefield, they must take a medical and often a physical test. If passed, they may begin primary training. Some soldiers can get medical exemption if they fail the medical test, but it will be hard for them to get a job or driving license.

The primary training is recruit training. Recruit training attempts to teach the basic information and training in techniques necessary to be an effective service member.

To achieve this, service members are drilled physically, technically and psychologically. The drill instructor has the task of making the service members fit for military use. Those who have been in the military especially at the time of Shah (the King), are aware of this process.

After finishing basic training, many service members undergo advanced training more in line with their chosen or assigned specialties. In advanced training, military technology and equipment is often taught. This kind of strong discipline and training was mostly inspired by the US to rebuild the Shah's military at that time.

Iran, at the time of Mohammad Reza Shah was the biggest recipient of American and British military equipment in the 1970s and quickly became a major power. The Shah bought some of the most advanced weapons from the West for the Iranian military as a defence. He in fact succeeded in making Iran one of the best equipped militaries in the region, in terms of both quality and quantity. Projections from the 1970s made it clear that he had innovative plans to make Iran into one of the most powerful conventional military forces in the world.

On the eve of the Iranian Revolution, the country's army (previous army) was described as the fifth largest in the world. If the Shah's ambitions were fulfilled, it would likely have been far larger with an enormous fleet of modern tanks and helicopters. Because of the same military equipment the country survived for years during the Iran–Iraq war. Military training in such advanced military equipment was indeed systematic and sophisticated.

However, because we were supposed to serve in the villages as teachers, we did not need to have advanced training, but training in garrison duties was compulsory for every recruit. We were in fact ordinary soldiers during the six months of basic training which were hard and arduous. We were not given any training in advanced matters, of the kind taught in many military academies.

Sepah-e Danesh, a part of white revolution[21]

The time in the villages was spent as teachers – what is known as 'Sepah-e Danesh' or the army of knowledge. This initiative was a part of the 'White Revolution' of the Shah and the People in order to educate villagers all over Iran. The White Revolution aimed at pushing the villages of Iran onto the level of the most modernised countries in the process of time.

According to some statistics, in Iran nearly 41% of villagers were illiterate at that time and thus could not foster productivity. There were more reasons as to why the Shah initiated Literacy Corps to reconstruct the villages. I'm not going to go to the details as there are books written in this field.

Failure in converting the villagers to Marxism

We were appointed as teachers in villages working as the representatives of the Shah because we were literate soldiers known as Literacy Corps, and our rank in the military was higher than ordinary soldiers. With my interest in the ideology of Marxism, I thought this would be a good opportunity for me both to educate the villagers as part of my duties and to awaken them to their rights according to the Marxist ideology in which I had been trained. I tried my best in different ways to convince the farmers of their rights while I was with them during my service. I was supported by my friends in different villages, but fortunately or unfortunately the villagers did not show any interest in this and they did not respond to my initiatives in changing their present status. Perhaps it was not a proper or suitable time to awaken them to the Marxist theory of revolution or maybe they were satisfied with their way of living and did not want more than that. Anyhow, I loved them and I wanted to help them by some means or other. Ultimately, however, I got disappointed with my efforts to introduce them to Marxism, so I tried to educate them in accordance with the syllabus which I had been appointed to teach by the government. I had to teach two different classes in the village. These classes were: 1. Day classes for children. 2. Night classes for adults. I not only performed my duty to educate them, but I also helped them in agriculture, making bridges and roads. Being the representative of the Shah in the villages, I could get financial supports from the government to help the villagers to develop their villages.

---

21 The White Revolution or the Shah and People Revolution was a reform in Iran organised in 1963 by the late Mohammad Reza Pahlavi and lasted until the beginning of Islamists' revolution. It consisted of several elements including land reform for the farmers, sale of some state-owned factories to finance this land reform, construction of an expanded road, rail and air network, a number of dam and irrigation projects, the eradication of diseases such as malaria, the encouragement and support of industrial growth, liberation of women, nationalisation of forests and pastures, establishing of health corps (Sepah-e-Behdasht) and literacy corps (Sepah-e-Danesh).of several elements.

I found some leftist friends in other villages who had encountered the same problems and same difficulties to enliven the villagers' movement. They had also tried to organise a syndicate to unite the peasants, but found no way at that time to stimulate the peasants to bring them together to demand their rights. This was not because of our lack of knowledge or our inability to propagate the theory of Marxism, but the circumstances in the villages of Iran were quite different from those in China or Cuba. For the same reason the intellectuals and freedom fighters, all the dissidents of that time failed in fulfilling their ambition in overthrowing the government. There was no interest in hearing about the doctrines of Marxism–Leninism, let alone any ideas of organising a general uprising of the villagers or farmers. I could see that these theories were not an immediate prescription offering a solution to every problem of village life. They did not promise to perform miracles which would transform every aspect of rural life. My friends (comrades) and myself did our best to awaken the villagers to their rights but it was all in vain. Being disappointed with the reaction of the villagers, I used to contact my comrades in different villages, both far and near, where they were on duty in order to discuss our problems and difficulties. I had meetings with them occasionally just to develop our mutual understanding and to increase our knowledge in this field. We came to understand that the circumstances in the villages could not be changed as quickly as we had hoped, and our motivation was not strong enough to make them move. Even our comrades in the cities did their best, but with no result.

Therefore, when we met each other from time to time, we discussed our own affairs and how to make plans for the future of Iran. My friends and I were not key directors among the Iranian Marxists, but simply true and faithful members of a group. We did our best to demonstrate our sympathy with the organisation of which we were members by offering to help wherever we could. Although we were committed followers, we never saw our leaders at all and we had no idea about their future plans. This was a point which always occupied the minds of myself and my friends as we wondered why we had no contact with the leaders whose plans were passed down to us as commands which must be obeyed without question. For example, we received pamphlets, newsletters, bulletins and other Marxist literature from unknown messengers (couriers) without knowing about the source. When I asked my close comrades about these secretive communications being sent to their own supporters, my friends convinced me of the importance of keeping the leaders safe, even though our own lives were more in danger than those of the leaders because we were moving to different places and distributing revolutionary bulletins by day and by night. In all circumstances we had to obey the rules under which we were trained. Some Marxist groups were active in cities, both in Tehran and the North, but we did not have access to them for security reasons. For the first time I felt a kind of dishonesty in the leaders who were unknown and we (the sympathisers) were in danger. I belonged to the Marxist group in my own city of Abadan.

After 18 years of servicing and teaching in the villages, my friends and I left, but with the help of the villagers and with the financial contribution from the government we could help them build some bridges, develop agriculture and we also educated the children and the adults. We failed in bringing Marxist-Leninist theories in villages, but we succeeded in helping them in education and development.

Some points from this chapter

- I was appointed as a teacher to educate the villagers.

- My military service divided into two parts: six months in garrison, and eighteen months in villages.

- Military education and training taught a useful discipline, even though it was very hard.

- Rigorous military training makes a man strong in body and mind.

- The Knowledge Corps or 'Sepah-e Danesh' were initiated by the Shah of Iran as part of the 'White Revolution'.

- The Shah's army was built and inspired by the US army.

- In the villages I thought I could stimulate the villagers with the introduction of Marxist theories.

My Journey to Zen

- I was hoping that I'd put the theory of Marxism among the farmers and the villagers.

- At that time the villagers were not so mature in politics to be able to comprehend this 'theory'.

- Apart from Marxist theory, I helped my people in the villages in other respects.

- Literate soldiers were appointed as teachers to educate villagers in many ways.

- My commitment as a Marxist was to awaken the villagers to their rights.

- Marxist theory was not a prescription for immediate results for Iran's proletarians.

- We received commandments from leaders unknown to us.

- We were obedient to our Marxist's superiors.

- We, the committed followers, were more in danger than the so-called the leaders.

- It was not fair to know nothing about the leaders for whom we sacrifice.

- A suspicion of dishonesty about the Iranian Marxist leaders started in me

Chapter 5

Travelling to India

After I finished my military service of eighteen months in the villages, I decided to go abroad for higher studies. I would have been happy to stay and study in my own country. However, due to a shortage of places in the universities, the entrance exams were deliberately made so difficult that the vast majority of applicants met with failure. For example, there might be 500,000 applications for only 20 places. This represented a great waste of talent and this policy forced many graduate students to go to other countries where they found it easier to obtain a university place. I decided to go to India for my postgraduate studies. I chose India because 1. It was cheaper compared with European countries. 2. It was near Iran and it was easy to visit my family. 3. India is a land of wonders with many outstanding thinkers. 4. There were no entrance exams.

Training in a Christian college

In the year 1968 I set out for India. When I arrived I did not know much English. In order to join universities, students have to learn English as a preparatory subject. In the city of Pune[22] there was a cheap, religious college called Spicer Memorial College. This was a Seventh Day Adventist Christian college providing holistic education for their church members, not very far from the centre of Pune. A six-month English training course plus studying the Bible were compulsory subjects at the college. The students of this church college had to attend classes both in English and the Bible, the holy teachings of Jesus Christ.

---

22 Pune is the second largest city in Maharashtra state. Pune University is very famous and it is known as the 'Oxford of the East' because of its many educational institutes.

The college was indeed a good place for students to come to know about Christianity and simultaneously to improve their command of the English language. The atmosphere there was friendly and instructive. Some foreign students were not interested in attending church to hear the evening sermons. They thought it was waste of time, but for me it was a good opportunity to learn something more about another religion. As a matter of fact I was indeed fortunate to come closer to another school of thought to learn and to experience more which was a part of my research. Brian Herbert says: "The capacity to learn is a gift, the ability to learn is a skill; the willingness to learn is a choice." In fact I was hitting two birds with one stone, learning English and acquiring the wisdom of Jesus Christ.

I thought to know something is better than to be reluctant to a good teaching, the teaching of a great religious leader. I found moral points in Christianity which are similar to other religions. I came to appreciate the moral teaching of Christ and his life story, and the kind of enlightenment he introduced to the world. Out of my love for true religious leaders, I have deep respect for Jesus Christ and the principles of Christianity.

The gist I learned from Christianity

Christianity is the world's most popular religion by number of his followers. It is a religion of those called Christians and a moralistic like other religions, with only one God. It is the largest religion in the world and is based on the life and teachings of Jesus Christ.

His followers called him a preacher, teacher, healer, and prophet from ancient Judea. Moreover his disciples believed him to be much more than that: they believed that Jesus was the only son of God who was sent down to earth to guide people to a true life.

Jesus is a religious leader whose life and teachings are recorded in the Bible's New Testament. He is a central figure in Christianity and is emulated as the incarnation of God by many Christians all over the world.

Jesus led a morally perfect life with moral teaching. He was the embodiment of all virtues that he preached during his successful and eventful ministry for years.

Similarities

Later I came to know about the moral similarities in Buddhism and Christianity. Both religions stress ethical living, compassion/love to other people.

Like Buddhism, Christianity also encourages followers to take steps to improve their wellbeing. Like Christianity, Buddhism has a strong devotional aspect. This is characterised by faith in the Buddha. Both of them preached the Truth without any distinction

They taught the importance of love, compassion, brotherhood, enlightenment through prayer and meditation, and other important moral points.

Here is a story which illustrates the similarity of good moral points of the Bible with other religions:

A university student while visiting Gasan (a Zen master) asked him: "Have you ever read the Christian Bible?"

"No, read it to me," said Gasan.

The student opened the Bible and read from St Matthew: "And why take you thought for raiment? Consider the lilies of the field, how they grow. They toil not, neither do they spin, and yet I say unto you that even Solomon in all his glory was not arrayed like one of these…Take therefore no thought for the morrow, for the morrow shall take thought for the things of itself."

Gasan said: "Whoever uttered those words I consider an enlightened man."

The student continued reading: "Ask and it shall be given you, seek and you shall find, knock and it shall be opened unto you. For everyone that asks receives, and he that seeks finds, and to him that knocks, it shall be opened."

Gasan remarked: "That's excellent. Whoever said that is not far from Buddhahood."[23]

This story tells us the path of enlightenment is one but the ways are different.

I was able to gain valuable experience at Spicer College, where I was taught that Jesus is the central figure of the Bible. His birth as the Jewish Messiah and Saviour of the world was prophesied by Old Testament authors.

Continuous Marxist Activities: the influence of Marxism

But to be honest, my mind was so influenced by Marxist ideology that it was hard to replace Marxism quickly with some other ideas. Frankly the notion of Marxism followed me like a shadow. I had worked in Marxism for years both in theory and practice and was not so easy for me to suddenly jump to another doctrine in a couple of months or so. I did not want to boast about myself of having this or that faith temporarily. In fact there was not enough space to plant all these new ideas in the old soil of my mind. On the

---
23 *Zen Bones, Zen Flesh.*

other hand, I did not want to jump from one branch of practice to another without full knowledge of what I was doing. I was not a tourist, wanting to add different events or information to my diary of life just for fun. In simple words, Marxism had already occupied a strong place in my mind and could hardly be replaced by another teaching unless the new teaching was clearly superior to the older ideas or gave me a deep shock to jolt me out of my established way of thinking. Although I attended the church classes almost every day, they did not affect my previous, established way of thinking. During my six months' training at Spicer College I was able to gain a good knowledge of Christianity and I was happy that my English was good enough to join a university. I thanked a lot to the Spicer College, the manager, the priest and those who arranged facilities to learn Christianity and others and to improve my English language there. I never forget their sincere cooperation and compassion.

My Marxist organisation

After finishing the English course at Spicer College I joined Pune University. There were many Iranian students studying in Pune. Most of them were 'leftists' and opposed to the policy of the Shah. I joined the Iranian Marxist Association in Pune which had many active members who had links with other organisations all over India. We belonged to a Marxist group known as 'The Organisation of Iranian People's Fedai Guerrillas'. This organisation emerged as a radical Marxist–Leninist movement in Iran in opposition to the Shah of Iran, intending to overthrow the Pahlavi regime. The group fought against the government of Mohammad Reza Shah. The organisation was the product of the merger of two smaller groups of revolutionaries, the Jazani–Zarif group and the Ahmadzadeh–Pooyan–Meftahi group. The Jazani–Zarif group's members were former members of the youth organisation of the Tude Party of which I was already aware when I was living in Iran. The second group's members were mostly followers of the National Front and its affiliated organisations.

The first meeting was organised in 1963 by Bizhan Jazani and his comrades. By 1966, when Hassan Zia-Zarifi and Jazani got together, they had reached the conclusion that the powerful American influence in Iran and the repression of liberal dissidents in Iran had made peaceful activism entirely ineffective. Armed struggle was therefore viewed as the sole effective way to liberation. After the subsequent arrest and murder of some of these guerrillas, the two groups officially united and the Organisation of Iranian People's Fedai Guerrillas came into existence.

In the meantime, internal discussions on the issues of revolution and the regime's nature were under way amongst the Fedaian which resulted in several rifts in the Organisation. The means and methods of struggle, together with policies towards the expected new government were the top priorities. Later some members were scattered among different countries and some remained in India – a 'democratic country'. India was a safe place for their activities. Having had a background in Marxism, I also joined them in different activities and attended their meetings. There were many Iranian associations all over India and I belonged to the Pune branch. Many Iranian students resided in this city because of the good climate, stimulating cultural atmosphere and the well-known university.

For several reasons I had to move to the city of Hyderabad in the south of India. I was transferred from Pune University to Osmania University and I studied philosophy in that university. I had my links with my communist brothers and sisters (the comrades) throughout India. I was a key element in their activities in Hyderabad. In Hyderabad, I not only contacted the Iranian association, but I was also drawn to the Indian pro-Maoist organisation that was active in the villages. This link was both political and philanthropic, working in the service of the people. For example, in 1977 there was a cyclone and heavy rain in Andhra Pradesh, including the state capital, Hyderabad. It affected eight districts, caused the death of 10,000 people and damaged 1,014,800 houses. All the Iranian leftists gave charitable help to those people who were affected. They all came to Hyderabad with presents to offer to the affected people as a direct donation given out of sympathy.

Helping the flood-affected as a philanthropic act

Many university students all over India gathered in Hyderabad and we all went to the affected area. The cyclone was very destructive and we went in among the people to distribute donations, such as rice, grain, dried bread, clothes and medicine. Later, lunch was served to the cyclone victims by the local services. The food was not regarded as edible by ordinary people, but the famine-stricken ate it so voraciously that it showed they had not eaten anything for days. To show my sympathy, I also sat beside them in a long line on open ground in order to taste the food they had been given. It is true to say the food was so horrible that only a starving person would dare to eat it, but they just needed something to fill the stomach and prevent them from dying. None of the students or the new visitors wanted to sit with the suffering people in order to taste the food they were eating. I was not hungry because the students were served separately. The purpose of eating with them was to show them that I was one of them and not separate from them. I wanted to show solidarity. Besides, I was curious to taste the food that starving people eat. I wanted to be closer to the affected people. My friends were surprised by my action, but at the same time they appreciated it. Indirectly I wanted to tell my friends that if they are aligned with the masses, they needed to be closer to them in order to understand them. It was a precious experience for me. To shout slogans without knowing the feelings of the masses shows only superficial sympathy and is no use in the depths of a crisis. To realise a farmer's problems or to understand the condition of a worker is to feel them, to be closer to them or to work with them. To understand about starving people, you need to live with them, eat with them and to develop sympathy with them. This is what differentiates between a true devotee and an ordinary person.

In the evening after the dinner we had a big gathering and some of the students had articles to read, sent by other students. I also had a poem in my mind. I expressed it wholeheartedly and it was welcomed by the students. When we left the village, it was clear that the inhabitants were happy and thankful for the donations they had received from us. Our act was both political and philanthropic.

A panic in the hotel

Being very tired by my long exertions in this field, I decided to go to a neighbouring country for rest and study. Afghanistan was nearby and relatively cheap to visit. So during our college holidays a friend, Abbas, and I decided to go to Afghanistan for some recreation and to see some of the ancient monuments there. In Kabul we hired a room in a delightful hotel outside the city. This cheap hotel was not far from the city in beautiful surroundings, including fruit trees which covered the whole compound. This hotel was not very busy, in fact as far as we could tell the rooms were almost empty. So we enjoyed a pleasant environment which was suitable for study and relaxation. We had brought some of the revolutionary books from India to study during our holiday. We thought that Afghanistan was a democratic country like India. All the books were in the Persian language, including a famous work written by the renowned Iranian Marxist–Leninist Mr Parviz Pooyan, *Armed Struggle*,

Both Strategy and Tactics. This book was encouraging people in various ways to overthrow the government. Among other books we had brought were some works by Marxist extremists, encouraging people to start an armed struggle against their capitalist government. I should mention that in Afghanistan Zaher Shah, the King, was ruling and the government was strictly against Marxism and extremists. We also bought some books from booksellers in Kabul. It was holiday time in our college, so we had time to read. Sometimes we used to sit with the manager of the hotel discussing the political situation in Afghanistan without knowing that the manager was a dedicated supporter of the government. Thinking the hotel was a safe place, we put all the books on the shelf of our room, where they were clearly visible. One thing we were not aware of was the peculiar behaviour of the hotel manager during our stay there. We never suspect him as a government informer. We used to answer almost all his suspicious questions frankly.

The manager of the hotel used to come to our room time to time asking us about our student's activities in India and probably in Afghanistan. We had nothing to tell him about Afghanistan but from our simplicity we told them about the political situation of Iran not knowing that he was cautiously and mysteriously acquiring information from us. He was pretending that he was against the tyrannical regime of Afghanistan to see our reaction and our comment. He sometimes looked at the books to know about them. He was not so educated and seemed to be illiterate but he was curious to know more about us. Neither Abbas nor me suspected him as a government informer.

Some days later in the evening we happened to hear the noise of a car outside in the compound. We were at the first floor of the hotel. I went to the window and saw a car with three men in ordinary clothes talking to the manager. Their behaviour and their way of talking to each other seemed strange and peculiar. Sometimes they looked up at the room where we were residing. I suddenly felt we might be in danger and asked my friend to come and check whether I was right. He also agreed that their behaviour looked strange. I was sure they were about to come up to our room. We feared that if they found the books about revolution we really would be in trouble and might not get back to India to our college in time or most probably we were put in detention for unknown period with no support even from our own government as we were dissident to them, and if that happened our circumstances became more complicated. I immediately took down all the revolutionary books from the bookshelf, but I did not know where to hide them in just a few minutes in that small room. An idea came to my mind and I told Abbas to check whether the next-door room was empty. He said nearly all of the rooms were empty. So we went to the next empty room and pushed the books as far as possible up the chimney of the fireplace and came back to our room. We washed our hands, which smelled of smoke and were black with soot, then we sat down in our chairs and looked relaxed apparently listening to Afghan music from radio. We could control ourselves with no fear or excitement, waiting for them. About a few minutes later three policemen knocked at door. Before we opened the door, they again pounded more firmly. We calmly opened the door, and they showed their identity and rushed into our room checking everywhere and everything. They went through our library but fortunately all they discovered were ordinary books which could be found in any bookshop. We had bought the books in the city and they were all about psychology and philosophy and had nothing to do with politics. However, they were looking for something more, books, pamphlets, arms, and other illegal materials which could be used against the government. They even pushed their hands up the chimney of our room, but they found nothing. Finally, they started questioning in a sweet language of Afghan-Farsi to us as to why we were in Afghanistan.

- Are you Iranian brothers?
- We happily said, yes
- What are your names?
- Khosrow, Abbas, we said
- How long have you been here?
- About two weeks
- Where are you coming from?
- India
- What are you doing here in Afghanistan?
- We have come for recreation Sir, and we are going back about next two weeks
- What are you?
- We are college students
- Your ID please
- We showed them our university ID and told them that we had come for a short holiday.

We were happy that they could find no incriminating evidence. They took all the ordinary books with them, saying they would investigate them, then they left us. We immediately went to the manager and complained about the police behaviour. He tried to pretend that he knew nothing about the matter, but we were sure that it was this manager who had reported us. After a few days we immediately changed our hotel and hid the books in a safe place.

Meeting Afghan friends

We had still 15 days more to stay in Kabul but we did not want to stay in hotels any longer. After the incident in the hotel we needed some recreation to come out of the bitter experience we had. We were looking for a safe place to spend our remaining days, and while we were walking in a park in Kabul city we came across some young boys (of our age) in a park. When we said we were Iranians they felt happy and we became friends as if we had known each other for ages. We told them that we had come to Kabul for a short visit and we were going back to India to continue our studies. We also told them that we did not like to stay in hotels any more. We preferred not to tell them about our problem in the hotel or other issues.

The Afghans are indeed a kind and warm-hearted people. Their culture is somehow close to our culture and our language is same. They respect foreigners and they have especial respect for Iranians and their neighbours. They do not think of Iranians as foreigners to them, they think of Iranians as their brothers and sisters. We were called 'Iranian brothers' by them. We felt relaxed while we were with them. When we told them we had no place to live and hotels were not suitable place for us, they offered us a room belonging to their relatives to stay in without charging any money. We had two weeks more to stay in Afghanistan. They took us to some places of interest outside Kabul which we liked. They sometimes invited us to their house to introduce us to their family. Then they suggested taking us to some places of interest in Kabul. First we visited Mohammad Nadir Shah's Tomb. His tomb sits atop Maranjan Hill or (Tapeye Marajan), home of the annual Nauroz kite-flying festival. Then we visited Kabul Zoo. It is the most popular attraction there. It is said that the pairs of lions were donated by China. We also visited Kabul Museum which was interesting and beautiful. We had lovely days with our Afghani friends. Before leaving them, we bought a beautiful bookshelf for them to appreciate their hospitality. We said goodbye to them and set forth for India. We were happy that we could overcome the stress and the anxiety of the hotel incident.

Panic again, this time in the custom duties

According to a proverb, "When misfortunes come, they come one after another."

We were happy that we passed the danger we had in Afghanistan, and had some fun and good days with our Afghani friends before we went back to India. We never knew that we were about to experience another misfortune.

While going back to India we were checked at the Afghan–Indian border by the officials. We did not know that they might check us because we were not checked when we entered the country. The customs officer checked everything and finally he found the illicit books. As a matter of fact we could have destroyed the books before leaving the country, but the books belonged to the Iranian library in Hyderabad and we had to return them safely for the use of others.

"What are these?" the custom officer asked us.

"Books."

"Where did you get them?" My friend and I looked at each other and said nothing.

"You! I'm asking you. Where did you get these books from?"

"We bought them from bookstalls in the city." But the customs officer knew that books such as these were never sold in bookstalls or bookshops.

"Which bookstall did you buy them from?"

"Sir, we are not familiar with this city. We are university students and we bought these books very cheaply."

"Cheap or expensive, these are illicit books and you are not allowed to have them."

"Yes, we know and it is our mistake, we confessed."

Then the officer ordered one of his subordinates to take us to a room for further investigation, although our bus was waiting to take all the passengers across the Afghan border and back to India. We were young and started requesting the officer to let us go free, telling him that we had to be in our class at the university on time and we might miss the bus which was waiting for us at the border. We asked him again to release us. The chief officer came to see us for a second time and he said that we had to stay there till the main investigator came. A good idea came to my mind. I told my friend to offer him some money to buy something for his family as a gift from the friendly Iranians – of course, not in the sense of offering a bribe. My friend did not dare to do this, so I called the main police officer and asked him to listen to me for at least five minutes. I explained to him that we were students and did not know that these materials were forbidden. I said we had to go back to India and we had to catch this bus in time. I told the customs officer that we had some Afghanis (Afghanistan's currency) and we could not use them in Afghanistan. I asked him to accept the money as a gift from his Iranian brothers. This offer delighted him and impressed him. He accepted our offer and let us go free. He said that I could give the money to his colleague so that they could share it with each other. So we were fortunately allowed to get out of there. The kind bus driver was still waiting for us and we could catch the bus in time outside the Afghanistan border. The bus left the border for Amritsar, the city on the Indian side of the border. We did not enjoy our trip, but we certainly gained some useful experience and came back to India.

Herman Hesse says; "I have always believed, and I still believe, that whatever good or bad fortune may come our way we can always give it meaning and transform it into something of value."

Dangerous activities

The Iranian followers of Russian Marxists and Chinese Marxists were cooperating with each other both in Hyderabad and other cities, but with a little conflict in strategy and tactics. Their relationship was friendly but also secretive. The theory of Mao was to seize the cities via the villages, and our duty was to awaken the villagers to their rights and to stimulate them into an uprising. However, both the Indian and Iranian students concentrated their activities on cities. Although this was more dangerous, we believed it would be more effective. The strategy to be followed was one of attack and escape (a sporadic fight). As a matter of fact, I was unknowingly getting involved in the violent part of Marxist theory as interpreted by the so-called theoreticians, but I was not aware of it being put into practice.

At the initial stage of our activities, we were ordered to operate at midnight according to a methodical, clear plan. We had to prepare the revolutionary materials to spread to different parts of Hyderabad city where the majority of people could see them. It was a risky and dangerous task because at that time the State government had imposed a curfew at night. The reason for the curfew was that the Maoists were expanding their activities over a wide range in the city. In defiance of the curfew, we had to paste the posters of the martyrs and the pictures of political prisoners on the walls of the city, and to distribute Night Newsletters all over the city centre as a way of making our protest. We were cautious and kept away from police or patrols. We were also commanded to confront the police as violently as we could, unless the circumstances seemed too risky or dangerous for us. We were trained in a system of intermittent fighting. I was young and full of energy, and indeed a zealous follower of the ideology. Slowly I was going deeper into the revolutionary system. During this process, we were becoming a serious and tight-knit band, preparing to go against our so-called enemies and working out how to confront them.

At that time violence was a part of the doctrine of both Marxist–Leninists and Maoists without exception. This made me think about the 'Way' which I had been following with my comrades for years with constructive expectations. I needed to sit and think deeply about where I was going. I was so involved and so overwhelmed by the revolutionary movement that I did not know what my purpose was and where I was going. I had become like a storm-tossed ship with no compass, riding on the waves going nowhere. I forgot my own identity, my character and my morals. I was in fact following the team blindly with no aim and with no intelligent plan behind me. As a matter of fact, my first interest was in the scientific importance of Marxism, but now I found myself in a sticky marsh of grudge, aversion, revenge and maybe something worse. This kind of imposition and absolute obedience was shaped in me gradually, which made it hard to escape from this predicament. I started to think about the way I had chosen and to question myself. In fact, questioning oneself sincerely leads to improvement.

Only by taking responsibility for oneself, to the greatest extent possible, can one ever be free, and only a free person can make responsible choices, between right and wrong, true and untrue, human or inhuman. Now I found myself heavily involved in Marxist-Leninist doctrine with Mao's motto of liberating the people through the use of violence. I could not avoid the issue any more. I had to stop and think before entering into the harder parts of this path. I had either to accept a policy which would cause conflict and confrontation, or I could choose to attend my college regularly and concentrate on my studies instead. Saving people at the cost of killing the same people was not logical and to my mind this seemed unacceptable. On the one hand, the aim of Marxism seemed to be democratic and rational, but on the other hand I did not want to use force at the cost of harming or killing human beings. For me, a human being is a human being whether he is a policeman, a soldier or an ordinary person. It was hard for me to condone violence or to harm others in order to achieve my aim. I was working for the people, not against them. This was the way I was choosing in my life. I had this conflict going on within myself for months. It seemed to me that Marxism was like a very beautiful flower, but it was also full of thorns. If one approaches too close to the flower or grasps it in the wrong way, one may be terribly hurt. The following incident affected me so badly that I decided to reassess my ideas about Marxism forever. The story goes as follows:

A curfew had been imposed at night in Hyderabad city of Andhra Pradesh as an emergency measure by the state government. My friends (the comrades) and I were to carry out our operations at night. The whole group was divided into two separate units, each one to carry out its duties in different parts of the city without the knowledge of the other. We started pasting posters on the walls of important places in the city in support of our comrades who were either in jail or who had been killed both in Iran and Hyderabad states. But according to the rule of the state government, disobedience to the law meant the likelihood of severe punishment, especially during a state of emergency which had already been declared by the government. As usual, we dressed all in black with soft shoes, carrying with us buckets of gum, bundles of posters, and big brushes to paste the posters onto walls, and to distribute the bulletins where necessary. At the same time, we were to spread newsletters throughout the city centre. We started in a certain place and slowly marched towards a big state bank. We began pasting the posters onto the big walls of the bank in front of the Iranians' meeting place in the centre of the city. It was nearly 2 am While I was busy pasting the posters outside the bank, two night-policemen saw me and became suspicious. At the same time my friend was in the bank's compound getting the posters ready. As I was walking away, the policemen ordered me to stop and stand still. If I stopped they would certainly arrest me, beat me severely and take me to the police station. They were even allowed to kill me. I preferred to run away from the scene, but my friend who was round the back of the bank was stopped by another policeman for investigation. He did not want to be arrested by them and he wanted to get away from them. As a result, he scuffled with the police, injured one policeman very badly on the face with a knuckleduster and then he ran away. He was lucky he was not arrested or killed. I also ran as fast as I could in the lanes of the city which I was quite familiar with them. While I was running fast, the night's dogs (vagrant dogs) which usually appear at nights started chasing me incited by the police in the zigzag lanes for my unusual run, but I could get rid of them anyhow. Seeing my friend beating the two ordinary policemen in front of my eyes was a shock to me because I did not expect this violence to happen so brutally. I never expected my friend to use force to save himself. I had already been advised by our team to use weapons such as a knife, knuckleduster or a club against our so-called enemies in order to defend myself, but I never obeyed this command. For months I felt regret about the policemen who were injured by our team. This incident made me think seriously to decide whether I wanted to continue to be involved with this organisation or not. One problem was that the team might suggest the use of lethal arms, such as a revolver, gun, rifle or grenade, and other deadly weapons, depending on the decision of our unseen leaders.

Breaking off relations

In our special meetings which were held usually once a week, I dared to criticise the team although it was usually forbidden to criticise in the framework of such organisations. Out of my sense of compassion I told them that violence was totally inhuman and might cause the downfall of the organisation before long. But my criticism had no effect on them. To my surprise they reacted negatively and called me a coward or timid, and showed no response to the sympathy which I showed for the policemen injured by one of our comrades. I felt very badly humiliated by the group who commanded me harshly: "If you don't beat, you will be beaten. If you don't kill, you will be killed. If you want to stay with us, you have to follow the same procedures as we do." This was the warning I received from one of the comrades. It was hard for me to go along with such violence from the group of which I was a member. I had been with them for years and had gathered a lot of information. As an intimate member of the unit it was not easy for me to leave their organisation, even though I was finding some of their principles horrific. I needed to bring up some excuse to free myself from their absolute domination. My friends demanded more reasons from me as why I should be kind to the enemy who had confronted us face to face. But I could not make them understand my own reasoning and how I wanted to express my sympathy for the police. According to them, being kind to one's enemies was not the way to liberate the masses. They would certainly laugh at me for being so kind to these people. I could not convince them of my own views, but I could not accept their reasoning either. It is like two persons in front of each other with two different languages and they want to convince each other on a matter of logic.

In order to reduce my contact with the group I had to approach them with care and respect. Therefore I made myself very busy with my university studies. This was the best indirect way to withdraw from them. Gradually I concentrated more and more on my studies and rarely saw my 'comrades', and in this way my connection became less and less. It was not very easy to sever my relationship with them, but eventually I managed to cut all my ties.

I do not personally want to criticise Marxist theory although it has been subjected to widespread criticism and most of Marx's ten cardinal points (*The Communist Manifesto*) are now being questioned. I was not a Marxist theoretician, but I was a true devotee for years who gave some of his life to the cause but with no spiritual benefit neither for me nor for other. During the course of human progress, we now find that the ten points of Karl Marx have brought no practical benefit. Regarding religion, Marx said that religions are the opiate of the masses. He might be right to some extent regarding some reactionary religions, but Marx wanted to criticise all the world's religions without exception even though he had no knowledge of some of them. Dalai Lama says; "Love and compassion are true religions to me, but to develop this, we do not need to believe in any religion."

Some points from this chapter

- In 1968 I went to India for postgraduate studies.

- I came to appreciate the moral teaching of Christ and his life story, and the kind of enlightenment he introduced to the world.

- Out of my love for true religious leaders, I have deep respect for Jesus Christ and the principles of Christianity.

- The code of conduct in Christianity is the same in many religions.

- I obtained some knowledge about Christianity at Spicer Memorial College.

- I never wanted to jump from one branch of practice to another without full knowledge of what I was doing.

- Coming out of the framework of Marxist organisation is not so easy.

- Marxism was so deep in my mind that it could not be replaced by Christianity.

- I continued my revolutionary activities with the Iranian Association in Pune City, India.

- The most active Marxist branch in India was the Organisation of Iranian People's Fedai Guerrillas. I supported them.

- I had to go to the city of Hyderabad to support my comrades there.

- To understand workers or farmers properly is to feel for them and to work with them.

- The villagers were happy and thankful for our donations.

- I was associating with both Russian Marxists and Chinese Marxists.

- I encountered violence in Marxism. Violence was a part of the ideology at that time.

- I got involved in violence but this happened unexpectedly. I did not anticipate that I would be involved in violence.

- My mind could not accept violence of any kind.

- I needed to reconsider my relationship with the Marxists.

- I was always criticised by my team whenever I spoke out against their violence.

- I did not want to harm human beings in order to attain my purposes.

- In our revolutionary training, we were instructed in systems of guerrilla warfare.

- Marxism could not lead me to the 'Way'.

- I withdrew from my team and concentrated on my university studies.

- Using force or injuring and killing people did not agree with my nature.

- If a religion does not cope with modern scientific needs it'll of course be the "opiate of the masses" according to Karl Marx.

- It is said that, love and compassion are true religions, but to develop this human characteristicy, we do not need to believe in any religion.

Chapter 6
Theory and Practice

*"In theory, theory and practice are the same.
In practice they are not."*
ALBERT EINSTEIN

The power of mind in serving oneself and others

The mind is not a thing or an entity with separate existence but that which arises dependent on conditions. Mind is an energetic intelligent force, which arises in an individual and which can be cultivated to develop positive human values such as kindness, sympathy, compassion and love. These values can be used to serve the world. A powerful mind, fully developed can even purify the atmosphere. It means its vibration can reach and can affect everyone positively. On the other hand when abused by developing negative qualities like hatred, enmity, jealousy and ill-will it can become a potent destructive force. A mind like many dictators of the world (past or present) can be a source of great misery and suffering to living beings. On a smaller scale, individual humans can also create suffering to those around them. A mind which is not properly guarded and trained, can become a dangerous force.[24] Our mind is like an elephant, both destructive and constructive. An untrained elephant can destroy many things and itself. A trained mind can serve society with all its power and energy. Our mind is indeed more powerful than an elephant.

---

24 Abhidhamma is higher Dhamma or higher teaching of the Buddha. Abhidhamma is the philosophy and psychology of the Buddha. It is a complete system of mind training, and an analytical doctrine of mental faculties and elements. It is the 3rd part of the Three Baskets of Wisdom in the Pali Canon. Abhidhamma deals with karma (Action), Dhamma (Doctrine), Paticca Samuppada (Dependent Origination), Sankhara (Mass of Volitional Activities and Past Memories), Samsara (Cycle of Birth and Death) and Nirvana (Absolute Calmness). Abhidhamma is a scientific teaching, analysing mind–matter scrupulously. Abhidhamma was first translated from Sanskrit to Chinese by the Persian prince, monk and translator, introduced it to the Chinese in AD 148.

In modern times, great minds are being exerted to discover many truths about the working of the universe through science. But if these discoveries are allowed to be used by untrained mind, great havoc can result. We only have to consider how the discovery of nuclear fission led to creation of the most horrible weapons of destruction in our own time. The human mind is capable of great achievements that benefit all human beings, but conversely, it can also be the source of untold suffering. In trying to explain the tremendous power of the mind, Einstein said, "Science may have split to atom but it cannot control the mind." What he meant was that mental energy was far from more power than atomic energy. The only way this tremendous energy can be harnessed and controlled, is by adopting the age-old mind controlling techniques developed by the ancient sages of the past, like the masters of meditation.

They analysed the workings of the human mind, its function and its development. They then showed how, given proper spiritual guidance, the mind can be directed to work for the benefit of all living beings.

Those who have felt and touched reality in a practical way use the human mind, refined through meditative practice, as the primary instrument of investigation into the nature of reality. While this method of investigation is based on observation, seeing the things as they really are, very rigorous logic and experimentation, science has traditionally viewed it as subjective and at odds with the objectivity of the scientific method.

In the past 25 years or more, an extraordinary confluence has emerged, the converging of the streams of modern science and medicine on the one hand, and the venerable and long-flowing stream of meditative investigation and inquiry on the other. These streams are flowing into the greater river that is the human longing for deeper understanding of what it means to be, and to be human, to be aware, to be alive, and to be healthy and whole, to know who and what we are and how we might live in greater harmony and wisdom, the vital states of mind which human beings should maintain them to promote their spirituality for their own benefit and benefits of others.

This much we need to remember – that we have a high standard computer in our skull that controls everything we do and it is nonstop functioning days and nights. This complicated human computer needs to come under our control. If we take the brain as a hardware, then the mind which spring from it can be software. In the hardware (the brain), we have all the power connections, wiring, storage, memory and processing power we need to function as a human being. In our software mind we have operating system that gathers, stores and manages information, using the massive processing resources of our brain.

As a matter of fact, our brain and our mind are inseparable – they're part of the same entity and one can't operate without the other. We in fact don't have to be a brain surgeon or neuroscientist to be curious about the contents of our mind functioning. The human brain is the most complex thing in the universe and we all possess one – how amazing is that? And I'm not so interested to go in to the details of the differences between the brain and the computer, but to point out briefly that our brain has billions of neurons that convey and analyse electrical information. The brains do a lot of things that computers cannot. Our brains feel emotions, worry about the future, enjoy music and scenery , arts, taste the flavour of different fruits, are self-aware, and fall in and out of love.

This much is enough to explain how to take the control of our mind rather than explaining it in words and letters. We need to look for the easiest way to control this complex machinery of our own computer, that is, 'mind' as how to train it to be aware, vigilant, energetic, and penetrative of the present moment, here and now.

Studying of the human mind – training the mind

I was studying Indian philosophy at Osmania University. It was an interesting subject and while I was studying at university, I had opportunities to put some of the subjects of my studies into practice in different ashrams and centres with different, qualified teachers. Now this was the time of seeing another side of our existence. This experience encouraged me to study something more practical than the mere interpretation of the abstract texts. In addition to find, an intellectually stimulating theories, I wanted something which would be of practical benefit to me and the mankind as well. During my studies I had the profound realisation that a human being is not merely a body. He has a mind and everyone is unique. Our university masters emphasised this point and encouraged us to put the Indian philosophies in to practice where there were a variety of centres for the practice. Most people may share the same concept of mind, regarding it as something mysterious or mystical, but this idea is generally superficial and not of much practical use. I learnt at university that to understand the mind we must first understand what causes and connects the mind with our common experience of other material bodies (including other humans and their minds) in the space around us.

To do this we begin by showing that in all living beings' minds evolved together with physical reality, the body. All our minds experience the same things, such as sleep, hunger, passions, feelings, sexual lust, etc. The origin of these things has been explained by Darwin's theory of evolution which I was studying at university. He says; "My mind seems to have become a kind of machine for grinding general laws out of large collections of facts."

Then we consider the mind in terms of the simplest solution for describing physical reality, founded on the one thing we all commonly experience, space, and the structure of matter. If we examine matter, we see it has a wave structure which is always changing. This understanding leads to solutions to several important problems of the mind and its relationship with matter. We come to realise that mind is not a fixed or stationary phenomenon. We need to consider several points: 1. Sometimes the mind cannot control the body. 2. What is the effect of matter on mind? 3. What are the problems for the mind when it is affected by matter? 4. Both mind and matter are in a constant state of change.

Studying about the speculative study of mind and matter encouraged me to be more curious about the practical aspect of it. When we realise that we have minds, then we are bound to know how it functions, where it goes, why is unstable, what it desires, how it is to be harnessed, etc...

A unit of mind changes 17 times more rapidly than a unit of matter, which has been explained in Abhidhamma.[25] Both change millions of times in a split second. We can say that all our problems in life can be traced back to the mind. The mind has three root defilements from which all other negative states can arise. These are greed/attachment, hatred/aversion and ignorance/non-understanding. But this theory which I learned at university needed to be put into practice in order to develop proper comprehension. Observing things lead us to reality of the world, internal and external.

Self- observation – knowing the mystery of the mind

My studies led me to investigate the main idealist philosophers/philosophies and their types of idealism, showing how mind can be used to solve their

---

25 Abhidhamma is higher Dhamma or higher teaching of the Buddha. Abhidhamma is the philosophy and psychology of the Buddha. It is a complete system of mind training, and an analytical doctrine of mental faculties and elements. It is the 3rd part of the Three Baskets of Wisdom in the Pali Canon. Abhidhamma deals with karma (Action), Dhamma (Doctrine), Paticca Samuppada (Dependent Origination), Sankhara (Mass of Volitional Activities and Past Memories), Samsara (Cycle of Birth and Death) and Nirvana (Absolute Calmness). Abhidhamma is a scientific teaching, analysing mind–matter scrupulously. Abhidhamma was first translated from Sanskrit to Chinese by the Persian prince, monk and translator, introduced it to the Chinese in AD 148.

respective problems. This teaching encouraged me to go into the depths of the science of mind and body. I felt convinced that there must be some techniques, tools, or ways to understand the mystery of mind out of the books and theories. Knowing the function of mind at the intellectual level is necessary but it is not sufficient. We need something more than our speculation (theory). We need something tangible. We are usually at the mercy of our mind, allowing ourselves to be blown in whatever direction our mind decides to go. We are at the mercy of our prejudices and preconceptions, established patterns of thinking which have grown up during our lives and which rob us of true freedom and the ability to make logical, rational decisions about what is best for us and others. Every minute of every day, mind is active, making decisions and directing our bodily and verbal behaviour. We are obedient to its commands, telling us what to do, where to go, how to behave and what decisions to make. For me, there was a burning question: Could I find a method, or tool, or technique which would allow me to take control of my mind, rather than be passively obedient to its whims and fancies? In other words, is it possible for me to command my mind according to my wishes?

Understandably, we give importance to the outer world. However, we should give even more importance to this inner world of ours as it is the chief commander of the body. According to the ancient wisdom: "Mind is everything; what we think, we become." Everyone is aware of the benefits of physical training, but a good physique is ill-matched if accompanied by a weak or untrained intellect. We are not merely bodies, we also possess mind. If that mind is untrained, little used, or wrongly used (as I experienced during my teenage years) then we may fall into the trap of following wrong ideologies and be led into unseen and harmful ways of thinking, which can cause many problems to both ourselves and others. However, with skilful practice each bad quality can be tackled and transformed into something useful, admirable, and dynamic. It is very important that we should pay attention at all times to the state of our mind. Centuries ago there were wise men who came up with special tools for the training of the mind, and it is this mental development which is the key to self-mastery and the transformation of the world into a better place for all of us.

Men have always debated whether the mind governs the body or the body governs the mind. Philosophers have joined in the controversy and taken one position or the other; they have called themselves idealists or materialists; they have brought up arguments by the thousand; and the question still seems as vexed and unsettled as ever. Perhaps individual psychology may give some help towards a solution; for in individual psychology we are really confronted with the living interactions between mind and body. Someone's mind and body may be in need of treatment; and if our treatment is based on wrong ideas, we shall fail to help him. Our theory must definitely grow from practical experience; it must definitely stand the test of experimental application. We are living amongst these interactions, and we have a strong challenge to find the right point of view.

My subject at university was theoretical and not practical in the way I was searching for. It was also a subject which was both open to discussion and relevant to our daily life. In addition, I was in need of some practical techniques, firstly to give my mind something much more objective and concrete than the speculations I learned from my university masters, and secondly to calm it down, as I had been involved in violence and other unskilful thoughts for many previous years. Frankly to say I have had an injury mind during my research in Islam and Marxism and needed to be healed. I needed to purify my mind of my past, unwholesome memories which lay deep in my subconscious mind. Now, I came to the conclusion that the subject of mind-training and mind-development should be my priority. Although it had taken me some time to reach this conclusion, I felt convinced that this was a proper course of study for me to follow and one which would certainly have an important impact on the way I lived my life. India has been a suitable place to reach this ideal and my mind was quite ready to grasp it.

Spiritual Trainings

Entering in the field of different spiritual practice
Now it was the time to experience another side of existence. Something practical which needs persistence, perseverance and hard work to come closer to the reality of ourselves? for me to put all the theories in to action in order to develop my mind after passing experiences in the past with no proper effect was indeed important.

1. Maharishi T.M. meditation
At university I found some of my college-mates were talking about an easy meditation practice applicable to everyone. It was said to lead to mastery of the mind and was called T.M. In 1975 I became acquainted with T.M.

(transcendental meditation) and tried out its techniques. As a matter of fact, T.M. was my first meditation experience. Near my residence there was a scientific ashram which was run by the expert students of Maharishi. T.M. stands for transcendental meditation as taught by Maharishi Mahesh Yogi. It is a simple technique practised for 15–20 minutes in the morning and evening, while sitting comfortably with eyes closed. During the practice the mind effortlessly transcends mental activity and experiences pure consciousness at the source of thought, while the body experiences a unique state of restfulness. T.M. is a kind of mental practice based on Indian philosophy and the teaching of Krishna, Buddha, and the Yoga Sutras of Patanjali. Like other systems of meditation, this technique brings its own special benefits. I personally derived benefit from it, so a new door opened for me as far as mind training was concerned.

It was a new experience to practice this kind of meditation for relaxation. I attended the ashram regularly and followed the instructions given to me by the experienced students of Maharishi. I practised accordingly, but in the end I found that it could not fulfil my expectations. The meditation is based on mere mantra-meditation to develop concentration. This involves the silent repetition of a special word or phrase. However, for me, the T.M. practice had some drawbacks:

1. The duration of the meditation practice was not long enough to bring the mind into a state of deep concentration.
2. Mantra as a kind of spiritual relaxation was impermanent.
3. Mere mantra is an obstacle to pure concentration.
4. The aim of T.M. is limited. Basically, it aims at the achievement only of some partial or temporary relaxation. It does not go beyond this. However, I continued to practice T.M. until I took up another kind of meditation.

2. Satyananda yoga meditation

Many concentration and meditation techniques have been developed by Satyananda. It could help me concentrate my subject of studies to some extent. The practices of *pratyahara* (stilling the mind) *dharana* (concentration), *dhyana* (meditation) and Laya Yoga techniques, derived from the Upanishads.

Here, I'm not going to go in to the details of this technique. In brief, there are three common Satyananda Yoga meditation techniques are:

a. Antar Mouna deals with the activities of the conscious mind, awareness of the thoughts, and mental activity and also control of thought processes.
b. Ajapa Japa is a mantra repetition practice with breath awareness in the psychic passages. The mantra is somewhat similar to that of T.M., meditation with some differences.
c. Trataka: Is another technique which involves gazing at one point, generally a candle flame, or an external object for relaxation and concentration of mind.

I worked with the students for a few weeks but no proper result as I expected. Besides, being a university student, I could not attend the classes regularly and to follow their special asceticism. I did not continue with the technique but I was benefitted by some techniques fragmentary.

3. Bhagvad Osho Rajneesh meditation

The most powerful and dynamic meditation known to the people of India at that time was the Osho Rajneesh meditation. Osho had recently come to Pune to propagate his teaching. His teaching prevailed in some parts of India; this was a new technique introduced by Osho. The main centre in Pune was known as Osho's ashram. Osho started his teaching in Pune in the year 1975. Many foreigners and local people participated and were attracted to the practice. Osho was full of energy to spread his teaching.

In the summer in 1975 during the college term I had enough time to join his ashram in Pune so that I could receive the teaching directly from him. In order to stay in his ashram one has to become a neo-Sannyasin (Osho's monk) and to practice his techniques regularly in the ashram itself. No formal ordination was necessary to become a Sannyasin. Wearing his special clothes with a long rosary around the neck and serving in his ashram for the rest of the visitors was enough. The Sannyasins were given special training by Osho himself. Osho had many techniques of meditation, but among them I was attracted to three important and effective techniques. I concentrated on these:

1. Dynamic meditation: It is practised for one hour and consists of five stages. The first three stages last for ten minutes each and the next two stages fifteen minutes each. Then there is sitting meditation in a large hall altogether.
2. Kundalini meditation: Kundalini is known as a sister meditation to the dynamic technique with four stages of ten minutes each.

3. The Mystic Rose meditation: This is a 21-day retreat. I was fortunate to receive these techniques directly from Osho himself in his ashram in Koregoan Park, Pune, 1975. I do not know whether these techniques are still teaching in his ashram. It seemed that one could find something new and original in his meditation techniques. I personally found it more dynamic than other forms of meditation. So, I practised the techniques in my daily life. Osho's technique was more physical and less meditative. However, there was no quiet, undisturbed place suitable for long mental practice. Besides, the length of sitting in meditation was not enough for deep introspection. Therefore it did not affect all the students profoundly, allowing them to penetrate deeply into their minds.

In order to reach the states of profound concentration known as Jhana or Samadhi, one needs to sit for long periods so that deep states of concentration can be reached. No deep state of concentration can be obtained by short practice. This kind of deep concentration with long sitting may affect the novices to come to themselves to some extent. The sex-meditation of Osho, which plays an important part in his teaching, was not applicable everywhere because of religious fanaticism and lack of religious tolerance found in some societies. Osho's theory of sex was somewhat similar to Freud's theory. Sigmund Freud, the famous psychoanalyst, was a revolutionary in this field. He developed the theory of the unconscious mind, as well as psychosexual development and the Oedipal complex. Although his sexual theory was later criticised by some of his colleagues, others found some positive points in the Freudian theory of sex. It was too early to adopt Osho's open sexual theory in a society which had not yet digested the science behind it. Therefore I preferred to rule out the sex part of the practice and to concentrate on the main techniques.

My own conception – constructive criticism, negative criticism
I am not going to condemn any techniques, teachings or beliefs. It is true that there was also criticism of the sex theory of Sigmund Freud, but this does not mean he was absolutely wrong in all respects of his theories. I would like to offer honest criticism which should be seen as constructive. There is of course a difference between criticism and condemnation.

There are two kinds of criticism, positive and negative.

Positive criticism contains helpful and specific suggestions for positive change, constructive criticism is highly concentrated on a particular issue for better. When someone is giving destructive criticism, it can hurt our pride and have negative effects on our self-esteem and confidence

Criticism need not be either condemnatory or negative. Creative criticism comes out of compassion, but condemnation stems from hatred and ignorance. The purpose of criticism is to awaken; the purpose of condemnation is to destroy. The objective of criticism is the discovery of truth, but the objective of condemnation is to destroy the idea. Criticism is to seek the truth; the diamond has fallen in the dirt, now let us wash it, let us cleanse it.

Criticism is deeply friendly. No matter how hard it is, it still contains friendliness, but condemnation is poison. It is poison covered with sugar. The sex-meditation of Osho has got different meanings in different cultures. This does not mean to condemn it. I derived some benefit from Osho's techniques but I was not awakened by them. In other words, the techniques did not jolt me from within.

Osho's techniques are so varied that some of them are quite enough for someone who primarily wants to experience relaxation, and I benefited from his three important techniques. Compared to T.M., Osho's practice was more dynamic. I preferred to practice Osho's techniques in my leisure time and to add them to my knowledge as a positive experience. The fact is, in my general teaching, I did not change the essence of the meditation, but I did change its form.

Albert Einstein believes that "The only source of knowledge is experience."

These spiritual experiences were helpful and valuable to me. I learned a lot from them. I learned the differences, the values, the intrinsic values of the different teachings and trainings. Through experience, we touch the reality as what it should be. Experience is to feel things, to see them it in a proper and powerful way. Experience is a good teacher. Therefore I gained knowledge and then I transmitted to others insisting them to evaluate themselves.

In fact my preconception became concrete and tangible. Even bad experience can give a good result and can bring about a new recognition which leads to subsequent reality. Learning from experience is one of the ways in which we decide to cultivate more of what we like about ourselves as opposed to just randomly accepting every way in which we react. The most important thing is to have an ideal and have something to create. That is important if we are a researcher or a truth seeker. That means we have to experience the world to choose the best. And as Patrick Henry says, "I have but one lamp by which my feet are guided, and that is the lamp of experience."

Some points from this chapter

- My subject at university was theoretical but I was looking for something practical.

- We must give importance to the inner world too.

- The life of man is the life of a moving being, and it is not sufficient for him to develop body alone.

- While we are feeding our physical body, we are also responsible for our psyche.

- We are not merely body. We are not merely mind either. Mind and body are inseparable parts of a whole structure.

- We see that both mind and body are expressions of life: they are parts of the whole of life.

- We need something more than our speculation (theory). We need something tangible.

- Knowing the function of mind at the intellectual level is necessary but it is not sufficient.

- We give importance to the outer world. However, we should give even more importance to this inner world.

- If mind is untrained, little used, or wrongly used then we may fall into the trap of following wrong ideologies

- I felt convinced that there must be some techniques, tools, or ways to understand the mystery of mind.

- For mind training I first started with T.M. (transcendental meditation).

- T.M. was not very meaningful and fruitful for me. I expected something more shocking.

- Osho's techniques were more dynamic and effective for me.

- Criticism is useful and creative. Criticism is not the same as condemnation.

- I would like to offer honest criticism which should be seen as constructive.

- Osho's teaching is a part of the truth and not the absolute truth.

- The purpose of criticism is to awaken; the purpose of condemnation is to destroy.

- The sex-meditation of Osho, which plays an important part in his teaching, was not applicable everywhere.

- No deep state of concentration can be obtained by short practice.

- I resolved to direct my efforts to the process of mind training.

- Mind training needs an effective tool or a technique to be activated.

- Our destiny can be changed for the better by assuming responsibility for our own actions and not relying on any external source or authority.

- Good physique is ill-matched if accompanied by a weak intellect.

- We must penetrate our mind in order to develop it.

- The mind is the most important part of achieving any fitness goal.

- Mental change always comes before physical change.

- If we look after our mind, we can never be a puppet to anyone.

- Failure in material world may lead to success in the spiritual world.

- Mind training is an ancient culture.

Chapter 7

"As long as we are persistence in our pursuit of our deepest destiny, we will continue to grow. We cannot choose the day or time when we will fully bloom. It happens in its own time."
DENIS WAITLEY

A rumour – a decision

In 1976 I graduated with a B.A. in philosophy from Osmania University in Hyderabad. I wanted to go back home to Iran, but being known as a Marxist activist and due to my past activities against the regime of the Shah, I was barred and it was risky to enter the country. It was rumoured that the opposition that had participated in anti-government activities was being persecuted and prosecuted by the authorities in Iran.[26] During the period of my studies in India I was among those students who were very active in their struggles against the regime of Shah. I was involved in all kinds of activities against the regime and in support of those who attempted to overthrow it. There were also rumours that the torture of dissidents by the government was being permitted. Some forms of torture were intolerably painful I was told. I wanted to go back to my own country, but at the same time I was one of the most active dissidents against the government during my stay when I was studying in India. Nevertheless, I firmly intended to go back home and I was seeking a way out of this difficulty so that I could return without fear of finding myself in trouble with the government. At the same time, I did not want to commit treason against my old comrades with whom I had cooperated for years. With these thoughts in my mind I decided to go back my country. At the university I set forth the matter before some of my good Indian friends. I was told by one of my classmates that there were ways to

---
26 It was in fact a rumour by the Shah's dissidents. Some believed and some did not.

appease the pains of torture if I was arrested in Iran. The ways were either Yoga practice or hypnosis. At that time I did not have access to hypnotism, but there were many yoga classes in Hyderabad. "It is said that in highly developed yoga mental practice, or hypnotism a state of trance arises in which the mind can be diverted in a new direction and pain can be ignored. It is a temporary mental condition in which someone is not completely conscious of and/or not in control of himself or herself. It was said that skilled yogis could perform a kind of self-hypnosis if they practice systematically and skilfully. In this high state of hypnosis the mind can transcend the physical body and no feeling can be felt.

This advice encouraged me so that before going to Iran I decided to re-start participating in the Yoga practice again with the purpose of making myself impervious to torture. The breathing exercise known as 'pranayama' was practised as a first step although, I had already practiced this kind of training. I was able to perform this exercise without difficulty, but the fasting rules which came with it were a bit difficult. For some weeks I practiced pranayama with hard breathing exercises. In further training, we were taught how to stop our breathing for a few minutes. My yoga master said that this kind of breathing exercise might be prolonged for half an hour or more, but it takes time and it needs patience. But I did not want to become a yogi master. I did not have the time or the interest. I wanted only to learn enough in order to satisfy my needs.

I used to go to the ashram regularly and I practised sincerely. Later, I learned Kundali yoga from the famous yogi master and his students. I was fortunate to have such a good master in Kundali yoga. I found Kundali yoga deeper than I expected. I was happy going for the yoga practice regularly. I practiced both in the ashram and at home. I did this practice continuously according to the instructions given by the teacher. I kept on practicing yoga until an unexpected event accidentally changed the whole course of my life. There is a definition of destiny, luck, doom, fate, etc. as: "Something to which any person or thing is destined, as predetermined by the divine human will."

Sometimes it is believed that when destiny wants to show its face, it shows it in disguise and it can pass many barriers and obstacles to go through. Sometimes the cards of life are reshuffled; a new card comes to the top of the pack and directs life in a new direction. It was well said by William Shakespeare that, "It is not in the stars to hold our destiny but in ourselves." There is also a quotation worth mentioning here which is attributed to Lao Tze:

"Watch your thoughts, for they become words.
Watch your words, for they become actions.
Watch your actions, for they become habits.
Watch your habits, for they become character.
Watch your character, for they become your destiny."[27]

Some points from this chapter

- After graduation I decided to go back home to render service to my people.

- My past activities against the government meant I was risking persecution and prosecution.

- It was a rumor that the even the ordinary opposition groups who had participated in anti-government activities are tortured.

- I started practicing yoga in order to learn to tolerate torture.

- Practicing yoga draw me inevitably in a completely different and unexpected direction.

- This new development sprang from my own desires.

- I came nearer to my goal spontaneously.

- Sometimes it is believed that when destiny wants to show its face, it shows it in disguise.

- Our destiny is not in the stars, but in ourselves.

---

27 It is believed that the following precepts were declared by the Iranian sage Zoroaster in 600 to 1000 BCE. They are:
1. Hovamettah – good word(s), 2. Hovakh,tah – good thought(s), 3. Hova,rashta – good deed(s).

Chapter 8

Karma Makes One's Future

"Shallow men believe in luck or in circumstance. Strong men believe in cause and effect."
RALPH WALDO EMERSON

Karma makes destiny

Then started a sequence of events which I firmly believe can only be explained as the results of some previous actions I had performed, if not in this life, then in a previous one. William Jennings Brayan says, "Destiny is no matter of chance. It is a matter of choice: It is not a thing to be waited for, it is a thing to be achieved."

In Hinduism and Buddhism there is a doctrine called karma. The basic principle is simple to state: our actions have results. Our good actions produce good results and our bad actions produce bad results. Our actions in the past create our present, and our actions in the present will create our future. The intricate workings of this doctrine are too complicated for us to see, but the theory is not difficult to understand. Karma is a natural law, operating by itself in its own field without the intervention of an external, independent agency. The law of karma can explain what mankind and many religions generally call the mysteries of fate and predestination. Our actions in the present will lead us to future retribution or reward, either in this current life or in a future one. Everything that happens to us, without exception, we ourselves, directly or indirectly, partly or entirely, set into motion at some time in the past. The doctrine of karma can explain what happened next in my life to bring about a change for the better. This may have been the result of some good action I performed previously.

One day I went to the yoga ashram as usual but to my surprise I found no one in the ashram. I asked the watchman and he said they had already moved to a new place. He gave me a new address which was far away from the present location. At first I decided not to go there, but an inner voice forced me not to give up and to look for the new place because I wanted to continue with the practice I had started. The address the watchman had given me was a little strange. I went to the exact address he wrote down, but there was no sign of a training centre there. I could see no ashram of any kind there. I asked in the neighbourhood about a yoga centre and no one had any idea about yoga practice or yoga centres in the vicinity.

I had been drawn to yoga for reasons which I believe had been rooted in my previous karma, now a new development was about to take place. At this new address I did find a gathering in a vast compound, but it did not seem to be a yoga centre. The people gathered there had some application forms in their hands, waiting to fill them in, but I could see no sign of any yoga practice at this new location. I was drawn to this place because of my interest in yoga, but I found nothing there which was related to yoga. I had gone to the correct address, but the people there were not students of yoga. This was a riddle and I did not know the secret yet. Robert Brault says, "Sometimes, perhaps, we are allowed to get lost that we may find the right person to ask directions of."

In an open compound some people were sitting calmly in meditation style and some others were filling in forms to enrol their names. When I asked one of the visitors about the purpose of their being there, he simply said, "Vipassana."[28] The word Vipassana was vague to me. I certainly did not know its meaning. Then I noticed that some buses were parking outside the centre. These buses seemed to be waiting to take the visitors somewhere. I knew nothing about the gathering, but I thought it might be a new place outside the city which had been allocated to yoga practice. I also asked for the forms and after filling in the details, the man in charge announced that the buses would start within one hour's time. They advised us to take our essentials with us, such as towels, a small mat, torch, clothes, bed sheets, etc. I immediately took a rickshaw (a three-wheeled motorbike) and fetched my things from home. I came back in time and the buses soon left the city in the direction of a place unknown to me. I still did not know where I was going. However, I thought I was going to a new place for yoga practice.

The buses left the city and, not very far from it, they turned off the main road onto a gravel road which ran towards a calm, green, quiet, remote

---

28 Vipassana in Pali language: Intuition, insight, intuitive vision or introspection. A system of meditation practiced in the Theravada School of Buddhism.

place far from the city. The name of this place was Dhammakhetta. Soon we reached the training place. We disembarked and the buses left the place immediately. We were told by the manager that there was no way back home. No noise, no traffic, no means of contacting the outside world and, above all, Noble Silence was the dominant characteristic. It was indeed an ideal place for everything connected with mental training and practice. Dhammakhetta, or Dhamma field, was inaugurated in 1976 by the late Sri S.N. Goenka, who planted a bodhi sapling brought from Bodhgaya. It is situated on 5.6 acres of land in Sahebnagar, about 12 km. from the city of Hyderabad the capital of Andhra Pradesh. The manager of the training centre announced that we were supposed to stay and practice in this place for ten days uninterruptedly, observing Noble Silence, a system of training which I had never experienced before. This rule made us concentrate on practice moment to moment and nothing else. I was happy I had come to a place suitable for spiritual practice. I always welcome such an environment for practice. We have learnt that recognition springs out of practice and when this initial recognition is put into our experience, then, new findings appear. New, complex discoveries have different properties, which can be screened and developed by further practice. Therefore, practice took priority over mere theory in this system of mind training. These processes can gradually lead to a kind of mental development with new and wholesome characteristics arising. Our spontaneous action is always the best and authentic. We cannot, with our best deliberation and heed, or pre-planned mind, come so close to any question as our spontaneous glance shall bring us. In spontaneity, no plan is designed.

Now I was in a place about which I knew nothing to practice. It was a beautiful experience to learn about something of which I had no prior knowledge. I experienced the magic of spontaneous discovery, by which I mean that it was not pre-planned by me. The essence of the teaching arose by itself. When you have seen no adverts, heard no sermons, nor met other forms of propagation, when your mind is quite empty about the subject, then you realise it through your own sense organs which means you realise it thoroughly and genuinely. In order to settle something in our mind we need to empty it first. The following story is narrated in Zen Buddhism:

"Nan-in, a Japanese master during the Meiji era (1868–1912), received a university professor who came to inquire about Zen. Nan-in served tea. He poured his visitor's cup full, and then kept on pouring. The professor watched the overflow until he could no longer restrain himself. 'It is overfull. No more will go in!' 'Like this cup,' Nan-in said, 'You are full of your opinions and speculation. How can I show you Zen unless you first empty your cup?"[29]

This simple story describes a state of consciousness before the division into duality, created by thought, takes place. No mind means no-mindness, or no-thinking, as the unconscious behind all conscious activity. Yet this unconscious is at the same time conscious, a mind conscious of itself.

This is a paradox which cannot be understood except by direct spiritual experience. The Zen master may create some mind games in order to challenge our thinking. The purpose of Zen practice is to achieve and maintain this state of mind. At that time I had no knowledge of this kind of thing, but my mind was open and ready to try all sorts of new experiences.

Mind training

Before starting the practice there was small ceremony in the Dhammakhetta Vipassana Centre arranged by the teacher, the late S. N. Goenka. In the ceremony, he planted a bodhi tree sapling which had been brought from Bodhgaya. Bodhgaya is the place in India where the Buddha attained enlightenment, and this sapling had been taken traditionally from the very same tree under which he sat during this momentous event 2500 years ago. All of us participated in that ceremony and the sapling was planted there in 1976. In the evening Sri Goenkaji explained the technique of meditation without mentioning the name of any particular person as the discoverer or inventor of the practice. This emphasised the importance of the technique, shorn of any relationship to a particular person. He explained that the technique was divided into concentration (Anapana) and introspection (Vipassana). We were told that the course would take ten days. It was divided into three and half days for concentration and five and half days for introspection or insight. I understood that the main factors for Vipassana meditation, or any spiritual practice, to be effective can be enumerated as follows:

1. The location should be a calm, quiet, remote place with a natural environment. It should be so calm and so peaceful that one can hear the songs of the birds and the sound of streams in the heart of nature.
2. There should be no talking, no telephone, no radio and no T.V. Therefore each student has to concentrate only on the technique, continuously and uninterruptedly and nothing else.

---

[29] *Zen Stories.*

3. There should be no gaps in the practice. The days and the hours are linked with each other with no interruption, completely focused on the suggested practice. That is practice with no interruptions or diversions.
4. No books, no letters and no discussions are allowed.
5. Every day the waking bell is at 4 am and bedtime at 10 pm Eleven hours are spent sitting attentively either in the meditation hall or in the individual cells.
6. Continuous practice moment to moment, and constant awareness on the technique. One become with the technique only.
7. Two times a day light food is taken, in the morning and lunch.

One and a half hours are allocated to a Dhamma talk given by the teacher in the evenings to explain the technique.

And also some other strict rules to support the practice in a successful way.

Working in accordance with this schedule all of us students sat in the meditation hall keeping a Noble Silence. The teacher explained the technique. In the beginning he simply explained the technique, the rules of the ashram and how to concentrate on the technique. His primary focus was the technique. The founder or discoverer of the technique was not important. It is like a person wanting to learn how to fly an airplane. First he/she has to practice how to fly. Later, they may ask about the inventor of the plane, but sometimes it is not necessary. The students had come to learn about 'body–mind' practice. Naturally the name of the founder will be introduced later for guidance if necessary. I also knew nothing about the practice and this is the beauty and the purity of a non-attached technique. Our initial recognition started with practice. We were told to watch ourselves – our body, our mind with full awareness. This can be interesting and can produce spectacular results. I always practise such techniques seriously and faithfully to give them the best chance to create changes in me. I also had a background of other meditation and concentration practices. So it was not the first time I found myself sitting in meditation.

In the Dhammakhetta training centre we were not required to obey any divine messenger or divine beings. It was not rite, rituals or religious activities. We only had to follow the rules of the technique in order to get a proper result. I was sure I did not want to deceive myself by following a false or bogus practice. I never wanted to jump from one branch of a technique to another one. I always wanted to observe a teaching thoroughly, to see it, to observe it and see how it could change my past patterns of behaviour into something new and better. How could this teaching make me understand myself better? The entire teaching and the technique which I encountered were natural and unforced, arising within me like a spark of light, with no ulterior motive or purpose behind them. In any system of mind training I expect to develop peace of mind and tranquillity, something to create a change for the better within me, and to change my speculative or deluded thinking into a true vision of reality. I was expecting that this technique would impact on me to see the differences, to push me towards my goal. I was enthusiastically made myself ready to follow the rules and the technique as a committed devotee.

Some points from this chapter

- I was directed to a wrong address but I was drawn to the right path.

- Moving from yoga to introspection, 'Vipassana', was not predetermined.

- What is variously called karma, destiny, fate, predestination, doom, or luck is shaped by the type of thoughts we have.

- Our futures are not the result of an accident, no matter whether we are directed onto the wheel of salvation or the wheel of misery.

- Our actions in the present will lead us to future retribution or reward, either in this current life or in a future one.

- A predetermined course of events is usually inevitable or irresistible.

- – Body–mind science was ultimately put in to practice.

- Dhammakhetta is a lovely, calm, quiet, natural place for any mind-training practice.

- A bodhi sapling, which was brought from Bodhgaya, was planted in front of us to inaugurate Dhammakhetta in Hyderabad city.

- Knowledge springs out of practice and when this initial recognition is put into our experience, then new experiences appear.

- Both yoga and introspection 'Vipassana', are meant for mind training but there are some differences.

- Practice took priority over mere theory in this mind training system.

- The beauty of any creed or technique is to be comprehended by each individual for him- or herself.

- In order to allow something new to take root in our mind we need first to empty it of our old extraneous thoughts.

- Teachers are merely messengers. They faithfully pass on the authentic teachings of previous teachers for the benefit of present and future generations.

- I attended the opening of Dhammakhetta inaugurated by S.N. Goenka in 1976.

- The beauty of learning something of genuine value is that I started with no prior expectations or preconceived ideas. When I made a start, I did not know where this path was going to lead me.

Chapter 9

The Technique of Self-Knowledge Inward Journey- Bare Observation

"Often, even after years, mental states once present in consciousness return to it with apparent spontaneity30 and without any act of the will; that is, they are reproduced involuntarily."
HERMANN EBBINGHAUS

Spontaneity

Zen literature represent spontaneity as follows:

"A centipede was running along quite happily until a frog asked him jokingly: can you please tell me, how do you know which leg to put down next? This question so confused the centipede that it sat in a heap, wondering how to run."

Spontaneity in Zen, means to be natural, ordinary, unprejudiced, and without a prior plan or intention. Spontaneity is the first principle of Tao proclaimed by the Chinese sage Lao-Tzu or Laozi.[31] For the Tao does not 'know' it produces the universe, just as we do not 'know' how we construct our brains. Spontaneity is not by any means a blind, disorderly urge, a mere power or caprice. Spontaneity is not subject to any rules, laws or commands. It is

---
30 – Wu-Wei (Chinese), Lit Wu means 'not' and Wei means 'action': non-action, as distinct from no action. A Taoism term which is used in Zen Buddhism, is action karma-less, not bearing fruit for the doer because performed without thought of self; hence purposeless of having no-mind for doing things.
31 Lao-Tzu: A philosopher of ancient China (600 BCE), the founder of Taoism.

absolutely natural. Where spontaneity occurs, Mind-Body behaves according to the laws of its own nature and the fruit of this is real and authentic.

Most of our experiences in life occurred spontaneously with no detailed planning. We have no systematic timetable for them. We have no preconceived strategy at all. When there is no predetermined for them then they are genuine and unadulterated. I feel that this exactly happened to me too. Even this technique of 'introspection' came into my life by accident. This means I had no other source to tell me about the technique, or to induce it into my mind before practicing it. You may call it an accident or destiny, but I am not a believer in such mysteries and I do not have much knowledge about them either. This means I never had a methodical schedule to discover any technique or undergo a specific experience. So the purity and the beauty of all of my experiences are that they appeared naturally, based on my curiosity or, you may call it, my past karma or whatever.

Inner journey- self awakening

During the first day of the Vipassana retreat I tried to understand the essence of the teaching and started working on it seriously. It was the first time that I was working on my mind in a practical way so seriously in a wonderful environment. In fact the conditions and the environment of the training centre were ideally planned in order to make it possible for the serious students to work uninterruptedly and seriously in order to get a good result during the ten-day retreat. It was possible to direct all one's efforts to the practice, without having to spend time dealing with mundane problems such as business, relatives, and other activities, at least during the ten-day course. The excellent conditions and ambience of the centre helped me to concentrate on one thing only: practice. At the beginning of the practice we were told by the teacher to sit crossed-legged, or in the half-lotus or full-lotus position, or any comfortable sitting position with the right hand resting flat on the palm of the left hand, to close the eyes lightly and to keep the back straight, then to start breathing naturally and normally. The posture was easy for me because I had already practised some kinds of meditation before. Full attention on the breath going in and out of the nostrils, concentrating on the point just under the nose where the breath enters and leaves was recommended as the best place. This kind of breathing practice made me pay no attention to what happens outside; I simply watched the breaths going in and out of the nostrils in accordance with the natural rhythm of the breathing. Here I would like to emphasise a point that some students may find it difficult to make progress because they have only a limited understanding of what the teaching is saying. I was indeed enthusiastic and curious to practise the technique as best I could without wasting a single time during the practice, and I was always successful in learning the training given by the master because I was very serious, putting the whole effort to the technique as if I was aware of the technique beforehand.

The purpose of this practice is to gain concentration which is a prerequisite for the learning of another technique. Concentration was a means or tool leading to a different practice called 'introspection'. Nearly ten hours every day are spent in alternating periods of sitting meditation and walking meditation (Kinhin)[32] with no outside disturbance, cutting all connections with the outside world. This is an effective way to come closer to the inside world, to know about this 'I', this 'Me', as the combination of 'mind-matter' putting them on the path to the purification of the mind and the realisation of 'Self'.

In the second stage of my practice my mind tended to wander, which is quite usual for the beginners. Then we were asked to mentally 'follow the breath' down inside to a spot just below the ribcage, the solar plexus, and back out again, repeating the process over and over. I tried to follow the instruction correctly. Then I directed my concentration to the area followed by each breath, that is from my nostrils through the chest and down to the solar plexus, then back again. These were the limits emphasised by the teacher and nothing further than that. The purpose of this stage is to establish automatic 'consciousness' of the breaths going in at the nostrils and down to the midriff, then back again. In the next stage we were told to place our attention on the breath as it was entering and leaving the nostrils. This resulted in increasing calmness of the mind. It is as if one were a watchman at a city gate who examines those entering or departing, but who does not worry or concern himself about those inside or outside. This simile of 'watching at the gate' can well be applied to the breaths entering and leaving the 'nose door'.

This form of concentration, which is called 'Anapana-sati' in the Pali language, will prevent the waste of energy on passionate thoughts and obsessive thought conception, clearing the mind in readiness for the next step, called Vipassana. Vipassana means: to penetrate deep into our mind, and to spread the calmness throughout the body. Vipassana means introspection, soul searching, pure observation of what is happening outside and inside of the body. It is mind–body analysis, observing every movement of the complex

---

32 Kinhin is the walking meditation that is practiced between long periods of the sitting meditation known as Zazen in motion.

machinery of our mind–body. By surveying the whole body in microscopic detail, we can see how the mind controls the whole body. This experience helps the meditator to proceed to the next stage. The result is the progressive weakening and eventual destruction of the ten fetters of the mind[33] to leave it pure, wholesome, and under full control. This leads to investigation of the entire body. The great differences between this form of meditation practice and other practices are many but I can summarise them as follows:

1. This technique is systematic and disciplined.
2. The process of breathing is entirely natural; there is no attempt to control or exaggerate the process.
3. The duration of the practice at every stage is quite suitable for the beginners.
4. The effect of the technique can be observed during the meditation practice.
5. The practice starts systematically and leads to a successful end.
6. The object of meditation, Kammatthana, becomes so refined and subtle that breathing apparently tends to fade away.
7. The continuity of practice uninterruptedly with no gaps in between the practice which plays an important role in the whole technique.

In the fourth and fifth day when the Vipassana technique was given, I went deeper into myself and found that things began to surface in my mind which had been long forgotten and buried deep in my memory. The entire practice was centred on understanding myself, my mind, my body, and how they work with each other. The meditators were asked to watch the sensations arising in their body consciously and attentively, using the power of concentration which had already been sharpened in the preceding practice of mindfulness of breathing. Whatever arises is watched without interference, leading to the understanding that everything is impermanent and changing. In this kind of practice the changes can be felt vividly. At the stage of introspection (Vipassana) I felt that my subconscious mind was shaken and due to this inner earthquake and my thoughts started coming up to the surface of my conscious mind. It was a fantastic mental game which led to basic realisation of my true nature. I had no knowledge about it and how it was functioning. The thoughts appeared arose in my consciousness and then disappeared. In

---

33 1-Self-Illusion, 2-Doubt, 3-Attachment to mere Rule and Ritual, 4-Sensual Lust, 5-Ill-will, 6-Craving for Fine-Material Existence, 7-Craving for Immaterial Existence, 8- Conceit, 9-Restlessness 10-Ignorance.

this way I could recognise the events (or thoughts) which were the cause of my suffering. These thoughts are like intruders which have lain hidden for years and suddenly show themselves, so that you can recognise them for the first time. The more I tried to get rid of them, the more they appeared. However, according to the advice of the teacher we have to observe them dispassionately and let them go away by themselves, without judging or condemning.

Sitting for one hour or more was now becoming easier. The restlessness of mind was getting lesser. Sometimes my mind was out of space and time and sat for more than one hour. I found I could remain without moving for as long as two hours at a time, scanning my entire body and observing the sensations as they arose and passed away. Suddenly I felt deeper sensations inside me. Unconscious things started coming out of me[34]. Fear, anxiety, enmity, jealousy and hatred arose in my mind, taking the symbolic form of serpents, scorpions, tarantulas, centipedes and other awful things, one after another. Where had all these things had been hidden up till now? I had no knowledge of them. During the hard practice, my normal sleep was also disturbed and more or less the same thought patterns started appearing in my sleep as nightmares. I had to train myself simply to observe them without reacting, just allowing them to arise and, eventually, to pass away. My entire attention was directed to what was going on inside me, not outside. Then for the first time I felt a kind of lightness, happiness and relaxation after each process of observation of the body. The burdens which I had carried for years were becoming lighter right in front of my eyes. My first understanding of Buddhism regarding the analysis of body–mind started with the Vipassana technique, without observing precepts, without reading long Sutras or obeying a supernatural being for salvation. This was the beginning of an inner journey. Prof, D.T. Suzuki says, "Awakening (Satori) is like everyday consciousness but two inches above the ground."

Conquering the self

From time to time we met the teacher. He encouraged us to continue the practice, emphasising that "the continuity of the practice is the secret of our success." When I told the teacher about my experiences, he smiled said that I had found the 'Way'. I was also appreciating myself and kept on practising for the rest of the course without interruption.

At the end of the seventh and eighth days, my mind was full of equanimity, and I was able to observe with complete calm profit, loss, happiness,

---

34 Charles Bowness, the writer of *The Practice of Meditation*.

unhappiness and other mundane subjects. I felt that my mind was frozen, my body in dissolution, my flesh and bones all melted together. I was wholly unconscious of what my body was resting on, or what was under my feet. This kind of reaction may happen to anyone who practises seriously and I am not exceptional in having these experiences or distinguish myself from others. When you observe or scrutinise your mind, you surely experience something within. When you concentrate your mind-energy uninterruptedly on your body, you certainly feel something real with no imagination. It depends on your effort and pure observation in an appropriate environment plus full energy giving to the technique. To some it is deep and to others it is shallow, but anyhow something keeps on demonstrating inwardly and starts appearing at the conscious level. Mind and body interact so rapidly that it is difficult to see the changes with the physical eye. When the mind is sharp enough, when it gets concentrated in principle, then it can feel different kinds of reaction and sensations throughout the body which are not encountered in normal daily life. What I had previously observed subjectively I could now regard objectively, with real peace and relaxation without tranquilisers. My mind stuck to nothing, like a drop of water on a leaf. Thoughts were flowing peacefully through mind, like deep, tranquil water. At the end of the ninth day I had reached a state of perfect relaxation which I had never experienced before in my previous practices. I found that useless and extraneous thoughts were the source of my suffering and fortunately they were getting less and lesser. The technique was helping me to remove the weeds which were growing around the sapling of wisdom which was beginning to flourish in me.

How can this spiritual awakening happen? Can it happen to all of us? The answer is, Yes, absolutely, if one wholeheartedly ready for it, then it can be achieved easily. This is the way of conquering oneself. I understood that self-control is the ability to subdue one's impulses, emotions, and behaviours in order to achieve longer-term goals. The Buddha says: "It is better to conquer yourself than to win a thousand battles. Then the victory is yours. It cannot be taken from you, not by angles or demons, heaven or hell."

Choiceless awareness
A spiritual awakening can happen spontaneously or as the result of systematic practices of meditation. Awakening is not a celestial gift given to some qualified meditation masters or religious persons. Those who have worked on it have no doubt about it and they have certainly felt this inner awakening to

some extent. These experiences vary and are unique to each person according to his/her observation with persistence and perseverance, and unquestioning belief. Belief about what? About this physical phenomenon, this psychic phenomenon which make this complex machinery of 'Man'. In general, a spiritual awakening tends to broaden the types of things someone is capable of experiencing. Each person might have different experience with others. They might feel more sensitive to their outer and inner worlds and may also have experiences that are difficult to communicate in words. According to the scientific research, this is because all spiritual experiences are the result of biological evolution. This process of evolution is what causes spiritual awakenings and genius. When this process does not work correctly, insanity can occur in some rare cases.

This is a very practical technique. One uses one's own mind and body as a laboratory in which to conduct this experiment of 'choiceless awareness'. This is not just a theoretical study, it is direct personal experience. How do mind and body interact with each other? My mind started boiling within and I had to channel the energy into my body. Scientifically point of view, concentration and introspection can affect everyone and it had a deep effect on me too. Concentration helps us to go into the depths of our mind and introspection helps us to develop our insight, feeling every sensation in the body and coming to understand the true nature of the body–mind as impermanent and always changing, not at the intellectual level but by bare observation, seeing in to the depth of the body. Two major factors are necessary to reach this point. 1. A true teaching of Vipassana by an expert master. 2. A true devotee who gives his/her effort to the training wholeheartedly as if their inner fire is going to ignite and permeate their entire being. The major factor in this interaction is nonstop practice without any impediment or disturbance. Free association, as found in the recent theories of Dr Sigmund Freud, really comes from a teaching which goes back to several hundred years BCE. Free association is a technique used in **psychoanalysis** (and also in psychodynamic theory) which was originally devised by Freud based on the hypnotic method developed by his mentor and co-worker, Josef Breuer.

Both old and new Freudians say that the importance of free association for Freud is that the patients speak for themselves, rather than repeating the ideas of the analyst; they work through their own material, rather than parroting another's suggestions. But in the Vipassana technique all the events are seen and understood by the individuals themselves without any outside guidance. According to James Strachey, "Free association is the first instrument for the scientific examination of the human mind." Although I admit the James Strachey doctrine, I believe that introspection performed by oneself in accordance with the right technique is more profound and effective in treatment.

The first stage of my inner journey was started by this bare observation, but this does not mean that I've accomplished the job. According to Zen, ' Satori', the flash of awakening, is the beginning of Zen and not the end of it. And according to professor D.T. Suzuki; "The first awakening (Satori), is just like the first candle illuminate a large dark hall to some extent. The second candle is more brighter and so on… until the full awakening."

When we start practising meditation or any spiritual training with strong motivation, persistence, belief, perseverance and right effort, we naturally experience some results leading to a feeling of lightness and natural relaxation. This leads to tranquillity of mind without requiring any drugs such as tranquillisers to overcome tension, stress or depression. This can help people to come closer to their innate mind – if that is what they are aiming to do. During this process, we forget how long we have been sitting because our restlessness is getting less and less, and finally fades away. It is true that even the easiest work can be hard and beset with difficulties in the beginning, but the toughest work can be accomplished as a result of determination and persistent effort. When we are truly concentrated on the present moment, we go beyond the limitations of time and space. This practice of mind training which I had encountered unexpectedly was essentially different from all my previous experiences. This was what I was looking for. I can refer to this as an 'inner journey' but without the involvement of any God or prophets.

In each period of sitting in meditation I observed new things which were hitherto unknown to me. Forgotten past events, which I knew nothing about showing themselves vividly and disappearing on the scene of my mind. The more they were coming out the more I felt relaxed. I had never seen such a horrible nightmares in whole my life but took them as good omen. Most of the negative state of my mind which were unseen in my life now started appearing on the surface and disappearing like bubbles just in front of my eyes. It was exciting and interesting for me to see another side of my existence. I had never noticed how my mind and body work. These experiences were enough to teach me about a practical way of 'self-knowing' and how the 'Self' can be brought under our own control. However, to reach such exalted states of mind, one must strive hard and seriously. At the start of this practice, I had to set aside all my theories and speculations about the past. I had to watch, to observe things with my sense organs, as they arose, with bare attention, free from prejudices and assumptions, and not be influenced by the second-hand knowledge I had received from books or other people. I wanted to become a swimmer in order to save my life out of books and scriptures. A good swimmer does not limit himself/herself merely to books, theories of how to swim. In order to learn, he/she has to plunge into the water even at the risk of drowning in order to save himself/herself. Skill or creativity is the result of sincere practice. In a true practice the creativities are put in to appearances.

Returning to the inner self one needs to see clearly as a result of direct, personal observation. To accept these things as facts is easy but to feel these facts as the reality of life with our third eye (inner eye) is different. The latter needs courage, faith, hard work, and persistence with a definite purpose.

There are of course negativities existing in our minds and we know nothing about them or, perhaps, it is more correct to say that we choose to disregard them or deny their existence. They are hidden deep in us but suddenly they get shaken inside our psyche and start springing up into our consciousness. For me, I got shocked by facing such vivid visions which I had never seen before.

Interaction of Body-Mind

We are not only body, but also mind. There is a spiritual aspect to our mind living within a physical human body. I am not talking about having to believe in a religion or having to accept some beliefs imposed on us from an external source. I am talking about the science of mind. It does not matter whether it is spoken about by the Buddha, Christ, or a scientist, or the sages in the centuries before Christ. We should not make the mistake of connecting everything to religions. This may have a negative effect because we may be harbouring some prejudice against religion. Any science which can tell us about the practical functions of the mind should be appreciated and applied. The question is to tame this wild mind by any means. We must attend to the speech and not mind who is the speaker. It is the message which is important, not the messenger. We should imagine ourselves as an automotive in motion, the automotive is our body, the steering wheel is our mind, and therefore the driver is our spirit. All three of these key components should be present for the automotive to run, and to run properly. Our mind (including our thoughts) is only our steering wheel, whereas our spirit/consciousness is the driver. Sadly, in most cases, our spirit is mostly being controlled by our mind. But how can this process be investigated and understood? By mere studying books? By listening to sermons? By obeying the supernatural powers? Is it possible to stop our mind from thinking any thoughts for five minutes? If yes, how and if not, why not? I am not going to go into the details of how the mind functions. This is a job left to each of us who is willing to know about this machinery system of body–mind called a human being. This is not a matter of believing in anything, such as reports, tradition or inference. Neither should we depend on logic or plausible reasoning. None of these approaches will allow us to reach our inner self. What I want to say is, when we do not know about our own self, our own body and mind, about their functions and how they affect our environment and society, then all knowledge, belief, and ideas about things outside us are useless.

We usually spend a great deal of our life imitating the experiences of others without realising how our own experiences could be much more valuable than theirs. This makes the difference between those who are followers and others who are leaders. Most people, however, find it difficult to tie themselves down to their own, personal experiences. According to Charles Bowness, "We find it difficult to come down to the earth, to get our feet on the ground or to sit on this dirty earth for a while. It seems much more pleasant to live in reverie or fantasy, to leave decisions to someone else, often to political and religious leaders. This feeling, in part, is why a few people are wise and many are wanderers."[35]

At this time, in a constantly changing world, I had found a way to deal with 'Self' so clearly and honestly that it released me from having to obey the preaching and precepts laid down by others as a way to achieve self-knowledge. This was very important for me in my life. To know about this complex machine we call a man, one has to analyse it by placing it under one's own microscopic observation.

No doubt all of us possess minds, and the mind is a broadcasting system for receiving and reflecting our thoughts and experiences. But the receiving thought varies from person to person. We can neither deny our psychic phenomena, nor close our eyes to the past events which have already taken place. We have accumulated good and bad memories in the mind, not only in this very life but also in previous lives. This fact has received scientific approval and is known as the 'stream of consciousness', once proclaimed by William

---

35 Deep, long breathing, practiced in Zen

James, the father of psychology in America. The stream of consciousness refers to the flow of thoughts in the conscious mind. Stream of consciousness in the Pali language (the language of the oldest Buddhist scriptures), is 'Vinnana Sota'. This term occurs not only in early Buddhist scriptures, but maybe in other, earlier sources as well. The yogacara school of Mahayana Buddhism developed this idea into a thorough theory of mind. William James says, "The great discovery of my generation is that a human being can alter his life by altering his attitudes of mind." As we see scientific explanation of mind has been explained by two philosophers, William James (1878–1910), the Buddha (560 BCE)

None of my previous experiences and the teachings I had received impressed me so deeply and strongly as the technique of 'heart-searching' which let me observe myself so vividly and clearly. This is the true reflection of my heart with no exaggeration and trying to tell others to taste it, to experience it without obedient to any particular religious teacher or an invisible being. I am not going to merchandise my experience but my duty is to reveal it to anyone who wishes to share in its practical benefits.

Obvious changes

I completed the ten-day course successfully and I noticed changes in myself during the course, but generally it was the beginning of the 'Way' although it could awaken me to the reality of life (my body and mind). It is indeed hard to explain these changes and experiences. It is like feeling or seeing a beautiful flower garden or green scenery in horizon. It is indeed difficult to explain it in words. I realised that this technique, or any other technique, can be influential when it is presented in a methodical and organised manner, coupled with sincere instruction given by a qualified teacher plus the burning desire of the devotees who give all their efforts to the well-established technique with their whole beings. This technique led me closer to the idea or ideal that I had been pursuing for years. It opened my eyes to the reality of myself at the subtlest level. This means it showed me how to depend entirely upon myself and to know myself without being placed under any obligations or commandments from outside agencies. What is important for us is how much benefit a technique can give us. If it is good, we use it and if it is bad, we throw it away. The emphasis should be on the teaching, not the personality of the teacher or the discoverer. Many people use telephone and yet do not know about the name of its inventor, Alexander Graham Bell. We use science and yet we do not know about the inventors and discoverers. To follow blindly a person because he is regarded as a religious sage, or to count him as a divine messenger is not going to help a person who is suffering from a long sickness or serious illness. Believing in oneself is more reliable. When you have a headache and you visit a doctor, you do not expect the doctor to pray for you to cure your headache, or to give you books to eradicate your illnesses. He may laugh at you if you make such silly requests. Instead, he should prescribe proper medicine to cure you. If you follow the prescription, there will be good chances for recovery. It has happened that some people think that they have no psychological problems. They keep on living without knowing that the influence of past events, which have been accumulating in their mind for years, is not going to leave them very quickly. Hence, they need some means or other to get rid of such intruders in order to have a wholesome mind. I also had such problems and I did not know from where they came. I was young and innocent, but I soon realised my inner crises and started knowing them through the microscope within. Compared to other youths of my age, I outran them in having equilibrium of mind at the initial stage of self-knowing. Hence, I felt more vigilant, energetic, calm, and more enthusiastic than the others. To speak frankly, I felt more normal than before and this was acknowledged by those who knew me very well. Being normal is great gift given by our own self introspection. Some people imagine they are normal whereas they have not seen another face of their lives.

As a matter of fact I was immune to many mental illnesses as well. But in spite of all these positive developments, still other entanglements were seen and I needed to overcome them as well. For example, you start cleaning your house and soon will notice that many spaces are left to be cleaned. This means cleaning has not come to end yet. The remaining spaces need more careful attention. Lao Tzu says, "A journey of a thousand miles begins with a single step." The 'way' is easy but sometimes we make the journey more complicated than we need to. We will never make a journey of a thousand miles by worrying about how long it will take or how hard it will be. As a matter of fact we make the journey by taking each day step by step and then repeating it again and again until we reach our destination.

I needed a more powerful device to deal with other space of mine. My quest regarding the purification of my mind did not come to an end, but at least I came to know about my weaknesses and my potentiality. Many of my delusions about myself had collapsed and I understood that during the whole course of my life I knew only a little about myself. I had been mistaken about the totality of my mind. What I knew about my mind was limited to some speculative knowledge I used to get here and there, and not based on personal, practical experience. I realised incomparably more about myself than I had known before. This understanding did, in fact, come from my own inner feelings, and not from the influence of any particular religion or sect. I must first honour and respect myself because I had overcome some of the difficulties and knots in my mind by my own effort and persistence. When I am talking about a treatment it is in fact a prescription suitable for one and all. It is not limited merely to a particular person, while others are excluded or denied it. It is available to anyone willing to make the necessary effort and to practice diligently. This remedy is not something to be imposed on others or by others. I am talking about changes, changing from subjectivity to objectivity. Propagation of a religious teaching or praising some religious leaders is not going to create changes in people. Changes should be done by oneself, and no one else. Dictating something to someone is not as effective as realising or seeing something for oneself. The first step of self-knowing starts with introspection and this helped me to come closer to my true nature.

'Self-observation' – abstract

Self-observation is self-introspection, or you may call it self-knowledge or self-searching. One of the keys to personal development and ultimately self-understanding is observing how our mind functions. In this way our heart feels while our body experiences. This self-observing shapes our personality and our personal reactivity. Self-observation practice is beneficial and can help to develop our mental faculty.

Breathing and focusing which are the basic principle of the Buddha's teaching are components of self-observation because they can help direct attention inward and quiet the mind much easier and more efficient than other methods as explained in two different schools of Buddhism that is Mahayana and Theravada. As we put attention on the breath whether Sosakan[36] or Anapana, slowly our inhaling and exhaling become more sharp and receptive. The breath is a neutral force having no schedule of its own. As the breath deepens we feel more relaxed and the heart opens to be more receptive to ourselves and others. It is important to calmly and patiently return to the breath when we notice that we have given attention to some thought, feeling or sensation.

---

36 Deep, long breathing, practiced in Zen

Self-introspection requires practice and being present without depending on any spiritual leader. It also brings about compassion for us and others dispassionately. According to the enlightened persons, when we are 'identified' with our habitual ways of thinking, feeling and behaving we are unable to be aware and self-observant because we think that we 'are' the thoughts that float across the sky of our minds. This process of 'attachment' binds us and causes suffering. Through compassion we are less likely to judge ourselves and others, thus creating a more open, expansive inner landscape from which we can be engaged in the world but not totally of it because of the self-observing faculty. Monitoring our thought-life enhances our experience of reality.

In essence, when we practice self-observation, we are becoming more aware of the 'thinker' behind the thought. Who am I?

Our ancient teachers always encouraged us to be curious and to discover something because all scientific endeavours depend on observation and experimentation. Through such pursuits, anyone can find something new to science, and if it's truly novel, the entire construction of science might have to be restructured. Therefore, the touchstone of experience should be applied if we need to judge better, or as a proverb says, "It were good if the touchstone of experience were used."

After many years of misdirected effort which had brought only poor results, I was ultimately delighted that I had come upon a technique which brought genuine and tangible progress. Naturally, I wanted to compassionately share this with others.

Some points from this chapter

- Vipassana means; introspection, self-observation, deep thought.

- My first experience of awakening of my own 'Self' manifested in me as a result of the practice of 'introspection'.

- It was the first time that I was working on my mind in a practical way so seriously in a wonderful environment.

- Concentration is a means or tool leading to another end called 'introspection'.

- The free association technique found in the theories of Freud is not a new discovery.

- Free association can be accessed practically and very easily in a true meditation practice.

- This practice of mind training which I had encountered unexpectedly was essentially different from all my previous experiences.

- The great discovery of the century, according to William James, is that a human being can alter his life by altering his attitudes of mind.

- The stream of consciousness, flowing through many lives, is as changing as a stream of water. This has been declared by both William James (1842–1910) and the Buddha (560 BCE).

- Compared to my other previous experience, the technique of introspection was different for me.

- When you observe your mind and body, scrutinising them carefully, you surely experience something within.

- Mind and body interact so rapidly that it is difficult to see the changes with physical eye.

- We are a spiritual being within a physical human body.

- We know a lot about our body but less about our mind. However, we cannot consider body as separate from mind, or mind as separate from body.

- According to professor D.T. Suzuki; "The first awakening (Satori), is just like the first candle illuminate a large dark hall to some extent. The second candle is more brighter and so on… until the full awakening."

- In training this mind–body, the concept of God is of only marginal use.

- A true change is to change from subjectivity to objectivity, from abstract to concrete.

- Satori – 'awakening' – must be the outgrowth of one's inner life and not sermons, or verbal implantation brought from outside

- Awakening (Satori) according to Prof, D.T. Suzuki, "is like everyday consciousness but two inches above the ground."

- Verbal instruction and conceptual presentation as far as the experience of enlightenment is concerned is futile.

- A ten-day retreat is a lovely and indescribable experience which cannot be put into words but which reaches down into the depths of the mind.

- A true teaching should never be imposed by force, or though blind faith, indoctrination, sermons, religious affiliation, or from a demand for absolute submission … but from direct observation of the reality as it is.

- The Vipassana technique can be justified by itself. No external authorities have to be accepted.

Chapter 10

Working in the Islamic Revolutionary System

The Islamic Revolution occurred in Iran in 1979 and overthrew the government of Mohammad Reza Pahlavi. The revolution was bloody and many people were killed. At that time I was still in India preparing to come back home.

The religious government or the theocracy took the power. Ayatollah Khomeini overthrew the Shah and succeeded him. To many this was the people's revolution but Khomeini and his followers called it Islamic Revolution. In fact all groups and organisations, Muslims and non-Muslims, participated in the revolution based on the promises Khomeini and his supporters had given the Iranian people before the clergies took the power.

Anyhow, the so-called revolution occurred to change the system to an ideal one. The revolution came with the motto of fundamental change for the benefit of one and all. Their motto was that, "We change Iran to a Flower Garden."

1. Dominion of Islam and propagating it.
2. Freedom of speech and pen.
3. Justice and eliminating discrimination.
4. Economic and spiritual progress.
5. Efflorescence in economy, education, technology, etc…

And many other promises which is usual when the new government come to power.

I was still young full of energy and this kind of feeling sprang from my heart to think about those who were looking for the knots of mind to be untied whether my people or others. This idea was too early to be applied to my own people while they were in the fever of revolution. An appropriate time was needed to convey the message and I was patient for it. But it was necessary for me to maintain my progress and to develop it during my stay in India. The more I practiced the more I got established in the technique to teach. I was sure no one could teach me such a systematic technique in Iran. Therefore I did more ten-day courses both in Dhammakhetta in Hyderabad and VIA (Vipassana International Academy) at Igatpuri, Nasik, near Mumbai before going back home. I received the true teaching directly from S.N. Goenka and senior Burmese monks who used to visit VIA to give further teaching to support Goenkeji. Goenka advised me to spread the teaching to those who want it and need it. I asked him whether I can establish a Vipassana centre in Iran as a branch of VIA and he said that all other Vipassana centres would support such a centre and it depends on the necessities of the society. From my point of view, it should have been very easy to establish a branch of the VIA after my return to Iran from India in 1979. This would have been a centre which could connect us with other centres all over the world in a healthy atmosphere, but I needed to practice more. I strongly believed in the value of such a centre, but it needed approval from the Iranian government who has recently taken over the power from the previous government. I was not certain how they would react, but I was hopeful that I would get a positive response. I was quite confident that this kind of healing and moralistic centre could help people in many ways.

Furthermore, a few months before travelling back to my country, I stayed in Mumbai city (Bombay) for some time and one day, by chance, I noticed an advert in a daily newspaper about hypnotism. I had a vague knowledge about it from my studies at university, but I had no practical experience. I wanted to know more than I had learnt from books at the university. I wanted to know more about it in a practical way. Therefore instead of my wasting time I tried to make myself busy with something useful.

So I joined the hypnotism class during my free time. I underwent the training given by a physics professor of Mumbai University who had been attracted to hypnotism and was willing to teach this technique to others. The intention of the professor was to redeem hypnotism from the dark depths of sorcery and black magic, and give it the same respectability as any subject which may be read, mastered and taught. In the hypnotism class I noticed demonstrations of phenomena which seemed strange to those who did not know about the science of mind. A short course in hypnotism in Mumbai was enough for me to get a practical teaching of this science to add to my other experiences. Having practised T.M., Kundalini yoga, Osho Rajneesh's teaching, concentration and the Vipassana technique, the science of hypnotism satisfied a part of my curiosity and I regarded it as a form of research. Like other students I was eager to learn about the wonders taught by the professor. First of all, I would like to explain in brief what hypnotism is according to how it was introduced to me during my training in Mumbai expounded by the professor. Hypnotism is a relaxed, focused state of concentration. That is the definition, but the actual state of hypnosis is a little harder to define. Until recently it was assumed that it was similar to sleep, or that the mind was somehow unconscious. In reality, there is a specific state that the brain enters into when it is receptive to suggestion. This has been discovered on scans during hypnosis. It is not an unusual state of mind, and may not feel like you are in a trance, or in hypnosis. For most people they simply feel relaxed. My hypnotism teacher gave me some explanation which was scientific and specialty in its own. He told us to note down and instructed us as: "There is a change in the brain wave activity, similar to that time just before sleep when the alpha state is entered. Your brain's waking state is a beta wave, just as you are going to sleep it changes to alpha and then to delta and theta in deep sleep. The alpha state is a very dreamy, pleasant state. During this time the mind is very open to visualisations and creating a rich sensory experience. The more real the experience becomes in the subconscious mind during this state, the more effect it will have on your waking behaviour," the physic master suggested. It was the first time hearing about the science of hypnotism so vividly, clearly, and scientifically. Even the theory of the science of hypnotism explained by the professor was interesting and informative to all of us.

The physic master then put the theory in to practice.

He could put nearly all of the students into a hypnotic trance which was interesting and wonderful. Although I had practiced different kinds of meditation, this was something new to me and I derived a benefit from it. The difference between hypnosis and deep meditation (Jhana or Dhyana) is that in hypnosis the subject is not conscious of events which occurred in the past. The subject is under the command of the 'agent' and the stories get transmitted to the 'agent'. On the other hand, in the high meditation practice the events of the past are visualised by the meditators themselves. The meditators themselves are in control of what is going on inside themselves, without the intervention of a third person. In meditation no intermediary is needed. The master acknowledged that I might have practiced some kinds of meditation in the past. That was why he could not dominate me as he might have expected. I was resistant to hypnotic trance because my mind did not easily accept the commands of the hypnotist. Although the duration of the hypnotism training was short, I got the gist of the subject and I built on the knowledge I had acquired at university. The master advised us to keep on studying and practising this science. Although I studied and practiced self-hypnosis, I rarely used it as a serious therapy for either myself or others. To me meditation and entering the highest state of Jhana or Dhyana is more powerful than the practice of hypnotism.

After my graduation in 1976 and having gained experiences in different schools of thought in India and other countries, I was enthusiastically willing to come back home after eight years of being away from homeland and my countrymen. I was full of energy and emotion to find myself among my kind and perceptive people to help them promote their talents and build a sane society together at the cultural level. Eight years of fatiguing researches and study now an opportunity being given to me in order to share this much of knowledge to my people. I was happy that the fruit of wisdom tree will benefit my own citizens. People were expecting change according to the Islamists' promises and I was hoping for the same. I was sure my people are curious enough to take the best advantage of the gift I had brought with me from India and from different spiritual masters to encourage them to direct their mind to the reality of life or every acquisition. I was sure that they were clever enough to grasp it and apply it to their life. As a matter of fact, the Iranians with their high culture have already had such a background and been familiar with such teachings and techniques centuries ago, and it was easy for them to comprehend and to develop this education easily.[37] This was my pure intention and sincere wish to dedicate my achievement unconditionally to let them taste the experiences. I am (was) not a predictor or soothsayer to see the future that one day I may l face some ideological prejudiced groups who have no feeling and sympathy for their own people and their land but rather to propagate their putrid ideology all over the world at the cost of

---

[37] According to the researchers the first original school of meditation was Zoroastrian. Early records of the different levels and states of meditation can be found in the 'Gathas' of Zarathushtra even before, Vedanta and the Upanishads (see the book Zoroastrian Meditation by Dr. Jose Luis Abreau).

killing their oppositions inside and outside of Iran. And also I did not know I'd encounter with horrible pursuit and persecution for having an idea after years of research and studies. Not knowing all these obstacles, I was still full of hope and ambition enthusiastically went back home.

The words 'faith' and 'belief' can be defined as the confidence which comes from personal experience. When you see something for yourself, then you know it is true. The fact is this kind of 'belief' works like a powerful engine. If a teaching is well-established with faith, the results can even surpass a teacher's expectations. This goes back to the previous experiences of the novice and how well he has understood the teaching. Sometimes a true devotee receives the message even before it has been put into words. He/she displays their background openly. My Vipassana masters could see these characteristics as I grasped the technique in the first retreat at Dhammakhetta, in Hyderabad. I can say that my background for receiving the teaching sprang from my faith. Different people, in good faith, can look at the same fact and interpret it differently according to their own views. But that's where an interesting conversation begins.

Here is a Zen story which illustrates this fact:

Provided he makes and wins an argument about Buddhism with those who live there, any wandering monk can remain in a Zen temple. If he is defeated, he has to move on. In a temple in the northern part of Japan two brother monks were dwelling together. The elder one was learned, but the younger one was stupid and had only one eye. A wandering monk came and asked for lodging, rightly challenging the brothers to a debate about the sublime teaching. The elder brother, tired that day from much studying, told the younger one to take his place. "Go and request the dialogue be conducted in silence," he instructed his younger brother. So the young monk and the stranger went to the shrine-room and sat down. Shortly afterwards the traveller rose and went to the elder brother and said: "Your young brother is a wonderful fellow. He defeated me."

"Relate the dialogue to me," said the elder one.

"Well," explained the traveller, "first I held up one finger, representing Buddha, the enlightened one. So he held up two fingers, signifying Buddha and his teaching. I held up three fingers representing Buddha, his teaching, and his followers living the harmonious life. Then he shook his clenched fist in my face, indicating that all three come from one realisation.[38] Thus he won and so I have no right to remain here." With this, the traveller left.

"Where is that fellow?" asked the younger one, running into his elder brother.

"I understand you won the debate."

"Won nothing. I'm going to beat him up."

"Tell me the subject of the debate," asked the elder one.

"Why, the minute he saw me he held up one finger, insulting me by insinuating that I have only one eye. Since he was a stranger I thought I would be polite to him, so I held up two fingers congratulating him that he has two eyes. Then the impolite wretch held up three fingers, suggesting that between us we only have three eyes. So I got mad and started to punch him, but he ran out and that ended it."[39]

Benjamin Franklin said, "The way to see by faith is to shut the eye of reason." So, as our faith strengthens, we will find that there is no longer the need to have a sense of control, that things will flow as they will, and that we will flow with them, to our great delight and benefit.

There were many students in the training centre. In fact as many as 70 persons attended the Vipassana course each session, but only a few among them succeeded in understanding and following the 'subject matter' of the teacher. I was fortunate I did what the teacher and the rules of the environment wanted and I applied myself successfully to what he taught and organised. This was because of my confidence in him and my sincere endeavours.

When the revolution occurred in Iran in 1978–79, most of the people celebrated it all over the country with enthusiasm and great joy, hoping for golden days to come for them. With the help of different parties, different revolutionary organisations, different sects and creeds and more important, the presence of people, the revolution was achieved. This was mainly because of the continuous collective efforts of different opposition parties and intellectuals including some different Islamic groups. In fact, all the people of different classes, different ideologies and different beliefs participated in the revolution in order to achieve changes which would allow them to express freely all their diverse ideas. However, before long the revolution the ship of

---

38 – The triple gems in the Buddhist doctrine are: Buddha, Dhamma, Sangha.
39 *Zen Bones, Zen Flesh, 101 Zen Stories.*

the Islamic revolution hit the huge iceberg of failures. This power was taken over by prejudiced groups of Islamists known as 'Fundamentalists' who in my opinion knew nothing about the essence of 'Reforms'. Unfortunately they established a monopoly of power, to the exclusion of all other parties. As a matter of fact the people's revolution of Iran in 1979 was shamelessly hijacked (stolen) by these Islamic clergy. Some people would say that it was Khomeini coup d'état against the Shah of Iran by Khomeini and his followers. Gradually the revolution turned into a tyranny of the clergy and religious fascism.

There are in fact, two kinds of governmental systems: free and dictatorship. There are several kinds of dictatorship: communist, religious, feudal, monarchical, Nazi, etc. But there are two characteristics common to all of them. They are unethical and they put spokes into the wheel of human progress. They are unethical because they do not give equal political rights to all people. They are bigoted because they stifle human initiatives in order to propagate their own idea.

There is only one type of government that gives equal political rights to all human beings: free enterprise. Although all dictatorships are bad, they are not all equal. They are bad to some extent. But the worst of all is a religious dictatorship because it touches the pulse of the nation, conquers their spirits, and assumes control over everybody not in the direction of the people's benefit but to globalise their ideology even at the risk and at the cost of their people's lives and money. History shows that religious dictatorships are by far the cruellest, deadliest, most inhumane dictatorships. The dark ages were a long and deadly religious dictatorship.

Religious dictatorship strives to unify a nation through a totalitarian state the mass mobilisation of the national community through discipline, indoctrination, absolute submission, threats and physical discipline to make everyone subservient to their own purposes. Theocracy is a system of government in which God or the deities are held to be the civil rulers. Religious Fascism seeks to establish stable, lasting domination over the people. In order to do this, they use different means such as political violence, schism (dispersion) among the opposition groups, physical violence and also imposition of strict religious principles in order to conquer the spirit of the masses. Another tool and trick taken by the monopolised government was (is) to stifle the struggle of the dissidents by defamation or denigration them with their special methods they know. This has happened many times by the government to spoil them before the public. Many writers, journalists, artists, intellectuals, lawyers and other thinkers and dissidents were either killed or their characters were assassinated in an attempt to first spoil their reputation, and second to deter them from their constructive activities. This practice involves disseminating misleading and exaggerated cases or manipulating the facts in order to provide the wrong image of the targeted person. Personality assassination is a form of defamation that can include, in addition to the person, family and surrounding people.

Assassination has a historical background and has historically been used as a substitute for the physical removal of individuals. There are ample examples of these behaviour by the so-called government and I refer the aspirants to more than this in the media and authentic news which everyone can access them.

After the revolution nearly all the people were happy to build together a new structure in Iran which history would show to be a fair and just society. I was happy I could go back home and see my people after nearly eight years away from them. I was happy that I would participate in future changes in Iran to help my people to that much of my knowledge. I was not greedy to get a post or high position in the new government. Being a simple teacher would make me happier than getting involved in politics or other business.

Now it was time to enjoy the fruit of the Revolution Tree, which the people had planted after years of struggling. I would have a place and a position to water this tree in order that it could grow to maturity and bring benefits to one and all. I was hoping the revolution could open all the closed gates of the past to realise our hopes for the future, and illuminate Iran as a shining example for every country in the Middle East, the motto of which was reiterated by the Islamic revolutionaries after they came to power. It was my aspiration that revolution could change things and push the country to success in every respect, both materially and spiritually, and also to enable intellectuals to express their ideas freely after having years of hardship or being exiled from their people and their country. But our understanding of revolution and its future structure differed from person to person. It is obvious that a revolution must change a situation with the participation of people from many different walks of life. To me, revolution should change everything fundamentally, that is economic and social change, and to develop our culture, allowing the elite and the intellectuals to have their share in constructing the country. This means developing friendship with one's neighbours and other countries.

Revolution involves a fundamental change in political organisation, in government and the constitution, the overthrow or renunciation of one government and the substitution by another, by the governed. However, in the long run the dream of the Iranian people for their revolution never came to reality. Revolution does not mean to destroy the old structures but to renovate them in the best possible way. A true revolution must change things fundamentally, both outside and inside. To change the situation effectively, we must change ourselves too. To change ourselves we must change the habitual patterns of the way the mind works. We need to change our perception from delusion to truth. How is it possible to change forms without paying much attention to the content? How is it possible to pay attention to people, when the revolutionary leaders have not developed compassion, forgiveness, unanimity, true justice… at least for their own people? What plans or ideas do they have in their minds? If a new government tries to use its influence and power to overcome the will of the people and to make them obey, or to try to hinder the talent of the people, or to ignore their creativity in order to monopolise power by imposing their own ideology, sooner or later the new government will face opposition which leads to the annihilation of their authority and power. Each of us has many maps or plans in our mind which can be divided into two categories: maps or plans of the way things are, and maps or plans of the way things should be. We interpret everything we experience through these mental maps. Therefore, when I entered the country which had revolted against the inefficiency of the previous government, I was now ready to offer my full and effective service.

I remember while coming back after eight years being away from my homeland I was so excited and enthusiastic that as soon as I disembarked the plane I involuntarily started tearing of joy, bowed and kissed the land of Aryans, land of the sages and the nobles. This may happen to any patriot who loves their country. Some people around me thought I was praying because of the revolution success. They in fact didn't understand my inner feeling for this spontaneous act as the land was (is) important to me not the transient events.

At the beginning of the revolution, I was employed by the ministry of education as a teacher. To obtain such employment at the beginning of revolution was not so easy. I had two interviews and one written exam, and had to pass through the Islamic Selection Body which is a tough process. Soon after my arrival in Iran, my ideas were subjected to investigation and scrutiny by bigoted Islamic investigators. There is a proverb in Persian which is translated as "Coming events cast their shadows before." In other words "A good or bad beginning makes a good or bad ending – such beginning, such ends."

I was asked to tell them the details of my whole activities during my studies in India. It was difficult for me to tell them the details of my political activities there and it could create difficulty for me. Besides they did not know about my activities in India comprehensively. However, they usually bluff their way through the interview in order to trick the employee into revealing more information about what they were and what they did before they were given an appointment in the revolutionary government.

The second interview was about my obligation to the Islamic regime. It lasted nearly three hours and was full of ridiculous questions. I thought this kind of interview was normal at the beginning of each revolution but I did not know that it would lead me nowhere in the long run. Finally, due to my university degree, I was employed by the ministry of education to teach at university and in junior high schools. I had always wished to have a position which would place me very close to people. The post and position which was given to me was sufficient to allow me to draw the attention of my students to something new and creative, something about our inner world, to know how to succeed in life through applying systematic formulas for success, and how to stand on their own feet. This did not mean that I was working under the command of the new government, but according to my own experience and knowledge which had nothing to do with government ideology.

Philosophy and psychology have always been interesting subjects, open to discussion, and most of the students have shown their interest in them. Unfortunately, Western philosophy or general philosophy was immediately removed from the textbooks of the high schools by the Islamic Educational Bureau or the so-called 'plan-makers' under a new policy known as 'cultural revolution'. Instead of permitting academic freedom, an absolute Islamic philosophy was substituted and imposed on all philosophy teachers. This change was ordered by the Iranian Ministry of Education. I had some knowledge about Islam, but this knowledge was not enough to go into the details of Islamic ideology as demanded by the educational authorities. I could not deceive the students by calling myself an expert Islamic preacher. Besides, the form of Islam as taught in the texts and approved by the Ministry of Education was a narrow-minded form as put forward by a committee of Islamic zealots. It was really hard for me to choose between what I wanted to teach and what I had to do for the sake of my livelihood. I immediately told the educational authorities about my inability to teach Islamic philosophy or Islamic ideology. I had ups and downs, and finally I was appointed as an

English teacher in spite of my wish to teach philosophy. Although my English was good enough to allow me to teach, I was not happy with their decision because I had spent eight years studying and gaining precious experience in the field of my choice and which I was ready to teach with full energy and enthusiasm. Now I was being denied the opportunity to teach the subjects which I knew best and even at the practical level. However, I had to accept their instructions as I needed a way of earning a livelihood and to maintain my family who depended on me. It is indeed hard and painful for a person who is qualified as an expert in one field, and yet is given a job in which he is not interested. What the new revolutionaries did at the beginning of their administration to the educated elite was neither right nor wise. Senior posts and important positions were given to a few prejudiced groups who did not deserve them. However, because they were obedient to the government's commands, they were selected for important work and were given key jobs. And the highly educated people who deserved high-quality posts were put in lower positions. This was the first unjust decision of the government at the beginning of the revolution. Their decision was absolutely wrong and discriminatory.

It is narrated that Alexander of Macedon was distressed and felt a sense of hopelessness attacking Persia (Iran). He asked himself, "How can I govern and dominate the people whose talent and understanding is much more than my own people?"

One of his counsellors advised him: "Go and burn their precious books, kill all the wise men and women, violate the rights of women and children. Then you can continue your government." However, another senior counsellor of Alexander, seemingly his teacher, advised him: "It is not necessary to do all these things. In that land, you simply give the key positions and important posts to the illiterate and ignorant people, and give the low and menial jobs to the educated and wise. The ignorant and illiterate people would be always thankful to you and they will remain your slaves forever. They never rebel against your government. On the other hand, the educated and the wise people will either emigrate to other countries and will die in foreign lands, or get frustrated and hopeless till they die with no initiative."[40]

They wanted to establish a kind of ideology favoured by prejudiced groups but which was far removed from the demands and interests of the people. However, I was still hoping to awaken my people to reality even from my

---

40   This is translated from the Iranian's Weblogs on the internet.

position as an English teacher. At the beginning of the revolution everything seemed to be democratic and human. They wanted to pretend to respect freedom and human rights, but in the process of time when they dominated all parts of the country, things changed and some restrictions were imposed. The revolution started to turn to other tracks which had not been expected. So, the dream of the Iranians in building a sane and advanced society, after the revolution, failed totally because of promises which never came true.

Some points from this chapter

- I was expecting to establish a small non- profit cultural therapeutic centre at the beginning of the Islamic revolution for the benefit of one and all

- I always wanted to impart my findings, that is my happiness and peace of mind, with my people.

- Food for the mind is more vital than food for body.

- I did many Vipassana courses before going back to Iran.

- My ideas and my activities were scrutinised by the investigators at the beginning of my employment.

- Faith is believing in things that agree with one's common sense. Faith is confidence based on knowledge.

- Faith is a powerful engine. It is the knowledge within the heart, it may be beyond the reach of proof, but it must agree with experience, and be rational.

- The people's revolution in Iran in 1979 was shamelessly hijacked (stolen) by the Islamic clergies.

- History shows that religious dictatorships are by far the cruellest, deadliest, most inhumane dictatorships.

- Hypnosis is a state of mind which can reach the depth of the subconscious mind by its special techniques.

- The state of trance in hypnotism can also be gained through deep meditation.

- Although I studied and practised hypnotism, I did not count it as a real 'therapy'.

- The effect of hypnotism differs according to the different personality of the subjects.

- The same state of hypnotism can be obtained by Dhyana, deep, genuine meditation.

- I added the science of hypnotism to my knowledge.

- The Islamic revolution could not fulfil the demands of the majority of Iranian people.

- A true revolution must change things fundamentally, both outside and inside.

- It was my aspiration that revolution could change things and push the country to success in every respect, both materially and spiritually.

- My subject of study was philosophy, but I was forced to teach English at high schools and universities.

- In the Islamic government high posts and positions of authority were given to low, uneducated people and low work was given to highly-educated people.

- The Islamic Revolution turned into a tyranny of the clergy and religious fascism.

- After the Islamic Revolution high posts and positions were given to the ignorant and illiterate people, and low and menial jobs given to the wise and educated people.

- Before long, the dream of the Iranians in building a sane and advanced society, after the revolution, failed.

Chapter 11

The Ugly Face of War – Travelling to Japan

"What is absurd and monstrous about war is that men who have no personal quarrel should be trained to murder one another in cold blood."
ALDOUS HUXLEY

Before entering in to the Iran–Iraq war, I find it necessary to give a brief account on our nearest border to Iraq which was more highly destroyed than other cities during the Iran–Iraq war.

Abadan is an island in Iran. It is a city and capital of Abadan County, Khuzestan Province, which is located in the southwest of Iran. It lies on Abadan Island. The island is bounded in the west by the Arvand waterway and to the east by the Bahmanshir outlet of the Karun River (the Arvand Rood), nearly 53 kilometres from the Persian Gulf, quite near the Iraq-Iran border. The population has now reached almost 350,000 people.

The island hosted Anglo-Iranian Oil Company's Abadan Refinery, around which Mohammad Mossadegh's nationalisation movement was centred.

Abadan was (is) important not only because of its strategic position in the Persian Gulf but being an important industrial city with a huge oil refinery.

At the time of establishing the refinery, Abadan was divided in to two beautiful areas, labour and seniors. Brime and Bawardeh were the areas for senior and expert staffs of the Oil Company and working class with different privileges according to their eligibilities and positions. Both classes had good facilities such as different clubs (sports, and other clubs for entertainment) also, big hospitals for the treatment of all the members of the oil company. The senior personnel were living in that area. The working class had their own accommodation provided by the oil company. The inhabitants enjoyed living with each other harmoniously. Every New Year in (Norooz), Abadan was open to a large numbers of visitors from different cities to visit and enjoy the clubs, shopping, boating, swimming, equitation (horse riding) and other places of interest. Even the inhabitants of the Persian Gulf countries visited this small beautiful city. This is a brief version on Abadan before the Islamic Revolution. The people of the island were quite happy and satisfied with their routine life and their circumstances. But unfortunately this harmonious life did not last long for them.

In the year 1980, a bloody war started between Iraq and Iran. It was a long war of attrition. I do not want to go into the details but I would like to mention a few points of the war and to connect them to my circumstances at that time.

Iraq invaded Iran on 22 September 1980, starting a bitter eight-year war. The war was not of Iran's making, but it destabilised the entire region and devastated both countries. The Iraqi leader Saddam Hussein claimed as a reason for the invasion a territorial dispute over the Persian Gulf, a waterway which forms the boundary between the two countries. However, the conflict was rooted in a battle of ideologies rather than regional rivalry.

Saddam Hussein felt directly threatened by the Islamic revolution which had brought Ayatollah Khomeini to power in Iran the year before. Khomeini wanted to spread his Islamic ideology not only to Iraq, but also all over the world.

The Ayatollah, for his part, saw Saddam as a brutal Sunni tyrant oppressing the majority of Shia in Iraq. The Ayatollah did not hide his enmity to Saddam and even spoke of toppling him from power. He also encouraged the Iraqi people to rebel against Saddam's government. On the other hand, Saddam Hussein's purpose was pre-emptive: he wanted to overthrow the Khomeini regime before that regime could overthrow him.

Saddam thought Iran was weak after the revolution because many of the army's experts, pilots, and outstanding generals were unnecessarily executed by the Khomeini's followers immediately after taking power. Therefore Saddam believed that Iran was in turmoil and that his forces could capture at least Khuzestan province. No doubt it was Saddam who started the bloody war, but it was Khomeini who prolonged it. Thousands of very young Iranians were sent to their death in 'human-wave' attacks. Saddam also used chemical weapons against the Iranians and against his own people – the Kurds of Iraq. Four thousand of them were killed in one attack.

Then the 'war of the cities' was started and both sides pounded their adversary's civilian population from the air. In a city (Behbahan city) where I was living and teaching there, a children's school was completely destroyed by the Iraqi's airplanes and nearly 300 young students were killed atrociously. I was at the scene and helped parents to collect the pieces of bodies of their dear children. Having seen the scenes of the children's bodies, I was sick for about one week unable to go to my job to teach. In 1988 when everything was destroyed and many people were killed, Khomeini had to accept the ceasefire and to drink a cup of poison.

The economic loss was immense. Not only the huge oil refinery was completely damaged at the beginning of the war but also many cities were destroyed. Regarding the human loss, it is believed that one and a half million poor people died on both sides for a war which was pointless. It is said that this was the largest conventional war of the twentieth century, lasting from 1980 to 1988. Because the war was mainly ideological, neither side had achieved its war aims and neither side could claim outright victory. Khomeini had not overthrown Saddam. Saddam had not overthrown Khomeini or forced him to re-draw the border in Iraq's favour. The war of attrition lasted eight years.

Abadan and Khorramshahr were border cities and very close to Iraq. These two cities in particular were under heavy attack and bombardment by the Iraqis for many days and nights. They were both damaged seriously at the beginning of the war. The centre of the big education office in Abadan was completely destroyed by Iraqi airplanes and many teachers and staffs were killed on the spot. Many others were killed in different attacks. After a lot of casualties, the people preferred to evacuate the border cities because no parts of the city were safe and there was no mercy from Saddam and his military allies. Abadan was bombarded from time to time, so – like many others – I had to leave the city with my family to go to another safe city after the heavy bombardments. The fighting spread all over the country and a war of attrition kept on going here and there.

Based on hatred and enmity of both sides brought about ruinous war and as the result, destruction, homelessness, and enmity upon the innocent people of Iran and Iraq. This happened when the government was first established due to their wrong policies or most probably because of their desire to export their ideology all over the world, but they were defeated at their first attempt by the outbreak of the Iran–Iraq war. Eight years of war were long enough to impose different kinds of physical and mental suffering on people.

Right from the beginning of the war, the groups of prejudiced Muslims in charge of the government imposed their domination on the majority of the people in order to establish their absolute authority and give themselves a stable power base. As a matter of fact, war was a blessing according to the Ayatollah Khomeini's viewpoint. It was him who encouraged the youth to go to the front to either kill or being killed. He ensured his devotees that, if they killed or were killed, in both cases they'll go to paradise. The regime needed war for their survival. One of the actions was to use the war as a good excuse to suppress dissidents. The war meant that the government could assume unlimited control over every aspect of Iranian life. I had to conclude that this was hardly an appropriate time for me to be with my people and help them according to their needs and to my capacity under any circumstances. I was not happy with war because I had reciprocal sympathy for both the Iraqi people and my compatriots as well. Why the people suffer because of the ignorant of the arrogant leaders who even do not know what is beneficial for their people and their countries?

Islamic ideology was of vital importance to the new government of Iran. There were small groups of activists following a different ideology who had helped the present government come to power. Even these were either killed or put in jail. The nearest and dearest faithful disciples of Khomeini, especially those who were with him in Paris (Neauphle-le-Château[41]) day and night supporting him and propagating his ideas, were executed or vanished in order to create fear in others so as not to oppose them.[42]

The minds of innocent people became preoccupied with an unwanted war and its side effects. My compassion for my people was overflowing to do something for them, give them hope, encouragement, happiness and all kinds of wholesome actions and more important to sow the seed of wisdom in to their minds in order not to get diverted to wrong ideology. I saw them suffering but I did not know how to proceed. It was risky and dangerous for me to gather people together in one place and to speak about things other than political Islam. One thing, which was dominating the entire country was the clergy's policy to ensure its own survival at all costs. However, I was eager to teach my students about the things that could help them in their studies and in other ways. The so-called revolutionaries made all sorts of statements,

---

41   Neauphle-le-Chateau is a small village near Paris where Ayatollah Khomeini was moved to a house from Iraq in 1979. He was fully supported by his devotees who were later executed by Khomeini in Iran.

42   Similar story in *Animal Farm* by George Orwell.

promising many things including freedom of speech. Sadly, bitter experience was to prove how empty were all their promises. However, to begin with their sweet words were so enticing that I thought of establishing a cultural centre separately from my ordinary classes. This centre could also help other people in different ways in varying circumstances, some of which were of vital importance. I was sure they could find an outlet to overcome their initial difficulties. My teaching was neither political nor economic. It was a method of concentration, enhancing faculties, patience, energy, etc... and moreover a practice which could help them concentrate on their studies rather than thinking about how to die for those who propagating paradise for them. But the Islamic fanatics were thinking how to maintain and how to promote their own way of thinking. They needed to have their ideology firmly and well established at the cost of destroying all their opponents and other parties. This was so important that it seemed to take priority over all other things, including the needs of the people. Based on their paranoid ideas, the government feared the introduction of non-Islamic ideas from the West which would damage the pillars of their Islam. They believed all ideas except the Islamic ones were dangerous foreign imports, which should be prohibited in an Islamic country. Their policy at the beginning of the revolution was nothing but to deceive people in order to strengthen and stabilise their powerbase. I realised this fact at the beginning of the Islamic revolution. However, I had a strong desire to find an appropriate opportunity where I could introduce some of my ideas in order to help my fellow citizens. In such circumstances it was going to be difficult to introduce a new and novel teaching in a country with an inflexible government whose stability was based on totalitarianism. Naturally, such a government strictly opposed all dissidents with the use of force and violence, showing them no mercy. The government could use its position of dominance to oppose the spreading of any ideas which they felt would threaten their security. This included any teachings which they feared might raise popular awareness above the limited level of knowledge permitted to them by the government. It was obvious that rational, humanitarian teaching which I could teach would, even in unfavourable circumstances, help people to develop greater confidence in their ability to have a say in how the country was run. This, in turn, might provoke resistance to the authoritarian regime. The problem was that governments of this kind see things only from one point of view – their own. So they refuse to tolerate diversity and a plurality of ideas. They see themselves as having a monopoly on the fruits of the revolution.

However, a revolution which has mass, popular support means that every citizen has the right to enjoy its fruits. A government which deprives all its people of these fruits is worse than a common thief, stealing his neighbours' possessions. This is the height of arrogance and dishonesty.

In spite of these circumstances I did not want to give up notifying my people about the reality of life, about their potential and their talents. However, I realised that it was not possible for me to spread my message among my students and the wider community, so I decided I needed a period of reflection to consolidate all that I had learned from my time of hard study and many other experiences. Under these circumstances, I decided I needed a period of personal retreat in order to re-establish my equilibrium and stability so as to ready myself for the next step.

Therefore I decided to arrange a ten-day retreat for myself in a remote place. I had never stopped practising the techniques, and I used to do this private course from time to time. I practised to maintain the continuity of the techniques lest I might lose contact with my past experience. After the lapse of some time, and due to my efforts, I managed to find some of my school students who were interested in those teachings which were directly related to their studies. In spite of the lack of facilities for practice, we used to sit with each other in different places, cautiously and out of the sight of the Islamic zealots. In this way I started getting connected with some of my students who found the technique applicable in their own lives. It is indeed hard for a person who is enthusiastically willing to reveal the truth but he faces the blinds who oppose it.

Inspiration for an Iranian Zen writer

During my meeting with my students, by chance one of them introduced me to a book written by Dr Parviz Farvardin. It was about Zen (the Healing School of the East) written by him. The late Dr Farvardin was an Iranian writer, psychiatrist, sociologist, poet and close friend of the late Iranian poet and painter Mr Sohrab Sepehri. I read his book many times and I added something more to my knowledge of the awakening of the Buddha that I had studied in India and other places. Dr Farvardin's clinic was in Tehran and I was full of enthusiasm to meet this man. I finally found him in his clinic and it looked as if we had known each other for a long time. He was kind, congenial and relaxed with a glowing face. I told him about my education and experience in India and he told me about his writings and also his difficulties with the Islamic guards. He said that after the revolution many things were forbidden to him and his books were not allowed to be distributed, although they had already been published. On many occasions he was taken for interrogation by Hezbollah's boys and he was threatened if he did not stop writing books and was threatened not to propagate Zen any more. He also said that he had restrictions placed on his curing people using his form of psychoanalysis he initiated first. The Islamic guards thought that psychoanalysis, especially of women, was a disruptive therapy, which might deceive or corrupt women, like hypnotism. He was the first writer to introduce Zen into Iran, predating the coming to power of the Islamic groups. He wrote about Zen so beautifully and in such a genuine way that I thought he had been with Zen masters in Zen temples in Japan. I read his books again and again, and I got some tentative knowledge about Zen from him. Dr Farvardin gave me a book by Alan Watts, *The Way of Zen*, translated into Persian by Dr Hooshmand Vizheh, one of his close friends. Dr Farvardin was the only Iranian writer and researcher who knew about Zen. I used to go to his residence in Dizin, North of Iran, located in Alborz Mountain, from time to time to receive some knowledge about Zen from him. I got a genuine picture of Zen by his guidance and reading some books suggested by him. His books and the Alan Watts' book opened a new eye in my mind regarding the teaching of the Buddha Sakyamuni in a systematic form of Zen. I was told by my friend Dr Farvardin that I'll find something new, dynamic teaching of the Buddha in the form of Zen. He then encouraged me to see the Zen masters in Japan if I need to know about Zen in a practical way. I had studied Theravada school of Buddhism for years with the qualified masters in their temples and now a step to the field of Mahayana. According to a proverb, "Seeing is believing." After being attracted by Zen in theory by my learned friend, I had to put the theory into practice to know about it with my own body and mind. Curiosity is having a strong desire to learn or know something. Those who pursue answers to their questions for the sake of gaining more knowledge are differing from indifferent people. Those who are curious may also actively seek out challenges and new experiences to broaden their horizons.

Curiosity is the desire to learn, to understand new things, and to know how they work. It leads to knowledge but also to the ability to make connections among various pieces of information. Albert Einstein says, "I have no special talent, I am only passionately curious." I was indeed curious to know more about Zen and was willing to find places for practice under a Zen master.

At that time there were no meditation centres in Iran. I was in fact under the training of the late Dr Parviz Farvardin at a theoretical level. I had no knowledge of Zen except what I gained from my good friend. There were no teachers to teach Buddhism or the practice any kind of meditation. There were no mind-training centres either. Everything was dedicated solely to Islam and mosques to propagate it. Because I was seeking practical instruction, I decided to visit these qualified masters in Japan and to practise Zen-Buddhism with them and thereby to add more knowledge in the field of Buddhism. I remembered the good proverb which says, "Where there's a will, there's a way." This determination to investigate Zen arose strongly in my mind because of the influence of the secret formulas introduced by Napoleon Hill in his famous book, *Think and Grow Rich* which was fundamentally enriched and developed by my own knowledge and experiences.[43]

My curiosity was to learn more about the Mahayana school of Buddhism. In my opinion, those who are interested to learn about Buddhism it is indeed necessary for him/her to penetrate in to two side of Buddhism. Just as a coin has two sides so also the teaching of the Buddha divided in to two parts, Theravada and Mahayana. Walter Cronkite says, "In seeking truth you have to get both sides of a story." In other words, "Just remember there is always two sides of a story, just because someone tell you one thing does not make it always the true version."

A quick start to Mahayana

Hence, I was fortunate that 'Zen' was first introduced to me at the theoretical level by my good friend, the late Dr Parviz Farvardin in finding another side of the teaching of the Buddha. And finally, I was advised by the doctor to go to the Embassy of Japan in Tehran to get a visa. It was in the summer holiday for schools and universities, and I was firmly determined to go to Japan for more training. At that time the country was still involved in war and the government was encouraging teenagers to participate in the war in order to support their Islam. Neither the enemy nor the government authorities were willing to stop the war while many innocent young people of two sides were killed aimlessly by two selfish, ignorant leaders. War has always been a blessing for the Islamic clergies and their obligation to God is (was) used to prepare the youth, especially teenagers, to fight a Holy War to ensure their

---

43 In 1964 while I was studying in India I came to know about this book. Some of my own formulas and experiences were added to the book as ratification and were later used by my students as a shortcut to success in any field.

own survival. They demonstrated this during the Iran–Iraq war in sending unarmed (empty-handed) Iranian teenagers in the form of mass attacks (human waves) to the front lines to walk over the minefields. This caused many deaths. The Mullahs believed this kind of sacrifice (suicide) would be blessed by God to protect Islam. Destruction and death were the result of the war, the wise know it. Both sides were eager to continue the war for their own wrong reasons and young innocent people were their shield. There was no proper or sufficient reason behind the war.

First, I had to ask my education office to give me permission to visit Japan then to get ready for the journey. Therefore, in a respectful manner, I formally requested the education office to permit me to go to Japan for researches related to my studies for a short trip during the summer holidays, which might last three months. In my application I explained about my research and that I would come back to my duties within two or three months. Unreasonably, they refused to give me permission although the schools and universities were closed, but instead they encouraged me to go to the borders to fight against the Iraqis just as the Islamic soldiers were doing. It is true that one has a responsibility to fight against enemies and to defend one's own country. But this war was not patriotic; it was an ideological conflict between two rival leaders. I did my duty as an Iranian citizen and participated in the war activities to help my people. Along with my colleagues in the Ministry of Education (educational team), I went to the war zones to support the wounded soldiers by providing for their needs such as medication, nursing, food, etc. We came under heavy bombardment by the Iraqi army and, unfortunately, some of our colleagues were killed by one of the bombardments.

When a particular, narrow ideology is imposed on a group of people, giving support to that particular ideology at the cost of killing other human beings is neither wise nor reasonable. In this case, desire for victory is baseless. Therefore, I reasoned that my first priority was to help my people overcome a range of psychological problems and thereby to overcome some of their deep-rooted difficulties. I was eager to show my people an art of living rather than a way of killing or dying, to teach them the way of love rather than the way of hatred. Contrary to the fundamentalists, my training, which was inspired by my kind and wise teachers, was humane, non-violent and wholesome. I did not want to encourage the teenagers to make sacrifices for me or my way of thinking, but to find a way of life which was best for themselves. I did not want to light a flame of enmity in the hearts of my fellow citizens, making them think that they were being given a key to heaven by killing others or committing suicide. I wanted them to open the gate to paradise within themselves. I was willing to spread peace and tranquillity as I had been taught and practiced. The fever of revolution had blocked the power of the people to reason and to understand where they were going. One thing was supremely important to the new rulers: "Loyalty to sectarian Islam and blind obedience to our rules." This was their motto. An unwanted, destructive war was imposed on the people of Iran by a lunatic person called Saddam Hussain and it was welcomed and continued by his rival Ayatollah Khomeini for more than eight years and the people of two sides had to suffer in every respect. In such circumstances I decided to go away to learn rather than to get involved in their selfish policies.

First training at Hanazono College

I wrote a letter to the Embassy of Japan in Tehran and explained to them my eagerness to learn about Japanese culture and my desire to obtain access to the Zen training centres in Japan. The Embassy of Japan sent my letter to the Myoshinji Rinzai Zen Temple (mother temple) in Kyoto. From there my letter was forwarded to the 'Institute for Zen Studies' an independent research faculty at Hanazono College in the ancient capital city of Kyoto. It belongs to the Rinzai Zen sect. The university and the neighbourhood itself are named after Emperor Hanazono, who donated this place to make Myoshinji.

The Institute was established in January 1964 to promote interdisciplinary research into the thought, history, and culture of Zen, and through this to help define the essential features and contemporary significance of the Zen Buddhist tradition. The ultimate hope was to further Zen's contributions to world spirituality. These goals were being pursued through an active publication programme and an ongoing series of seminars and special projects.

Soon I received a formal invitation letter from Hanazono College inviting me to come to Japan for Zen practice. At that time, in 1984, no visa was required to visit Japan and so I set out. I was welcomed by the Ven. Kohtoku Noritake-san [kinmokotsu Roshi], the Zen master, the abbot of Hosenji Zen temple who was waiting for me at the college. There, I came to know about the basic principle of Zazen practice under the teaching of the Noritake Roshi. From there I was respectfully directed to the Hosenji Zen temple where he was teaching Zen. My further Zen training was held at Hosenji with my first Zen master Noritake Roshi in 1984. Hosenji was situated in a delightful area of Kyoto city.

I decided to visit some temples and Zen masters for a short training and then to go back home again to continue my duties at the Ministry of Education as a teacher. Once again I contacted my office in Iran and requested them to permit me to stay in Japan longer than the summer holidays. The authorities rejected my request and insisted on their previous condition. Having received this invitation from the Zen temple, I decided I had a good opportunity to start practising with these qualified Zen teachers. I did not want to miss this opportunity which the Japanese offered me. Hanazono College is affiliated to Myoshinji temple, giving Zen training to foreigners. So I undertook training under the Rinzai Zen teacher Ven. Kinmokotsu Roshi (Kohtoku Noritake-san). Although he was a monk, he also had a position at the college. I stayed with him at Hosenji temple in Kyoto for some months and received basic Zen from him in his temple. Noritake-Roshi treated me well in every respect and he kindly asked me to stay at Hosenji Zen temple for as long as I wished. I ran the temple for nearly three months while receiving Zen training from my first Zen master, Noritake Roshi. At Hosenji temple I welcomed visitors and some of the Zen masters from different temples in order to become familiar with basic Zen. It was a good opportunity and I found myself in the middle of Zen masters and Zen temples just as I had dreamed.

Request from my education office

After having such a good opportunity, I again wrote two letters to my education office and requested them to grant me at least one year off without salary to study Japanese culture and Zen in the hope that I would not lose my job in the ministry of education in Iran. I waited for their response. To my surprise, not only did they refuse my simple request, but also they reacted very impolitely and rudely. I did not know why and how their reaction could be so humiliating and unsympathetic. Later I discovered why they responded so rudely to my request. The story goes like this: I wrote two polite letters to the office of education where I was teaching. One letter was personal and sent directly to the president of the education office, explaining to him in a polite and friendly fashion the precious opportunity I had gained, and asking him to allow me to continue my cultural research. The second letter was an official request to the administration office seeking leave without pay for one or two years, which is the right of every teacher according to the rules of the Ministry of Education. When I had finished my letters and was about to post them, Noritake-Roshi gave me two printed envelopes. On the back of the envelopes the address of

'Hanazono Zen studies' was printed. I put the letters into the envelopes and sent them to Iran by post. The education authorities received the letters and on seeing the word 'Zen' their immediate reaction was one of fury. In fact they had misunderstood the matter. Two weeks later I received a fiery letter from the administration office as follows: "Mr Dehdasht Heidari the teacher of junior high schools and Azad university: Regarding your request for leave without pay from this office, we would like to say that we considered your request and it went to the executive department responsible for the employment of teachers. Because you are studying 'Women' at the time when the country is engaged in war, you have no rights to be granted leave from the office of education. Moreover, if you fail to come back within one week, your file (records) will be sent to the centre in Tehran in order to sack you from your job."

The letter was received by me within fourteen days and I felt sure they had already sacked me illegally from my job with the Ministry of Education. But I did not know why they mentioned 'Women' instead of Zen. There is no relationship between Zen and Women. As a matter of fact I was not studying 'Women' and there were no colleges or institutes in Japan to deal with 'Women'. Later I found out that they might have noticed the word Zen on the back of the envelope and they mistakenly translated the word 'Zen' as 'Women' because of their misunderstanding of the translation from English to Persian. Some educated people in Iran know that Zen is Zen and it is part of Japanese culture, but uneducated people mispronounce Zen as Zan and 'Zan' in the Persian language means 'Woman'. Because the authorities had no knowledge of Zen at all, they thought I was studying women at Hanazono College and for this reason I was cruelly sacked from my job. I felt defamed and humiliated because of this misjudgement.

I was qualified as a teacher and I wanted to work as a teacher, despite these setbacks. It would have been easy for me to get a job with the NIOC (National Iranian Oil Company) as I had been offered a job by the Employment Bureau because of my expertise in the English language and because my father had forty years of service at the Abadan Oil Refinery. He was paid a good salary commensurate with his experience. I could have had a promising future if I had been employed by the NIOC, but I preferred to be a teacher and thereby remain closer to my people. As a matter of fact, I had always been a teacher throughout my life. I had been a teacher in the framework of my big family, teaching the members of my family different subjects. I was a teacher in the villages for about eighteen months with Sepah-e Danesh or the army of knowledge initiated by the Shah of Iran. I used to teach basic English to the Iranian students in India to get them prepared for entering university. I was employed as a teacher at junior high schools and some universities appointed by the Ministry of Education, and now as a government teacher in close contact with the people. I had also been instructed and trained by my Dhamma teachers to teach Dhamma to people all over the world. I was happy to be a teacher because it gave me the opportunity to convey the wisdom of the sages and the patriarchs to other people.

Some points from this chapter

- A long, bloody war was imposed on Iran in 1980.

- The primary cause of the war was ideological.

- The war was started by Saddam Hussain but it was prolonged by Ayatollah Khomeini.

- Nearly 1.5 million people were killed and many cities were destroyed.

- There was no victory for either side.

- Abadan and Khorramshahr (border cities) were destroyed at the beginning of the war.

- I participated in the war activities not by arms, but providing facilities to help my people.

- The war allowed the government to dominate every part of people's lives.

- The war strengthened the grip of the Islamic clergies over the entire country.

- The nearest and dearest faithful disciples of Khomeini, especially those who were with him in Paris, were executed by the so-called revolutionaries.

My Journey to Zen

- My aim in serving my people was different from that of the government.

- What we've done for ourselves alone dies within us. What we've done for others and the world remains and is immortal.

- One thing was dominating the people and the country, and that was the clergies' policies to ensure their own survival.

- A totalitarian government needs to impose its dictatorship in order to govern longer.

- In 1983 I came to know about Zen Buddhism from the Iranian writer Dr Parviz Farvardin.

- I was deeply impressed by Zen and was willing to search out Zen masters.

- I was sacked from the Ministry of Education due to misjudgement of the Islamic authorities.

- Some educated people in Iran know that Zen is Zen and it is part of Japanese culture, but uneducated people mispronounce Zen as Zan and 'Zan' in the Persian language means 'Woman'.

- Misunderstanding of 'Zen' and blindly judgment in the education office made me sack from my job

- A book about Zen was first written by Dr Parviz Farvardin in 1972.

- I was invited to Japan by 'The Institute For Zen Studies', for Zen training.

- My first Zen training started at Hanazono College, Kyoto city.

- I started my further Zen training at Hosenji Zen temple in 1984 in Kyoto.

- The clergy's Islamic ideology was enshrined as a divine principle to allow them to govern people.

- Persian culture was gradually devastated by the political Islam

- The Iranian dissidents and activists were gradually suppressed and executed by the Mullahs who were brought to power.

- One and a half million poor people died on both sides for a war which was pointless.

Chapter 12

Training at Mahayana Schools – Practising Zen with Zen Masters in Zen Temples

"Accomplishment will prove to be a journey, not a destination"
DWIGHT D. EISENHOWER

In response to my request for leave without pay, the education authorities had sacked me illegally from my job and they sent my file to the Ministry of Education in the capital with their spurious reasons. Their unjust decision left me with little choice. Having had the good opportunity to study at Hanazono College and Hosenji Temple in an atmosphere of warm hospitality, with kind masters, in an ideal environment with wonderful training, I decided to stay in Japan to study and practise Zen in Noritake's temple Hosenji in Kyoto city. At that time I was the only person practising at Hosenji Zen Temple (1984).[44] Noritake-Roshi started to teach me the pure wisdom which had been handed down from the patriarchs long before I entered a monastery. At Hosenji temple we had a variety of practices, including special ceremonies, talks, retreats and different kinds of Zen activities. I was getting well prepared to enter the systematic method of Zen. After some months of training under the Noritake-Roshi, he found that I was quite qualified to attend monasteries for more hard practice. Therefore he introduced me to the Ven. Harada Shodo Roshi, the head abbot of the Sogenji Zen monastery at Okayama city. Noritake-Roshi told me that Harada Shodo was one of the best masters in Japan. Shodo Harada Roshi is a contemporary Zen master, born in 1940 in Nara, Japan. He began his Zen training in 1962 when he entered Shofuku-

---
44 At present Hosenji is one of the big Rinzai Zen temple for training.

ji monastery in Kobe, Japan, where he was trained under **Yamada Mumon Roshi** (1900–1988) for 20 years. He was then given Dharma[45] transmission (*inka*) and was subsequently made abbot of Sogenji Zen monastery in Okayama, Japan, where he has taught since 1982.

Harada Roshi is heir to the teachings of the Rinzai sect of Zen Buddhism as passed down in Japan from Hakuin (1685–1768) and his successors. Noritake-Roshi took me to the Sogenji Zen monastery in Okayama. After a simple ceremony held by the head abbot of Sogenji, Noritake-Roshi introduced me to the Zen master for longer training. Without his recommendation it was not so easy to join Sogenji. Besides, I had already practiced Zen at Hanazono college and also at Hosenji temple under the guidance of Noritake-Roshi for more than three months. Soon I became a fixed member of Rinzai Zen at Sogenji and started practicing with the Sangha. The more I practiced the more I got attracted to the technique. It was interesting and informative for me. I can say that I had come to a right place. Although the practice at Sogenji is (was) rigorous, but I felt complete satisfaction with the training.

Harada Roshi's teaching follows his old masters and the Zen patriarchs and includes the traditional Rinzai practice of the following activities:

1. Daily Sutra chanting for the Buddhist patriarchs, which starts in Hondo (Main Hall) first.

   Reciting the Sutras loud and together is important because they help us remain mindful of the teaching and disentangled the 'clinging' conscious mind. Besides it appeases the tension of the mind to some extent, especially in the morning when the mind is loaded with extraneous thought. The Ven. Hakuun Yasuntani Roshi says: "There are three reasons why we recite Sutras. First, we recite them to make an offering to Buddhist patriarchs; second, to create a noble relationship with all beings; third, to unite these first two actions with our Buddhist training."

2. Zazen (seated meditation)[46] which is quite different from ordinary meditation in both posture and practice. "Good sitting without movement provides good concentration," the Zen masters emphasise.

---

45 Dharma is the teaching of the Buddha, also a moral quality of righteousness, duty, law, truth, standard, ideal, events, phenomena, doctrine.

46 Za, in Japanese, means to sit and Zen means contemplation. Zazen is seated Zen.

In Zazen we try to let all thoughts find their way out of our mind using the very effective methods learned for this very purpose. We actually empty our minds in such sitting, rather than invite in more nuisance thoughts as new guests.

3. Sanzen (private interviews with the teacher twice or thrice a day) to solve the Koan given by the master and to clarify the technique.

4. Sosakan (deep breathing) which is a revolutionary technique among all breathing systems.

5. Using Koan[47] (a riddle) to reach sudden awakening.

6. Samu (work with mindfulness in conformity with the training). It is meditation in motion. This is a part of concentration practice.

7. Sesshin (intensive retreats). There are three sesshin in a month, one week intense practice and three light practice each five days with Samu.

8. Teisho (lectures by the teacher).

9. Takuhatsu (alms receiving) which is a good antidote to the refractory 'Self'.

10. Yaza (night meditation). It starts at 9 pm and lasts for an indefinite period. This is an ideal time for concentration and introspection.

Such a systematic of mind training can hardly find in other schools of thought. Although the training is tough and rigorous but it is ideed effective. For the same reason that Ronzai Zen is different with other schools of meditation in both form and content.

After practicing in the Theravada school of Buddhism, this time I went under the training of Zen at Sogenji. I need not give a detailed description of the practice but hint at the main points of the practice. This built on my experiences of Vipassana meditation. Posture in Zen is very important.

---

47 Koan (Chinese: Kung an) is a public case or document, or a kind of riddle used in Rinzai school. Koan, more gesture than word or phrase, appear nonsensical and cannot be expressed or solved by intellect or rational reasoning. Koan is a test set for the student by the Zen teacher to know whether or not the novice has really reached Satori (awakening). Helped and encouraged by Koan study, students of Zen may open their minds to truth.

There are two kinds of sitting. Full lotus and half lotus. Sit cross-legged, or in the half lotus or full lotus position, with the right hand resting flat on the palm of the left hand, with the ends of the two thumbs touching, with the eyes half closed. Keep the back straight. When one chooses a position, he/she has to stick to it. No change is allowed during the sitting. In Zendo 'meditation hall', the style of posture should be observed strictly. Good sitting brings long sitting and good concentration, the Zen masters confirm. Then we start breathing in gently and slowly to draw as much as air as possible into the lungs. Just as we blow a balloon filling it with air, so also we fill our lungs with air as much as we can. It is as if we are going to swallow all the air into our lungs, expanding or inflate it as much as we can. Then slowly and with awareness, we let the air out very smoothly either from the mouth or nose, releasing as much of it as possible. Even the stale breath should be exhaled. We should empty ourselves of as much air as possible. This kind of breath is called Sosakan which is practiced in the Chinese and Japanese temples. During the practice the body should be absolutely firm and steady in order to make the mind stable and unshakable. No movement while sitting. Mind get concentrated better when the body is stable and immovable. We can use counting in this practice using numbers 1 to 10 as follows: 1- breathing in, 2- breathing out, concentrating on the belly.

As usual, I was an industrious student following the instructions as best I could during the three courses which were held every month. This was a strict and rigorous practice. We had at least ten hours Zazen in a day (usually in O-Sesshin or one week uninterrupted retreat). Each Zazen lasted 40 minutes.[48] This was reinforced (fortified) in me with Zen practice. I felt the same experience which I had during Vipassana practice with some additional matters which are the characteristic of Zen, especially the differences in breathing exercises and some additional practices. But on the whole, I came to know that Buddhism in general and Zen in particular is nothing but practice, a technique, an observation based on experience. It is a way of dealing with one's problems, a way of gaining insight into one's own nature, a guide to discovering our true self. Practice is the most important thing; precepts are secondary as are the philosophy and the importance of human advice. No recitation of Sutras is required. In Zen the priority is given to practice. Awakening, tranquillity, peace of mind and unity with one's self can all be achieved without these additional practices. Only experience or

---

48   In my other books I have explained the Zen teaching and technique as compared with other non-Buddhist practices.

observation can justify or explain Zen. In Zen higher knowledge comes from personal observation. To enter the world of Zen, one must pass through the tunnel of experience.[49]

The outward appearance of this type of training may seem rigorous and Spartan to some. However, it is important to note that this system of mind training was handed down to Harada Roshi. It was formed by deep compassion and permeated by the simple and direct Mahayana doctrine that all beings are endowed with the clear, pure Original Buddha Mind. The purpose of our training is to realise this mind in ourselves and in all other beings. This is a practical and scientific way of 'self-Knowing', and in Rinzai Zen this can lead to sudden awakening or Satori.[50] Here, I'd like to reiterate the saying of the Prof. D.T. Suzuki regarding Satori: "The first awakening (Satori), is just like the first candle illuminate a large dark hall to some extent. The second candle is more brighter and so on…until the full awakening."

These techniques helped me to learn something more than I had learnt from the prevailing form of Buddhism as commonly taught in other countries. From this experience I came to believe that limiting ourselves to one particular idea or to a self-centred technique can bring about a prejudice against other systems of mind training." Dalai Lama says; "Open-minded people tend to be interested in Buddhism because Buddha urged people to investigate things – he didn't just command them to believe." With this all-embracing view constantly in mind, Harada Roshi has been training people from various backgrounds at Sogenji since 1982 and welcomes serious students (men and women, lay and ordained) from all over the world. Over the past 20 years, he has trained men and women, mostly from European countries. I was the only Iranian who underwent his training two to three years after he took over the Sogenji Temple for teaching.

When I first went to the Sogenji in 1984, there were less than ~~ten~~ eleven members practising Zen under the instruction of Rev. Harada Shoho Roshi (Hojo-san). There were four Americans, two French, two Japanese, one British, one German and one Iranian (myself) as the fixed members of the temple. The Roshi was happy that even Iranians had knowledge about Zen culture. I also told my Zen master about Iranian mysticism which is a powerful tool in the process of 'self-knowing'. I was the first Iranian Zen disciple, practising

---

49 More details about the practice in my book *Zen-mind, Arya-mind*, published in 2006, London.

50 Satori is a technical term used in Zen-Buddhism to describe a state of consciousness beyond the plane of discrimination. It may vary in quality and duration from a flash of intuitive awareness to Nirvana. Satori is the beginning of Zen and not the end of true Zen training.

Zen with other nationalities beginning in 1984. I was also happy to see myself practising with them. The schedule of Sogenji and the Zen practices of the Roshi were different from other forms of Buddhism. Discipline, Zazen (meditation), Samu (physical work), martial arts, Yaza, Sanzen and Koan.... are Zen practice in almost all Rinzai Zen temples. These are the characteristics of Zen practice which cannot be seen in Indian Buddhist temples and other monasteries. I do not want to infer the superiority of Zen to other techniques of Buddhism. Although I belong to a Zen community, Zen or Cha'an is not the monopoly of a particular master or a particular country. Rinzai Zen is a system of sudden awakening to the wisdom of the Buddha. We can admit that the way of sudden awakening has been inspired by early Buddhism and developed in China and Japan. There is some evidence which proves this fact.[51]

In my opinion, the experience of sudden awakening can happen to those who, enthusiastically and wholeheartedly, are ready for it. Although Zen is the flower of the Buddhist tree, we cannot ignore the possibility of sudden awakening in early Buddhism. Impermanence can be considered as one of the Koans for awakening too. I offer some examples which are explained in the book by the Ven. Narada Thera, *A Manual of Abhidhamma*.[52]

1. The sorrow-afflicted Patacara, who lost her dear and near ones, understood impermanence and realised Nibbana while reflecting on the disappearance of the water that washed her feet.
2. Culapanthaka, who could not memorise even one verse after four months of trying, attained Arhantship by comprehending the impermanent nature of a clean handkerchief which he was handling, while gazing at the sun.[53]
3. Upatissa, later venerable Sariputta Thera, realised Nibbana on hearing half a stanza relating to the law of cause and effect.[54]
4. Maha Kashyapa was awakened to impermanence and realised awakening when the Buddha showed him a flower.

---

51   An Shigao a Prthian Prince of Persia was the first and the most important translator who translated the most important Buddhist texts and Sutras in to Chinese in AD 148, two centuries before Kumarajiva of the fourth [h]century. An Shigao was the first who brought Buddhism in China. See the book about An Shigao, by the same author.

52   I personally have studied in two schools of Buddhism. Both schools try to reach the awakening of the Buddha in their own ways. The 'Awakening of the Buddha' is the goal of two schools but the ways to attain it, is slightly different.

53   Hakuin, the father of purely Japanese Rinzai Zen Buddhism, had his first experience of enlightenment upon hearing the ringing of the temple bell.

54   Hui Neng the sixth Zen patriarch, an illiterate peasant from Canton, is said to have had his first awakening when, still only a boy, he happened to overhear someone reading a stanza of the Vajrachedika (Diamond Sutra).

5. The Parthian prince known as 'An Shigao Bodhisattva' got his awakening by reading Abhidhammattha Sangha.

To some, a fallen, withered leaf had alone been sufficient to attain Pacceka Buddhahood.[55]

There are many other examples which show that, even in those days, sudden awakening was known. This awakening may occur at any time or any place to those who have already magnetised (occupied) their mind with a Koan or Kamaathana[56] (the object of concentration) by means of sincere practice to attain Buddhahood, just as Issac Newton discovered gravity in a sudden moment of realisation. However, the distinctive quality about Zen as a school of Sudden Awakening is that the Zen approach is systematic with special training using some different Koans, which are given to all trainees equally, but in Theravada this is not the case. Awakening in Theravada may happen once in a while, but in the Zen school it may happen at any time. Awakening in Zen is equal for all, and many temples and monasteries now exist for special training. In Theravada, however, it happens to those people who have applied themselves diligently to the prescribed training and who are prepared to dedicate themselves to the practice for as long as necessary to reach the attainment.

To me, strict discipline with a regular timetable and well-organised management, a qualified teacher plus ardent devotees are potentially important and necessary for any success, especially for taming the erratic mind. I found the discipline of Zen in the Buddha's awakening to be stronger than ordinary, common meditations or yoga practice.

The training at Sogenji and the teachings of Zen masters are different both in form and content from other schools. All the Buddha's teachings lead to one thing – Enlightenment, but the Zen school uses short cuts which can hasten one's journey to Enlightenment. This difference does not mean there is a deep gap between Zen and Vipassana – between Theravada and Mahayana, or even other techniques related to the Buddha's teaching. Compared to the techniques and teachings which I had learned previously, Zen was a new experiment which introduced the Buddha and his awakening in a special way

---

55 One who is enlightened by and for himself, one who has attained to supreme and perfect insight but who does not have the capacity to teach others what he has discovered. By comparison, a Sammasambuddha also reaches enlightenment without the help of a teacher, but he teaches his discoveries for the benefit of all sentient beings.

56 Kamaathana in Theravadian schools of Buddhism works like Koan in Rinzai Zen schools. It is subject of meditation for concentration and insight.

known as 'Zen-Buddha'; this refers to some innovations to reach awakening which were introduced by the Cha'an[57] or Chinese Buddhism. I realised that Zen is a powerful and direct way of turning the wheel of Buddha-Dhamma to realise the Buddha's wisdom more deeply and quickly.

There are in fact two kinds of school which developed in Japan, Rinzai Zen and Soto Zen. Although the purpose of both of them is to train the mind to the awakening of the Buddha Sakyamuni, there is a slight difference between Rinzai Zen and Soto Zen. Soto Zen is a school of gradual awakening, but Rinzai Zen is sudden. Rinzai Zen uses sudden and spontaneous sounds or motions such as shouting, odd questions or unexpected blows (with a stick or pushing). In Soto Zen there are no such surprises and shocks. In contrast to Soto Zen, Rinzai Zen uses Koans as a short cut to Satori (awakening). The breathing exercises in each of them are a little different.

The characteristics of Zen practice made me change my attitude towards simple sitting meditation. To me Zen meditation (Zazen) is somehow different from ordinary meditation because it approaches the mind innovative and ingeniously. I would like to say one thing about my curiosity and research. I am not someone to jump from one branch of a technique or teaching to another only for fun or out of curiosity. I taste each practice and this adds something new and good to my previous knowledge. I believe that the awakening of the Buddha is an ideal for which we can all strive, but there are different ways, techniques, and also teachers to show the 'Way' correctly and in a genuine fashion or an effective manner. I had already chosen my way of life from my great teacher 'the Buddha' who always emphasised to his disciples that they should rely on their own observations rather than having blind faith.

Technique as a medicine

From the above-mentioned explanation we understood that no external sources, no blind faith, no rituals, no sutras, no sacrifices can save a man from the entanglement he himself has created for ages. This is the gist of the Buddha's teaching in the form of Zen. A devotee firmly relies on his own effort and his creativity. He gains confidence through self-reliance He realises that the whole responsibility of his present life as well as his future life depends completely on himself/herself alone. Each must seek salvation for themselves.

---

57   Zen-Buddhism is derived from Cha'an Buddhism in China, founded in AD 148 by the Parthian prince An Shigao Bodhisattva. But traditionally, China Buddhism was then developed the by the 1st Zen patriarch Bodhidharma in AD 520, and formed into a school by Hui-neng and his followers in the eighth century. Cha'an Buddhism is a Chinese reaction to the intellectual Buddhism of India. About An Shigao, See the book, *An Shigao Bodhisattva*, by the same writer.

Achieving salvation can be compared to curing a disease: if one is ill, one must go to doctor. The doctor diagnoses the ailment and prescribes medicine. The medicine must be taken by the person himself/herself. He cannot depute someone else to take the medicine for him. No one can be cured simply admiring the medicine or just praising the doctor for his good prescription.

In order to be cured, he himself must faithfully follow the instruction given by the doctor with regard to the manner and frequency in taking his medicine, his daily diet and other relevant medical restrains. Likewise, a person must follow the precepts, instructions or advice given by a person or persons who have gone the 'Way' who gives prescriptions for liberation by controlling and subduing one's greed, hatred and ignorance. No one can find salvation by simply giving praises of the enlightened one or by making offerings to Him. Neither can one find salvation by celebrating certain important occasions in honour of the Buddha. Buddhism or Zen is not a religion where people can attain salvation by mere prayers or begging to be saved. They must strive hard by controlling their selfish desires and emotions in order to reach awakening or salvation. This scientific and therapeutic teaching made me to find the differences. The teaching of non-attachment made me to take Buddhism as my way of life and show it to others to test it practically and judge it dispassionately. This commitment to the Buddhist path should not be regarded as a form of unquestioning submission or undertaken out of fear, but as a result of my personal, dispassionate observation and experience. I can say that my wide, previous experience of different techniques made me immune to any form of fanaticism or bigotry. It is like a person who uses different kinds of strong compost to fertilise the soil of the tree of wisdom in his own garden. Then he suggests to others how they should feed their tree of wisdom with the right kind of compost. The quality of the compost and the way of enriching the soil are the factors for growing the tree of wisdom in the garden of our life. There are different kinds of compost and different ways of enriching the soil. To develop our mind we need to have technical devices in order to train it and bring it under our control. These devices should be tested by our own experiences, our own observation and own understanding. There are different ways to spiritual development and all experiences are useful as a basis for comparisons. It is not fair to condemn other opinions in order to prove the correctness of our own views, or to fill our own minds with prejudice so as to ignore other techniques and to give importance only to our own viewpoint or chosen techniques. If we do so, we have not understood the pure teaching of the Buddha about self-realisation.

Having experienced a variety of techniques and teachings, I had now come to a Zen temple to experience another method of mind mastery. I started practising 'Sosakan' as instructed by the Zen master. Sosakan is a penetrating tool of training mind which was explained in prior pages. It is tough but more effective. This form of breathing exercise was new to me since I practiced Zen. Anapanasati is a technique widely practised in Theravada Buddhism. Sosakan and Anapana are both breathing exercises practised to develop concentration and other attainments. Although the techniques are slightly different from each other, but to me each deep breath (Sosakan) is nearly 20 times longer than the normal breath used in Anapana. In Anapana there is no attempt to control the breathing and some breaths will be shallow and some will be deep. Also, ten deep breaths in the normal practice of Sosakan are nearly 200 times longer than one ordinary breath. In other words, Sosakan is deeper than Anapana, although both of them are used to develop concentration. In my opinion and based on my experience of the two systems of concentration, in Anapana practice, the mind of the beginner gets easily distracted and discursive thinking distracts the mind especially for the beginners, whereas in Sosakan, the mind gets concentrated more easily and there is no arising of distracting thoughts in the mind. Anapana is a way of thinking, but Sosakan is a way of 'No-Thinking'. In Sosakan, breath starts going in (inhalation) through the nose and out (exhalation) through the mouth, calmly and slowly.[58] Sometimes both exhalation and inhalation pass through the nose, or maybe through the mouth. In Zen when we talk about no-mind or no-thinking, it starts with a deep breath. Counting 1-10 and again 1-10 makes the mind concentrate easily and brings immediate relaxation. The results depend on the experience and effort of the meditator. This technique is indeed one of the wonderful techniques introduced by the Ch'an masters and Zen teachers both in China and Japan for deep concentration and sudden awakening (Satori). To me, Sosakan is a precise device for developing concentration, which helps to make one's practice of Vipassana more vivid. When these two are merged with Samu (work) or a martial art, then the result is sublime.

---

58 The two techniques of shallow breath and long breath explained by the Persian monk An Shigao in AD 148 in China. See, *Master Tang Hoi* by Thich Nahat Hanh, Parallax Press, Berkeley, California.

Dream to reality – the power of imagination

"A dream doesn't become reality through magic; it takes sweat, determination and hard work."
COLIN POWELL

We remember a proverb which says 'practise makes perfect', telling us the importance of continuous practise in any subject, any profession that makes the seekers perfect. There are many books written in his field and I need not to say much about this fact.

There is no alternative to the hard work and success. In order to reach exalted states, we are obliged to put our knowledge, our imagination into practice. By practice we can give value to our knowledge. The secret of any success depends on continuous practise with no gap in between. This continuity can make us able to reach what we dream, what we imagine. Speculative knowledge is essential to some extent but alone it cannot take us to our final goal. We have to convert our knowledge into action which needs a regular practise. Practising anything enthusiastically on regular basis indicates one's persistence and perseverance which leads to success. It is through practise which distinguish a man among many. To see the reality of life one should work hard, observing things with the eyes wide open. My power of imagination with nonstop experiencing, different participations helped me realise the matters better. This was the process which I underwent during my journey.

I practised Rinzai-Zen at Sogenji seriously. The Roshi was observing and examining each devotee carefully and with full awareness. In this new training centre I found myself different, with different teaching and discipline. Because we were few, the master could pay detailed attention to each of us to explain the true teaching of Zen. He patiently taught us both in groups and individually. Once a month some members of the monastery were allowed to visit their families or friends for one or two days. I used to go to Hosenji Zen temple in Kyoto to stay in Noritake-Roshi's temple. I stayed with my Japanese family and then went back to Sogenji for practice. I used to tell Noritake-san about my desire to become a Zen monk and he used to tell me that it would take time and that I must have patience to wait until the appropriate time came. He said that I needed more practice and experience, together with the master's recognition, in order to be admitted by the Sogenji

Roshi. I started practising with other members of the Sogenji Sangha. I did not find any difficulty in the hard teaching of the master because I enjoyed every part of the Zen activity. I was flourishing with other, older students due to the true teaching we received from the master, which we followed wholeheartedly. I did my best in every respect. In all the Zen activities I was energetic and faithful. After some months, Ven. Harada Shodo Roshi was preparing a ceremony to ordain a Japanese devotee, Doitsu-san, who had already practised Zen. Among the Zen students I wanted to present myself as another candidate for ordination as a monk. The Roshi used to pay much attention to me but it was too early to say anything about my ordination. My practice at Sogenji received the full approval of the Zen master and was appreciated by the Sogenji Sangha. I followed the rules and regulations of the temple diligently. I was also keen to become a monk, but it depended on receiving recognition from the Roshi and many other circumstances. Becoming a monk in a traditional Japanese Zen temple is not so easy and it takes time. My guardian and my first Zen teacher, the Ven. Noritake-Roshi, would be happy if I became a Zen monk but he could not force Sogenji to accelerate the date of an ordination ceremony.

Stephen Hawking says; "I have noticed even people who claim everything is predestined, and that we can do nothing to change it, look before they cross the road." A popular notion is that, change will not come if we wait for some other person or some other time. We are the ones we've been waiting for. We are the change that we seek.

Sometimes ordinations were held at Sogenji and many people were invited to the ceremony. There was a big ceremony on 24/3/1985 at Sogenji; many monks and nuns and other important figures were invited. I gave my room as temporary accommodation to two older monks who had come from Myoshinji Zen monastery in Kyoto. After the ceremony finished, the monks left Sogenji and one of them forgot to take his official robe (Koromo). He left it there in my room and he went off with just his simple ordinary robe. I do not know whether he had left it on purpose or if it was a game of a Zen master. If the old monk needed his robe, he could certainly have sent someone to fetch it, but no one asked for that special robe and I was happy I could keep it for myself. All the guests left the temple and everything went back to normal at Sogenji. One day after O-Sesshion (one week retreat) was over, I was free the next day and I preferred to put on the older monk's robe to give myself a brief moment of pleasure by showing off as a monk. Because my room was very near to the Roshi's room, I usually took some fruits or juice to him. In the afternoon, unaware of my dress, I took some fruit and juice to the Roshi. I sat down at the door, respectfully opened the door and offered him the tray of fruits and juice. He looked at me, gazed for a few seconds and said nothing. Then I realised that unconsciously I had come in disguise. After some days elapsed, the Roshi announced that Heidari-san (my surname) had been nominated for ordination and asked Mrs Prescilla Staurandth (Daichi-san), the 'assistant teacher', to speak to me to ask whether I agreed with the decision. It was the greatest delight and most wonderful news in my whole life and I welcomed the Roshi's decision with an open heart and appreciation. Noritake-Roshi had already been informed and he was my guardian who inspired me with his presence in the ceremony. He too did not know how the ordination had been announced so soon. He asked me if I had already spoken with the Roshi regarding my ordination and I said, "No."

The ordination ceremony was held on 05/05/1985 at Sogenji Zen monastery and Doitsu-San and myself were officially ordained as Zen monks at Sogenji Zen monastery by the head abbot of the monastery, the Ven. Harada Shodo Roshi. To be honest, I did not know how or why the Roshi decided to confirm my ordination so quickly, but I was very happy with his decision. Noritake-Roshi did not know either. It was a shock to all of us and the Sogenji Sangha. There were students who had started training in Zen earlier than me, but they were not fortunate to receive ordination from the Roshi. This incident was a turning point in my life.

Something had happened which changed my future, a future which might have been predetermined by unknown causes. So, some days before the ordination took place, Doitsu-san and I practised for the ordination ceremony with Daichi-san and with the help of other members of Sogenji (Daijo-san, Midori-san, Haidi-san, Domyo-san, and …). Many people participated in the ceremony and Noritake-Roshi as my guardian was also present. Finally we received official ordination from the Zen master the Ven. Harada Shodo Roshi at Sogenji Rinzai Zen monastery affiliated to Myoshinji (mother temple), and ultimately the robe (koromo), which I had dreamed of for years, was bestowed on me. Doitsu-san and I were the third Zen students of the Sogenji's Roshi. In the ceremony, the family of Doitsu-san had happily come to Sogenji to see their son's spiritual promotion. My Iranian family could not participate in the ceremony due to some restrictions by my government, but instead, Noritake-Roshi and his family participated in the ceremony and their presence gave me inspiration. In fact they were my family in Japan and their presence was the main factor in accelerating my progress along the path.

My commitment as a monk

After the ordination at Sogenji, I felt that my responsibility as a Mahayana monk to myself and other people was a serious matter in accordance with the oath I had taken in the presence of my Zen master. Based on that commitment I had to convey the 'Teaching' or the Dharma to others with no discrimination according to race or any other thing. This is a message of peace, harmony, friendship, unity and humanity to one and all, equally. This tradition is common in the Zen community, especially for the monks. The training of monks after ordination becomes tougher and some new responsibilities become obligatory. Both Noritake Roshi and the Ven. Harada Shodo Roshi advised me to convey the message of the Buddha and the patriarchs to other people by writing, speech, or any forms of teaching to those who needed it without harming even an ant. The Roshi advised both Doitsu-san (the Japanese monk) and me to carry forward the light of the Buddha's teachings. We are obliged to preach to everyone and to train them; we must wake up sleeping people; we must correct false ideas; we must help people have a right viewpoint; we must go everywhere to spread the teaching concerning the ending of suffering even at the risk of our own lives, but Buddhism is not a proselytising faith. My priority to this commitment is (was) my people and my country. I was sure that because of their cultural background of Iranians (past and present), they would able to understand it. For the same reason it has always been in mind to transmit my experience to them if they were allowed to be given rights to choose.

The Zen masters instructed us that no force or any kind of imposition should be used to propagate their teachings. In association with the Sogenji Sangha, I started receiving the Zen teaching from the Roshi during the Sesshins which were held every month with three short (Ko-Sesshins) of five days each and one long course (O-Sesshin) of seven days. The way and the method of monkhood were taught seriously and strictly by the master. The kind of practice in Zen, especially Rinzai-Zen, is different in both form and content from other schools, even from Soto Zen, not because it is superior to them but it is different in method. At Sogenji and under the instruction of the Roshi, there were three main factors of instruction, namely discipline, responsibility and serious effort. These three took priority over other rules.

I went under the tough training of Rinzai Zen taught by the contemporary Zen master, the Ven. Harada Shodo. We used to get up at 3.40 am every day to start our daily practice. Then we had tough Zazen practice for some hours a day, alternately sitting and walking. I understood that this kind of mind training culminates in both self-discipline and therapy at the first stage.

I understood that Zen works like a therapy before one can enter other fields of the practice which leads to awakening (Satori). Therefore without having a peace of mind (tranquillity) reaching the higher wisdom is impossible. Calmness leads to the first awakening, 'Satori'.

We practised Zazen for at least seven to ten hours a day (Zazen therapy). The other activities we engage in include light physical work as part of concentration training (labour therapy). There are meetings with the teacher in Sanzen at least thrice a day (oral group therapy). There is also conformity with the new environment (environmental therapy), new diet (food therapy), and practicing Tai-chi or other martial arts (sport therapy). There are two aspects of Zazen practice: 1- It works as a treatment (for both the prevention and cure of mental illness). 2- As a way to insight. These characteristics can be found in some Zen temples which can encourage people to test it for themselves.

I did rigorous Zen training successfully. Likewise, I did the same with the Thravadians. According to my teachers I was quite qualified to teach meditation and to run a meditation centre in Iran. But in spite of all these abilities it was wishful thinking to assume that the Islamic authorities in Iran could provide the necessary requirements for establishing a cultural centre in which people could develop their minds and allow their talents to flourish. As a government teacher in Iran, I could convey the message of awakening and deliverance more easily and effectively to students of different subjects and different people if the circumstances were suitable. It was easy for me to stay in Japan to develop my practice and experience, but I wished to spread my findings to give benefit to my own country first without expecting anything in return. I was thinking about how I could return to my previous job after having received such productive and rewarding training.

Therefore, acting on the advice of my masters, I decided to go back home to Iran as a committed monk. Before going I contacted my students in Iran and told them about my project and my intention. They became happy and welcomed my decision. They said that only a few people knew about Zen and its training and the teaching will certainly be welcomed by them.

When I returned, I dressed as a layman and not as a monk, being aware that according to Islamic rules the punishment for conversion is death. First I met my disciples and told them about my new experiment in Japanese temples and monasteries. They were happy that they come to know about the Japanese culture. In teaching Zen we need to have a structure similar to a temple for genuine training but in the Islamic republic of Iran it is (was) is absolutely forbidden.

I started teaching Zen Buddhism in the form of 'therapy' or 'psychotherapy' without using the word 'Buddhism'. Because of the training I had received, I felt that in accordance with my Mahayana vows I had a duty to awaken people to a new way of life, for peace, friendship, non-violence, unity, meditation and deliverance. The aim was absolutely human and humanitarian act.

I received wise advice from my Zen masters as to how I should proceed. Before going home I once again went to India and participated in a Vipassana course with S.N. Goenka at Igatpuri, Vipassana International Academy (VIA). Now that I had practised Zen for two years continuously during my first trip to Japan, the ten-day course of Vipassana seemed different to me compared to the hard practice of Rinzai Zen, both in form and in content. I believe that for all the methods, the goal is the same, but the ways of reaching that goal are different. For example, there are many ways to go to Paris from London. By train, by bus, by boat and by plane. The destination is one but the ways of reaching there are many. Some are slow, some are fast, and some shallow, others deep, and so on. If you have always been a train passenger and are unaware of other means it is not fair to judge other ways and you should not become attached to one particular 'Way'. This means that the train passenger, who has never seen an aeroplane in his/her life, may think the train is the only way. Therefore, objective observation and skilful selection are ways to make a person unbiased and objective in his assessments. The ways leading into the depths of the mind are different, but one can find shortcuts with a systematic way in order to get there. That is why it is advised by the wise that we need to have different experiences in order to see clearly which path we want to choose. Based on my different experiences in the practice of meditation, I realised that Sosakan breathing exercise and the way of Zen is a stronger and more effective way to reach the depths of the mind. In Zen training, concentration and relaxation can be gained easily and quickly. I say this not because I am supporting Zen, or intending to gather more and more people to the way of Zen. Zen is not a mere commodity, to be loaded on the back of an ass in order to find more customers for it. Zen is not a religion, as it is not a system of faith and worship and owes no allegiance to any supernatural power. If someone asks me what the Buddha taught us and what Zen is, I can answer him/her in a line that the Buddha discovered a tool, an appliance in which to penetrate in to our own mind and body to reach awakening, that's all. He did so and invited other to come and see, not to come and believe.

As a matter of fact, I am describing my own experiences after having observed other techniques and teachings. I leave the judgment to those who have practiced the discipline of Zen. Zen training is not as easy as other systems of non-Buddhist meditation, which require the practitioner simply to sit, meditate and let the imagination run free. In those systems we usually sit and think. In usual sitting more thoughts will be added to our previous thoughts, whereas in Zen we sit in Zazen not to think. No-thinking is a principle in the system of Zen practice. Zen practice is hard but the result is immediate and fruitful.

After having practised different breathing exercises in two schools of Buddhism, 'Theravada' and 'Mahayana', with different teachers, I personally found that Sosakan as a sharp tool of concentration and Vipassana as an effective way of introspection (self-analysis) are deeper, more practical and the results is more tangible, leading to the attainment of both concentration and relaxation, and also in the long run to solve Koans to comprehend 'Satori'. I believe that Sosakan can be regarded as a safe, iron bridge leading to the field of 'introspection'. To feel the sensations of the body, mind should be sharpened by an effective sharpener. Therefore I preferred to make the bridge strong for stepping forward steadily to the other shore. Moreover, Samu (physical labour), martial arts or other Zen tools make the mind more vigilant, and let the body move in accordance with the framework of Zen practice. This process is difficult to be seen in ordinary meditation. In fact, Zen is neither sitting nor working. It is both sitting and working. In other words, it is the combination of mind–body interaction. In Zen, sitting concentration can be merged with Samu (work) as 'Body–Mind' training. This combination makes the mind sharp and penetrative. It also brings a sense of calm to the mind, which then permeates the body. To be honest, having practised Zen I found it – in comparison with other systems of mind training – more dynamic, more practical and bringing more immediate understanding of the nature of our body-mind. Compared to other, normal meditations, Zen practice is different because of the above-mentioned explanation, although all the teachings of the Buddha are meant for awakening. With this experience of meditation in general and Zen in particular, I made ready to return to my country to carry out my sacred task to convey my people the wisdom in which they were familiar with, centuries ago.[59]

Some points from this chapter

- I started Rinzai Zen training in Japan in 1984.

- My first Zen teacher was the Ven. Noritake-Roshi and my first Zen training centre was Hosenji Zen temple, Kyoto city.

- I was sacked by the Ministry of Education due to their spurious decision.

- I found differences between Zen and non-Buddhist meditation.

- In 1984 I was the first Iranian to start studying Zen in Zen temples in Japan.

- All the techniques of the different schools of Buddhism are very similar with only slight differences.

- One destination, many ways.

- To some, Sosakan is more effective than Anapana in penetrating deep into Vipassana 'Introspection'.

- My first understanding into the Buddha's teaching came with the practice of Vipassana. My second understanding came through Zen practice.

- The sudden awakening can be easily understood and distinguished from other meditation practices.

---

59 – It was An Shigao who first disseminated the Dhamma in Persia and then transmitted to the Chinese intellectuals in 148 A.D.

- I was getting well prepared to enter the systematic method of Zen.

- My ordination as a Zen monk occurred sooner than I expected.

- As a Mahayana devotee I took an oath to help every suffering being.

- I was sent to Iran by my Zen masters as a missionary.

- Zazen is somehow different from ordinary meditation.

- Zen is the combination of Zazen, Samu, yaza, martial art and San-Zen.

- Training in Zen in coming closer to the realisation of the 'Self' is different

- The schedule of Sogenji and the Zen practices of the Roshi were different from other forms of Buddhism

- Sosakan and Anapana are both breathing exercises practiced to develop concentration, but Sosakan is deeper

- I found an effective way to reach the depths of the mind

- Harada Roshi is heir to the teachings of the Rinzai sect of Zen Buddhism as passed down in Japan from Hakuinzenji.

- In Zen, higher knowledge comes from personal observation. To enter the world of Zen, one must pass through the tunnel of experience.

- A golden saying by Albert Einstein is; "The true sign of intelligence is not knowledge but imagination."

- In my opinion, the experience of sudden awakening can happen to those who, enthusiastically and wholeheartedly, are ready for it.

- 'Awakening' in Theravada may happen once in a while, but 'Satori' in Zen schools may happen at any time.

- - To me, strict discipline with a regular timetable and well-organised management are potentially important and necessary for any success, especially for taming the disobedient mind.

- All the Buddha's teachings lead to one thing – Enlightenment, but the Zen school uses a shortcut.

- I believe that the awakening of the Buddha is an ideal for which we can all strive, but there are different ways, techniques, and also teachers to show the 'Way'

- The Buddha discovered a tool, an appliance in which to penetrate in to our own mind and body to reach awakening, that's all.

- I finally decided to return to my country to carry out my task for the benefit of my people.

Chapter 13

Returning Home with Mahayana in Mind – Dreaming of Establishing of a Zen Centre in Iran

"True sadness is when someone still thinks you are the same person after all these years. They brand you because of their own ego, fear and lack of spirituality. What's sadder is when they think they are wise and unprejudiced."
SHANNON L. ALDER

I continued nonstop Zen practice at Sogenji for the two years of my first trip. There are usually three training courses in a month at Sogenji and a gap of only one day in between each session. Nonstop practice should be observed as the rule of Rinzai Zen training. The continuity of the practice is (was) emphasised by the Zen masters as the secret of success which is essential for every practice. I was indeed well-established in the technique and day by day I used to get more and more knowledge about the system of training, continuous awareness in a calm, quiet environment of the temple and other associated practices could bring about the spontaneity for sudden awakening called 'Kensho'.[60] Kensho, is the first experience of Satori. Two years of continuous practice of Zen in my first trip to the Japanese temples and monasteries with strict discipline and rigorous practice was enough for me to collect more experience

---
60   Kensho: is simply seeing into one's own nature which is the goal of Zen teaching.

and to convey it to my own people in my own country. Honestly speaking, I was willing and enthusiastic to transmit the teaching of awakening and peace, not for name, fame, material benefits, supporting any groups or sects or propagating a faith or religion, but a message of sudden self-realisation for one and all. For example, you have tasted nice food full of nourishment which strengthens your body and mind. You have already benefited from it without knowing the cook or the cooks, but you cannot resist giving it to your fellow beings, especially your fellow citizens, so that they can at least get a taste of it. But the food for thought or the food for mental development is (was) much superior to the food for the body. I was in fact appointed to offer food for the mind. This was the A to Z of my purpose. It would have been selfish for me, as a Mahayana devotee, to keep this teaching merely for myself. It is about the purification of mind and no harm could come from teaching such a subject. If, for example, a scientist discovered or invented something, he is bound to offer his finding to the masses as a universal remedy and not keep it for himself or herself. So also during years of research and practice in different countries with different qualified teachers, my eyes opened to a reality which had remained hidden to me for years. I felt bound to share my experience with my nearest and dearest. Therefore I was impatient to bestow this knowledge first upon my own people.

This was always in my mind that positivity incorporate with positive thinking will push me forward. For the same reason I tried to stay positive and enthusiastic. To work hard and not give up hope, to face the obstacles and to overcome them, and keep on learning and experiencing the events, and moreover surround myself with my, warm, creative, and genuine people. These were the signs of my positivity and commitment.

Generally speaking, I am a positive person. I like to see things positively. There is nothing wrong with this view. In my opinion, to be positive is better than being negative, because it gives us greater energy for the idea or the purpose to be fulfilled. While negativity is exhausting and paralysing, a positive attitude gives us the will to work around obstacles and ultimately succeed. I was confident about my task, my purpose and the way I had found for better living. With so much confidence and energy I was coming back home to work for my people, to be with them and receive inspiration from them in a practical, human way. I was at least expecting my colleagues in the education department to support me and to cooperate with me in building a sane and strong society, as the revolutionaries repeatedly promised for the betterment of our society. I was expecting them to allow me to express my ideas as what was really needed for society and the people. I did not want to propagate diversionary idea or to strive for a position, to go against this or that. Very simply, I wanted to teach people to take a look into their mind, observe it and then change it for the better. This is applicable to one and all. However, I would be surprised if they (the rulers) thought otherwise. I did not know that I would face some sick and paranoid characters. There must be some special definitions for a kind of mental illness called 'paranoia' in the science of psychology or psychotherapy, but according to my knowledge and my own observation I need to describe some paranoid political people as follows:

1. They fear that something bad will happen to them if they do not prevent it.
2. They think that others are responsible and not themselves.
3. Their belief in what they imagine to be true is exaggerated or unfounded.
4. The central thought which is present with paranoia is a sense of threat.
5. A paranoid person is someone who knows nothing about the essence of reality. They act according to their illusion.
6. They think they are quite reasonable and their information about the 'suspect' is absolutely genuine.

The explanation above is not out of my imagination but the reality about those whose characters were shown during their interrogations and investigations. I directly reflect their innate characteristics.

Anyhow. I was still positive, optimistic and enthusiastic to work in my own country rather than to be a wanderer in foreign countries. Moreover the whisper of my Zen masters was still resounding in to my ears as to carry on the Bodhisattva's vow[61] to help people with what they need. This desire made me go back home confidently and happily.

I was happy that I was the only Iranian Zen trainee who wanted to introduce two system of mind training of two schools of Buddhism, Theravada and Mahayana, and to make the trainee choose between them. The techniques which I intended to offer to my people are indeed universal and the tools could be directed and taught by a person who have practically gone through

---

61 - The Bodhisattva's vow is: To liberate sentient beings, putting an end to desires, mastering Dharma (cosmic law and order), and striving to reach awakening.

long time experience in this field, a systematic and discipline method for one and all without imposing a conversion or proselytising faith. A specific technique brought about by any qualified masters of all time. My people also deserve this knowledge to apply it in their daily life, a teaching which has been inherited from our forefathers.[62] Two years of nonstop practice at Sogenji, as taught by the Roshi, encouraged me to go beyond my solitary practice and made me share my findings with my people. At first I started translating some booklets and pamphlets I had brought with me from Japan. I was hoping that theory would help the novice to understand the practice better.

It was my dream to establish a small centre for Zen meditation practice like other monks did in their own countries, inspired by their masters and supported by their wise government. Why not? What is drawback? Why should the Iranian people deprived of having such a constructive cultural-therapeutic centre to promote their talents and their creativities, while all over the world (except Iran and the Persian gulf countries) welcome such remarkable centres and do their best in setting up such humanitarian centres?

Such a centre would probably welcome not only in Iran but all the Persian Gulf countries as a wonderful system of mind training and also satisfactory relationship with other countries in this field. The same intention sparked in my mind at the beginning of the revolution when I came back home from India in 1978–79. But the monopolising revolutionaries were not so kind and so intelligent to understand this fact in order to think about the benefit of their country. They did not even want to know what this technique is and what is used for. They thought it was deviated and illegal only because it differs from Islam. This establishment is (was) not only my unquestionable right as a government teacher, but also as a committed Iranian citizen who compassionately willing to prove his abilities in flourishing the society, but it is the duty of the revolutionary government to provide facilities in making such a magnificent cultural centre for the interest of the people instead of denying it with baseless justifications. I was sure that this cultural centre could not only help all the students from different institutions and colleges, but other people in many ways. This was my ambition which is not far from reality.

When I came back home, I had no job and no means of livelihood. I had already lost my job due to a misunderstanding by the education authorities whose decision was not just. First of all, I strove to go back to my previous

---

62 – An Shigao, the Parthian prince from Persia of AD 148, was quite familiar with the techniques and the 'Teaching'. The Persians can account him as their forefather in the path of Dhamma (Dharma).

job by trying to convince the authorities that I had committed no acts of immorality during my research at Hanazono College or Zen centres in Japan. I did not believe I had done anything wrong, so I had nothing for which to apologise. On the contrary, it was for the authorities to apologise for their big mistakes and lack of understanding about things and ideas which cost me a lot. In democratic countries they not only have to apologise for their big mistakes, but also they must give compensation for their acts. Anyhow, I had to even conceal my conversion as a Buddhist monk. Therefore, I preferred not to mention my ordination to anyone as I knew that the Islamic fanatics were strict about it. It was hard to get my previous job back but I had to make an effort and to find a way to regain it by any possible means. If I could be given employment as a teacher, it would be a stepping stone to my goal of helping my people as a teacher again. This was my first step to carry out my duty as a Mahayana Buddhist. To return to my previous job, I had to go to different cities, and to see different officials to convince them of their mistakes. Being away for two years from my country, and being fully concentrated on the subject of my practice, things in Iran seemed different to me. The world of the past two years was different from the present one. I saw things and people differently. I was enthusiastic to help my suffered people to come out of their entanglements as much as I could. The government now dominated over the mind of majority of people through media and other means of indoctrination. Since the beginning of the revolution they were establishing their ideology more powerful. But having self-confidence I was happier, more positive and full of energy to convey the message in spite of hindrances because the truth surpasses all the facts and I had no fear to reveal the truth. This was handed to me by my kind and compassionate spiritual teachers without expecting anything in return. In Iran I could not reveal my status as a monk. I could not wear my robe either. I could not say anything about religion nor could I tell anyone my purpose for coming back home. If I did so, I would certainly receive severe punishment. I was aware of the rule of Islam about conversion and more than that propagating an idea except Islam. According to the rules of Islam if a person is born a Muslim and if he/she consciously gets converted to another religion, the penalty for their act will be death, even if he/she repents. For this reason I was careful to hide my identity as a monk or a religious activist. I had to make the government authority understand that I was an ordinary researcher and interested in traveling to gain more knowledge about what interested me. To do research is the right of every teacher or even college students, but in the Islamic regime the extent of one's researches is limited by the government's wishes; privileges are given to particular persons who show that they believe in the government's policies.

At first, my colleagues in the education office did not pay attention to me. Their behaviour towards me was strange and the atmosphere was not favourable and friendly. I felt that I was untouchable in the Islamic society. I was unnecessarily defamed and humiliated by my office. For some weeks my colleagues made fun of me as a 'sex-researcher'. One day one of my previous colleagues, a Mullah of the same university who taught theology and Islamic ideology, asked me out of curiosity to explain to him about women in Japan. Upon hearing this silly question a tear of regret came to my eyes and I sighed deeply about what kind of people were now ruling the civilised land of Persia, and that such men could occupy positions at the universities, which were supposed to be the highly-educated section of society. I honestly felt sorry for those who judge with their ears and not their eyes. I had to explain to them that I was practicing the Japanese culture, 'Zen' and Zen is not Zan (woman). It seemed to me that they had become obsessed with this matter. The initial welcome which I received from them was deceptive.

The government can create scandals about people easily and defame them if they disagree with their views. In addition, if the person is seen as a nuisance or dangerous to them, he/she will be either jailed, tortured or killed. Many writers, journalists, authors, artist and oppositions were vanished or killed mysteriously in the same way. In the city I was humiliated too on account of my research with their false accusations, whereas my research was human, cultural therapy and martial arts. And even more strange is that they did not allow a person to defend himself against their false accusations. The attitude of my colleagues showed how ignorant are those who knowingly pass judgment on things about which they know not even a word. In such a medieval, narrow-minded environment the Roshi and I were hoping to establish a small centre for training purposes, but this seemed impossible in a society where everything was under the tight control of a minority ideological group. However, even in such circumstances I had to investigate every possible opportunity and leave no stone unturned. A government with a monopoly of power tries to expand its own ideology, hypocritically describing its dissidents as full of deviations and apostasy.

My purpose was to make people touch the truth, which hitherto they had never seen. It was necessary, indeed essential, for my people to know about other cultures in order to see the differences from their own. This made me do my best to make a small place for Zen training, not only for my students but also for my colleagues to come and see the reality of life and to break out of the shell of ignorance which surrounded them, and as the proverb says, "Seeing is Believing." The fact is even among the well-educated, nobody knew what Zen was. In one sense I was fortunate that the Islamic authorities knew nothing about Zen, because Zen is fundamentally opposed to reactionary elements, deviational thought and it can remove the cloud of ignorance covering the minds of the charlatans.

For about three years, me and my family were vagrant and homeless, trying to find a way to go back to my previous job. I was finally able to succeed with the help of some of my old friends. This was made possible with the help of them who told me how to satisfy and convince the religious authorities (by bribes or other things) in order to return to my job. Upon my friends' advice I could finally contact my people again. I returned to my previous job after suffering a lot of torment, agony and pain. First, as a punishment I was sent to schools of low standard in the suburbs of Shiraz and then to Yasoodj suburbs in the east of Fars province. I felt that I was still being doubted by the authorities because the atmosphere in country was chaotic, with a strong inclination to war and an insistence on absolute obedience to the Islamic leaders and their way. Naturally I was not in conformity with their way of thinking, but I had to go along with their system while following my own precepts.

At this time of war the religious authorities tightened the ring of their licence for dissidents. The government called them the fifth column of the enemy. They dominated the people especially during the time of the war. When I was sent to Yasoodj, I found it to be a beautiful green city. The high school where I was teaching as a contract teacher (temporary teacher) was in a good place. I was in fact full of energy and confidence for change. Changing for better, for the people and the society where I was living. The windows of the classrooms opened onto a green garden with big trees, which was a beautiful environment, especially when the weather was fine. Sadly, the garden was always polluted with dirt and rubbish left by people living in the neighbourhood. They used to throw their rubbish into the garden until this beautiful area became filled with rubbish and nobody took responsibility for cleaning it. When the windows were opened, instead of being greeted with fresh air and the fragrance of flowers, one would inhale the awful smell of rubbish. I wanted to encourage the students to participate in some group projects in the form of Zen culture, the Japanese style which I had seen and practised in the Japanese family. During my stay in Japan I noticed that some Japanese set aside two days holidays in a month cleaning the whole house and the gardens all together. Even the children were taught to participate in cleaning. This culture is derived from Zen temples and monasteries and was brought to the society.

One day while I was teaching in class, I asked the students to think about the hygiene of the garden and how, as responsible students, they could change the environment. The garden could be used for study and play if they made it clean and beautiful. In fact, the place looked like a small park which all the school students could use in their break times. In order to encourage them to work together I had to explain the role of great men in getting the cooperation of their people in building their society. My favourites in this field at that time were the Chinese leader Mao-tse Tung and the Vietnamese leader Ho Chi Minh. During my Marxist activities I had studied their biographies and how they worked with their people apart from their highly position. They were great leaders although later they were criticised.

Inspired by the selfless example of these two revolutionary men, we decided that we would all work together during our holidays to clean up the garden. I did not know that my speech about the two leaders would create trouble for me. As long as the war was running, this provided an excuse for the government to suppress all dissident. Dissidents were kept under control throughout this time. Besides I was not a native of the borough. To them I was a stranger and this was another excuse for them to disrupt my life.

I was immediately called by the head of education. Usually the head of an office is expected to set an example and stand out as different from ordinary people in his behaviour, speech, dress and in every other respect. Unfortunately, he was not given the post and position because of his high university degree or his outstanding character, but because of his blind obedience to the Islamic regime. On entering his office my first thought was that I had come to the wrong room. The official was dressed in army uniform with a long beard, wearing army boots instead of ordinary shoes. He had all characteristic of a stand by soldier except having arms. It was not necessary for him to show off as a dedicated soldier because we were not in an emergency situation caused by the war. Yasoodj city was situated far from the frontier and had nothing to do with the war. There was no sign of war in that small city. All the cities were calm except for the border cities. There was no need to demonstrate in such a funny dress and make such an exhibition. The head of the education office could have been given a job as a low-class servant or a butler because of his inhuman behaviour and his illiteracy rather than having this important position. I knocked the door and entered the room and said hello to him but received no response, as if I had a deep hostile to him. His room was also full of the pictures of the Mullahs of the past and present. The room was like a mosque (shrine) rather than a cultural room.

He told me to sit and abruptly asked:

- Do you know we are in a war?
- Yes, Sir. It is a war imposed on Iran by Saddam Hussein, I said.
- And do you know what Imam (he meant Ayatollah Khomeini) said?
- About what?
- About Islam which may be in danger.
- In danger from whom Sir? I said
- By non-Muslims, and he immediately asked: Are you a communist?
- No, sir, I said.
- An atheist?
- No, Sir.
- Do you believe in God?
- Yes Sir, God is love, God is beauty, I answered.
- But you've spoken about communism in class, haven't you?
- No, Sir. I'm neither a communist, nor propagating a doctrine of communism.
- If you are not a communist, why, then, do you teach Muslim children about communism?
- Sir, I never teach communism because I have no knowledge of it.
- But the schoolchildren never tell lies.
- My intention has been misunderstood, Sir.
- What were you telling them? he said.
- I was telling about cleaning the garden of the school.
- It is not your duty. It is the duty of the janitor of the school.
- But I intended to change the environment for the better.
- This must be you trick, I know the tricksters.
- I'm not a trickster, Sir, I'm a teacher.
- You have a big mouth, enough.

I could not convince him that he had misunderstood the story which had been told to him about me. Because of this he had come to believe the accusation and to believe that I was at fault.

He then asked me a variety of silly questions for nearly two hours, thinking that is how an expert investigator should behave. As a matter of fact he seemed to be an investigator rather than the head of an education office, because the method of his questioning was of a crossexaminer. He warned me that their people were Muslims and believed in God. He said that the students hated atheists. He threatened me, with carefully chosen words, not to direct my students down a wrong path. After hearing such strong language from the head of the education office, I preferred not to stay in the city any more as I felt I was in danger by staying there, especially as I risked causing a scandal because of a rumour that I was an atheist. I was advised by my good friends to leave the city immediately because the authorities might accuse me of being an atheist in a society full of prejudice and ignorance. These prejudiced people had been told that shedding the blood of an apostate is legitimate if they are killed or executed. At about 12 o'clock at night I hired a truck and escaped from the city with my family. I went back to the city of Behbahan, where I was first sacked.

In the Islamic Republic of Iran it is not so easy to return to a job after one has been dismissed, especially if one is under suspicion of being a non-Muslim. I had ups and downs for nearly three tormenting years during which time I struggled to regain my former employment as a teacher. My return to my previous job was due to the efforts of my good friends about how to deal with some of the authorities concerned, sometimes with a financial inducement. I was happy to be coming back to my job because I felt that at last I was getting closer to my people and this would allow me to express my compassion for them and the problems they were facing. Besides, teaching is (was) a part of my life and I'm very interested in it.

During the first or second year of teaching classes, I could not resist telling my students about Zen, as the Japanese culture which was developed within a few centuries, as a form of therapy, creativity, energy, self-mastery and aid to concentration which was very important especially for the students in general. This was an open and honest way of contacting people who were curious to know about themselves and other cultures as well. After all, this is what school or education means. I talked about how to organise their minds the way they wanted, to apply formulas for success and how to have peace of mind by practicing the technique. As a matter of fact I necessarily needed a place for this project to be conducted genuinely and perfectly but no response to this demand. To me there was nothing wrong with giving this teaching and it could help students in whatever field of study they were engaged. Then I slowly started telling them how to concentrate on their studies using the technique of a simple breathing exercise. This technique was neither religious nor political, to be persecuted or prosecuted by the prejudiced Islamists. Most of the school students started showing interest in it. Next, they wanted to know whether there are things beyond this simple technique. They were curious to know more about Japanese culture and other schools of thought. Although I was appointed as an English teacher, sometimes at their request I told them about different cultures in different countries. I also familiarised them with the techniques which could help them to accelerate their studies. Here and there, I talked about Zen and how it had shaped the culture of Japan in different ways of life since it appeared in Japan and how it can develop the mind in a practical way. I told them that Zen had not been monopolised by Japan or China and that it belongs to one and all. To prevent misunderstanding about Zen as a foreign and imported word, I had found the equivalent in the Persian language. I told my students that Zen-therapy was also introduced by the Iranian sage Zoroaster in the form of Moraghebeh (sitting and doing nothing) more than 600 BCE.[63] Hence, Zen can be translated as Moraghebeh in the Persian language.[64] They understood that Zen is a practice by which they can improve their studies and is also a way to enlightenment in long-term practice. They liked the subject and they used to follow it as instructed. It was an interesting subject for them and I used to set aside some time to talk about Zen as an art of living. Based on my initiative I combined Zen with a formula of how to reach success by a short cut. In 1976 in Hyderabad in India, I was attracted by a book, *Think and Grow Rich* by Napoleon Hill. I found out if this formula mixed with Zazen or deep concentration would help the mind to become sharp and able to carry out everything efficiently. By adding or subtracting the content of the book, I changed the formula from accumulating wealth in to the formula to reach 'Satori'. This book had many recipes for success, but it made no mention of either meditation or concentration as an important part in achieving success. Besides, the power of

---

63 Sri Swami Shivananda, the student of Radhkrishna, believes that the Persian sage Zoroaster experienced deep Samadhi (meditative absorption) or communion with Ahura Mazda, the Supreme Lord of the Universe, on the top of Mount Sabatam. He had highly divine visions. He conversed directly with Ahura Mazda and received the wisdom of the Lord. He received seven revelations from Ahura Mazda. At the age of 30, he came out as a great sage. After receiving the divine light of revelation, he became the renowned messenger of Ahura Mazda. (This information is taken from the writings of Sri Swami Shivananda.) Also, see the book *Zoroastrian Meditation*, by Dr. Jose Luis Abreu.

64 Of course at that time I knew nothing about An Shigao, the Parthian Prince who established "Ch'an" in China. More details in my previous book *An Shigao Bodhisattva*.

imagination which has mentioned as an important formula for success needs a deep concentration (Zazen practice) as how mental images come to reality. I believed the formula should be taught in all public schools and colleges, and I expressed the opinion that if it were properly taught and practiced it would so revolutionise the entire education system that the time spent in schools, universities, and other cultural institutes could be reduced to less than half.

I did this during the time I was employed as a teacher by the Ministry of Education. More students came from other classes to learn about things they had not heard before. It was entirely confined to Zen but it was a new teaching which could help them to be more creative when entering universities and could bring success in every calling. In this way I could also divert the suspicions of various prejudiced groups from an understanding of my main task.

Their interest and their presence in my classes revived my energy to tell them more about my experience. This subject was more important to them than learning a foreign language like English. All this came about as a result of the interest they showed in the subject matter, and not because I tried to force it on them. However, I was happy to teach those students who were interested, what they wanted to hear. I was so inspired by the presence of so many students that I allocated most of the classes to Japanese culture and Zen as a part of my experience. One of the main characteristics of being under the control of that government was that they did not want people to know more than they were permitted to know, which is Islam. According to them, everything except Islam is considered to be deviant propaganda, supporting Western culture, and dangerous to the Islamic Republic of Iran. Unfortunately, this direct contact between me and my students did not last long and the reason was obvious. The fact was the interest of the students in a new way of thinking and a new outlook on life and success was increasing quickly and the number of students was multiplying. Wherever there was a gathering, the regime feared there might be a plot against them. So they had to meddle in everything in order to save their monolithic structure called Islam. A few days later I received an official letter from the education office to appear before their head. I did not know why I had been summoned because I had done nothing wrong during my teaching in classes. I did my job honestly and right. I thought they were going to award me something on account of my recent researches, or to increase my salary or give me some promotion. It was none of these. The chief seemed very fiery. After offering me a seat, he started his questions in this way:

"What do you teach at school Mr Dehdashti?" he asked in a commanding tone. I was surprised by this question because they knew I was an English teacher, as I was appointed by them. I said, "I teach English, Sir."

"Yes, I know you teach English. What else do you teach to our children at school in classes?" I was still puzzled about his line of questioning and again I said, "English, Sir."

"But you teach a kind of mystic religion," he said. Not knowing what he meant, I said, "What is that sir?"

"It is Zen", the chief said.

Immediately my inner computer started working and I wondered if some zealots in the class might have reported our discussions in the class, but at the same time I was sure that the president of the education office knew nothing about Zen or such a system of mind training. So, instead of answering him, I politely asked him, "What is Zen, Sir?"

He wanted to pretend that he knew something about it and confidently said:

"Conjuring or sorcery you've learnt."

I patiently said, "Zen is not sorcery, Sir."

"The thing which you learnt in India," he corrected himself.

"Zen is not from India either, Sir," I said confidently.

"I don't know where it came from," he said, "but this much I do know: you have spoken about Zen to the students."

I immediately said, "Sir, a mistake is to commit misunderstanding. When you do not know what Zen is, why have you brought me here to question me about something about which you know nothing? I am a teacher but not your teacher. Sad to say, we are infected by our own misunderstanding of how our own minds work. And because you do not know what Zen is, I can tell you whatever I want, no matter whether it is true or false."

Knowing very well that he did not know anything about the matter, he angrily and selfishly said, "What is Zen, then?"

I calmly said, "Finding your true nature, Sir."

He thought I was making fun of him, whereas in fact I was answering him truthfully and honestly. Suddenly he said, "Do you mean you are teaching the students about my nature?" He paused for a while and then said, "You'd better tell them about your nature."

"Yes, Sir. It can be about my nature or anyone's nature, it makes no difference," I answered him. These answers did not satisfy him and he coolly threatened me, advising me that I could find all the knowledge I wanted in

Islam. He then warned me not to divert the minds of the students onto such worthless ideas. I should stick to Islam or I would be in trouble. I preferred not to argue with him any more for fear that he would incriminate me with false charges which would put me in trouble again.

As a result of this experiment I learnt that I must be more careful about my activities as I was living in the middle of a group of prejudiced Muslims who knew nothing except what was allowed by their religious dictatorship. I tried to be more cautious regarding my missionary activities so as to avoid falling into any traps set by the Muslim fanatics. I resolved to speak only about the part of Zen which is concerned with treatment, concentration, moral conduct and inner mastery or to speak about the formulas for success. I also used Moraghebeh, that is, the Persian equivalent to the word Zen. I tried not to speak about Buddhism, but about Vipassana (introspection); not to speak about hypnotism but relaxation; not to say a word about my other activities, but instead to concentrate on my services to humanity. In this way I could survive and I could approach my students cautiously in order to convey the messages of the spiritual masters in a disguised fashion.

While I was practising by myself I had established contacts with other temples in Sri Lanka, India, Japan, Malaysia and other training centres. The war was still going on with the reluctant involvement of the Iranian people. I strove to provide a calm place for people to relax as a basic need, and as a step to higher relaxation and peace of mind. To have a relaxation centre was a must for them to immunise themselves against the circumstances and the events they faced from time to time. In this way I could help my people in accordance with my spiritual commitment. As an expression of this commitment, I had already taken oaths at Sogenji before my master and the Sangha.[65]

It is believed that a revolution must be for the betterment of society, helping people to avoid superstitions, violence, enmity and so on. The people should learn how to strive for peace, love, compassion, solidarity, wisdom and so on. Revolution means a fundamental change, from ignorance to social responsibility, from deficiencies to development, from suppression to freedom and creativity. In such circumstances people should understand the positive values they had in the past and how to maintain them in the future. This should be the perfect way for people to realise their potential. But if a revolution does not lead to inner revolution, or fundamental changes, or to training people about how to come out of their difficulties, the structure

---

65 Sangha: Buddhist monastic order, including monks, nuns, and novices.

of the same revolution will gradually collapse and the consequences are obvious. Since superstitions and ignorance dominate the country, we have to expect tragedies and disasters even worse than before. Victor Hugo said, "Superstition, bigotry and prejudice, ghosts though they are, cling tenaciously to life; they are shades armed with tooth and claw. They must be grappled with unceasingly, for it is a fateful part of human destiny that it is condemned to wage perpetual war against ghosts. A shade is not easily taken by the throat and destroyed."[66]

I wrote to the Roshis, both at Sogenji and Hosenji, about the situation in Iran and my cultural-therapeutic activities. The masters advised me to teach the people only concentration without mentioning the name of any particular master or religious leader. They also told me to come to Japan if I could. I followed their advice and I started teaching my students basic Zazen in the name of Moraghebeh as a way to control their minds. Then I arranged some group sittings with my students in their homes or in some remote villages. Someone may be surprised at how it is possible for an inclination to simple 'group sitting' should attract so much persecution and prosecution. There are many reasons behind it and one of them is: according to the logic of the prejudiced Islamic groups, those who are not with the Islamic government are against it, especially when a new way of thinking becomes fascinating and popular among the people. The Mullahs preached and propagated Islam simply in order to bring the youth to the mosques as a means of imposing the government's selfish ideals. My teaching, on the contrary, made the youth feel the reality of life and this can entice them away from the mosque to new worlds for their own benefit.

I had ups and downs along the risky road of being a committed monk, but I never felt exhausted although the circumstances were tough. In order to revive my own practice and to give inspiration to my students, I practised Zazen with some of my students in different houses at least once a week. Sometimes I used to go alone to mountains or remote places for a course of self-study or a ten-day retreat as personal practice. It usually gave me confidence and energy in my daily life. I always remembered the story my master used to tell his disciples: a student of Tendai, a philosophical school of Buddhism, came to the Zen abode of Gasan as a pupil. When he was departing a few years later, Gasan warned him, "Studying philosophical theories is a useless way of collecting preaching material. But remember that unless you meditate

---
66   Victor Hugo in Les *Misérables*.

constantly your light of truth may go out." Again, in this connection Mother Teresa says, "If you want a love message to be heard, it has got to be sent out. To keep a lamp of enlightenment burning within ourselves, we have to keep putting oil in it."

A ten-days retreat in the mountains

I used to set up a tent in a remote place and provide myself with some dates, dried bread, vegetables and nuts for a ten-day sitting in meditation (Moraghebeh). From my home in the suburbs of the city, I found a very good, remote place in the middle of the hills of Ramhormoz of the Khuzestan Province, far from the villages and the city, where there was nothing but silence. This kind of retreat usually gave me the patience and relaxation to continue with my duties as a teacher and to be more compassionate towards my students. The road to the meditation place which I had chosen was rough and far from the nearest villages. Therefore I had to use a donkey to carry my necessities there. There was no smooth road for vehicles except for motorbikes. As soon as I reached the place, I cleaned the area of big stones in order to set up my tent. The place where I set my tent was almost flat. It was located in a shallow valley, but for sitting in long periods of meditation I needed to find a proper place near my tent. I finally found a good place on top of the rock. I usually sat at the top of a huge, deep rock. There was a cavity on the rock which would protect me from the wind and the sun, and I had a view over my tent from the top. I usually sat at the edge of the cave, overlooking the scenery in front. The place was calm, cool, with no disturbances except for a few harmful insects. The absolute silence which prevailed made it a very suitable place for successful meditation. The first three days of my practice went well, and concentration was getting deeper and more subtle due to my sincere practice in a favourable environment. A kind of calmness started in me and permeated my whole body. This ecstasy helped me to sit longer in meditation and I was indeed happy about this sensation. But the fourth day, in the afternoon I heard some sound from the distance of small bells, which are usually hanging from the neck of some herder coming nearer to my place. I immediately discovered there was a shepherd approaching my temporary hideaway. I did not pay much attention to him and I kept on practising. However, I was expecting that the shepherd and his cattle would pass close by me and I hoped that there would be no disturbance. But the cattle were coming nearer and nearer. While the shepherd was making his way he probably noticed a tent in the middle of a mountain where no one had ever lived before. His curiosity was aroused and he wanted to see who was living there. He directed his cattle down to the tent. Then he looked into the tent, but he saw no one and so he started shouting: "Is anybody there?"

He paused and again repeated the same sentence louder. He shouted again and again. This in fact interrupted the continuity of my practice and I had to watch him and his cattle from the top of the rock where I was meditating. The tent was open and the shepherd let the cattle eat what I had in the tent. But the shepherd was not satisfied with this and he was looking for the person or persons living in such a remote place. Living in that area all alone can no doubt surprise everyone and make them wonder how long a person could survive in such a remote place where there were no trees, no pure water, no means of outside contact, or other facilities. The shepherd was holding a stick in his hand and looking for the owner of the tent.

"Is anybody here?" he shouted, striking at the sides of the tent with his stick. I remained silent, thinking that eventually he would leave the place with his cattle if he did not see anybody there. However, he did not want to leave the place without knowing who was living there. He walked around and suddenly he saw me sitting motionless on top of the rocks. As usual, I had covered myself with a white bedsheet while I was sitting still. The brave shepherd got frightened.

"Who are you?" he asked again in his folk language (Lori). I remained silent and kept on meditating, hoping he would interpret this as a sign that he should go away and get on with his own business, but he was insistent to know who I was, especially as I had covered myself in a white cloth and was sitting still like a statue of the Buddha. He started coming up to reach me, carrying his stick. While he was approaching me I could see a kind of fear in him. I think he had never encountered such a scene in all his life, although Iranian shepherds are famous for their bravery because they fear nothing. The hill where I was meditating was steep and in spite of its roughness he was cautiously coming nearer to me while controlling himself in order not to fall down. He finally reached me and sat in front of me nearly two metres away. I indeed felt his breath which was fast and abnormal and after a little pause he slowly said with fear, "Who are you?"

I remained silent and this made him more curious and with the stick he tapped me on the leg once or twice to know who I was. When he did not get any reaction from me, he dared to poke the stick into my ribs and pushed it harder to see whether I was a human or what. I could not tolerate this action anymore and I was sure that he would act even more violently if I stayed silent. He again prodded his stick into my rib and this time harder. Suddenly I reacted by shouting at him so loudly that he got shocked and nearly fell down from the top of the hill, but he clung to a big stone to balance himself.

I asked, "What do you want, shepherd?" With this sudden shock he was so scared that he started gazing at me for a while to see my face properly. As he was grasping a big stone so as not to fall down the steep hillside, he noticed that I was speaking in a human language. I then smiled at him to show him that I was friendly towards him but that I did not appreciate his extreme curiosity. When he saw me behaving like an ordinary human being, he was happy and relaxed and he found he could speak to me freely with his sweet folk language. Then he asked me a variety of questions such as why I was there, what I was doing in a remote place, how long I had been there and my purpose in staying in the mountains. I could not answer all his questions because he would not have understood me. Finally he strictly advised me not to stay in such an environment any longer. When I asked him to tell me the reason, he started telling me stories about ghosts and jinni in which he believed strongly. I had to speak with him in his folk language, saying that I was here because my teachers advised me to come to a quiet and healthy place. In order to stop his questioning, I convinced him that I was a teacher and I had come for relaxation. The Iranian villagers have always been kind and amiable and on hearing this story he invited me to his house, and also offered me food from home to be sent to me by his son. I thanked him for his kindness and convinced him that I had to stay for six days more and then I would go back to my home. He finally agreed and preferred to leave me alone. While he was taking his cattle away from there, from time to time he turned back and looked at me with a mixture of astonishment and doubt.

It was hard for me to come back to the level of Samadhi (concentration) I had gained during four days of continuous practice. My mind had been distracted for a while and I tried to come back to my previous state of concentration. However, I was happy that there were still six days left to continue my practice, and I started again.

Panic at night
That night I went to my tent as usual. I sat in Zazen before I went to bed. I had a mat to sleep on. I always slept at 10 pm and got up early at 4 am Before

sleep I used to sit in meditation because I had nothing to do except practice. During the night, when I was in deep sleep, I was awoken by a strange noise around my tent. At first I did not pay much attention to it. I was sure no humans were to be seen in such a remote place. The sound became louder. It seemed as if someone was tapping on the sides of the tent. I tried to ignore it and decided to go back to sleep. Suddenly I remembered the story of the shepherd about ghosts and jinni. I did not want to believe such stories and at the same time I wanted to investigate the sound which was reaching my ears from time to time. If I slept without discovering the reality, my imagination would be filled by ghosts who would be just as true as the illiterate shepherd believed. First I shouted from the tent to ask if anybody was outside. There was a possibility of wild cats because I had seen them in that part of the hills as I was preparing the tent for the night. However, cats cannot climb tents or do not stay by the side of the tent for long. The sound was becoming more obvious. I was a meditator dealing with reality, the reality both within me and without. I had already practised Zen and meditation in various remote places, such as cemeteries, woods and deserts, and I did not want my mind to accept things which do not exist. I decided to confront this sound direct. It was nearly 2 am and it was a dark night without a moon. First I lit the small oil-light and opened the cord of the tent from top to bottom. The sounds could be heard from time to time. It was a windy night too. I checked one side of the tent but I saw nothing. I went to another side of the tent and the source of the sound became clear to me. I raised the oil-light onto top of the tent to see better and suddenly to my surprise I saw a big bird just in front of my eyes, probably an eagle or a crow. The bird needed a flat place to perch on, and from time to time it lost its balance and its wings impacted the sides of the tent, making the sounds I had been hearing. The bird had no proper control over its perch, but it flew away when I disturbed it. I was happy that I had finally found out the cause of my fear and I slept well till the morning. Some believe in ghosts and some not. I don't necessarily not believe in ghosts, but I've not encounter them to believe. To me, 'Seeing is believing'. Ghosts to some people are nothing but the creation of their own minds.

Here is a Zen story which illustrates my experience. The title is 'The Subjugation of a Ghost' and it goes as follows: A young wife fell sick and was about to die. "I love you so much," she told her husband, "I do not want to leave you. Do not go from me to any other woman. If you do, I will return as a ghost and cause you endless trouble."

Soon the wife passed away. The husband respected her last wish for the first three months but then he met another woman and fell in love with her. They became engaged to be married. Immediately after the engagement a ghost appeared every night to the man blaming him for not keeping his promise. The ghost was clever too. She told him exactly what had transpired between himself and his new sweetheart. Whenever he gave his fiancée a present the ghost would describe it in detail. The ghost would even repeat conversations and it so annoyed the man that he could not sleep. Someone advised him to take his problem to a Zen master who lived close to the village. At length, in despair, the poor man went to him for help. "Your former wife became a ghost and knows everything you do," commented the master. "Whatever you do or say, whatever you give your beloved, she knows. She must be a very wise ghost. Really you should admire such a ghost. The next time she appears, bargain with her. Tell her she knows so much you can hide nothing from her, and that if she will answer you one question, you promise to break your engagement and remain single."

"What is the question I must ask her?" inquired the man.

The master replied, "Take a large handful of soybeans and ask her exactly how many beans you hold in your hand. If she cannot tell you, you will know she is only a figment of your imagination and will trouble you no longer."

The next night, when the ghost appeared, the man flattered her and told her that she knew everything. "Indeed," replied the ghost, "and I know you went to see that Zen master today."

"And since you know so much," demanded the man, "tell me how many beans I hold in this hand!"

There was no longer any ghost to answer the question. All the man's anxieties had been figments of his imagination and had no basis in reality,[67] just like my uncertainties caused by the bird flapping its wings.

The Basiijis' paranoia

Two days later, after the shepherd's visit to my secret place and before my ten-day course ended, I had another disturbing experience. While restarting my meditation I heard another noise which seemed strange to me. There were sounds of motorbikes coming from a distance. This time it was my turn to be surprised by hearing motorbikes in this remote area. Two motorists stopped in front of my tent. They found me up on top of the rock and shouted to me

---

67 Zen Flesh, Zen Bones

impolitely to come down. I had to cooperate with them because they were armed with guns and there was a possibility they might shoot under the false impression that I might be dangerous to them or be their enemy. At that time of war these armed groups known as Basij[68] were allowed to do whatever they wanted if they saw unusual or suspicious things. I was not an unusual person, but they could suspect me. I slowly came down and immediately spoke to them in a friendly way. I did not have a suitable answer to justify why I was staying in that area. I had to create a story for them to let me free. I told them that I had come there because I was mentally sick and needed a calm, quiet place for relaxation. But they did not believe me. They looked at me and asked me what I was doing there. I knew that the shepherd might have told the Basijis (militia) about me as an act of kindness in order to help me. The armed men suspected that there might be other people there and waited to see whether any others were in the area. I assured them that I was alone there and that I had come for mental practice and nothing else. First they ambushed to see whether other persons are with me. I used to see such imaginary actions in the movies waiting for the criminals to arrest them but not in reality. I did not know whether I laugh at them or to lament them. I was not so dangerous to them as they imagined. Their behaviour was indeed ridiculous and lunatic. After an hour or so, they asked me to sit on the back of their motorbike and they took me to the nearest guardhouse (gendarmerie station) in the Jaizan village of Ramhormoz city. They brought me to a local police station so proudly as if they had captured the most important criminal in the area. Some Basijis even expected to be rewarded by their superintendents for their act of heroism. There, the army officer, dressed in his special uniform, asked me different questions and tried to incriminate me with false charges of being a spy or a fifth column of an enemy. Although they knew that I was a government teacher, I was beaten in order to make me tell them the truth as to what I was doing in the hills. I explained to them that it was not possible for someone to carry out espionage for an enemy while living on the top of a mountain where there was no means of communication or any other equipment. After being held in detention for a few days with no food and answering many silly questions I again asked them to contact my office in the Behbahan city which was not far from there. Eventually, one of my colleagues who knew the guard officer came from my office, showed the police authorities some documents from the education office confirming that I was a formal government teacher. The innocent shepherd had made the situation

---

68   Mobilisation Resistance Force- The oppressive Army of the Islamic regime. Preparing military forces and the like for war.

worse for me and this prompted the fanatics to create more problems for me. According to what I had learned from my studies, I understood them to have paranoid personalities. I have already explained the paranoid state of their mind in previous pages, but sad to say paranoia is a state of mind which distorts our attitude to reality. Paranoia is a mental state where one is suspicious without reason. The mind is full of delusions or hallucinations. One may feel that people are trying to harm them in some way or that something dreadful is about to happen. It is a thought process believed to be heavily influenced by fear and doubt, often to the point of delusion and irrationality. I found the same state of mind in most of the members of the groups of prejudiced Islamists. For the same reason I was unnecessarily beaten and kept hungry for days. Those who mistrust the way they view the world and its people are said to be suffering from paranoia. Arthur D. Halvaty says; "Paranoia is the delusion that your enemies are organised." According to my understanding, these men questioned me without good reason, with no understanding and in a rude manner although I was a member of the ministry of education. I was indeed fortunate that I was not killed by them perversely. The act that can be done easily and nobody is accountable. My tent, some books, and other belonging were seized by the Islamic militia (may be my insignificant belonging taken by them seemed to be as a victory or perhaps as warrior trophies according to their hallucination).

My bitter experience of how religious minorities (or other Iranian ethnics) suffer in the Islamic Republic of Iran illustrates the depth of ignorance in the high ranks of the government authorities. They persecute others on account of what they think and what they believe. They give importance to their own way of thinking, whether it is accepted by society at large or not. Their concepts are based on an unidentified source which is devoid of both wisdom and compassion. Their attitudes have been formed by the necessity of having to obey any command out of blind devotion. The Islamic regime has a fixed way of thinking based on the need to establish their fundamentalist ideology and to eliminate totally all other ways of thinking. It has always been their way to punish crimes not yet committed. Regarding these Middle Age's rulers Sigmund Freud says, "What progress we are making. In the Middle Ages they would have burned me. Now they are content with burning my books."

So my dream of establishing a temple, a Dhamma house, an academy, or a small centre for mind improvement, for the welfare of majority of people, was fading away in the face of these medieval attitudes.

Some points from this chapter

- Food for thought or food for mental development is much superior to food for the body, although we do need them both.

- We must distinguish between constructive ambition and destructive one.

- I tried to go back to my previous job because I loved teaching.

- I had to suffer a lot to regain my previous job as a teacher.

- I had to keep secret my ordination as a Zen monk to protect myself from persecution.

- After being trained in Rinzai Zen I came back home to teach.

- My ambition was to establish a cultural- therapeutic centre in Iran based on Zen discipline.

- The Zen monks and nuns showed their willingness to help me build a small Dhamma House.

- I was defamed and humiliated by the Islamic government for not cooperating with them.

- Staying and living in a totalitarian society is indeed painful for anyone who has independent ideas.

- My dream or to say, my ambition, was to establish a mind-training centre.

- To be cautious, I taught the Noble Teaching in an informal way.

- The students preferred to hear about the things they had not heard before.

- Most of the students wanted something more than the precepts as heard from or preached by the clergy.

- Initially, Zen Buddhism was taught as a form of therapy. In long-term training, Enlightenment.

- My Zen masters advised me to teach the Noble Teaching in a peaceful way.

- I used to report my cultural-therapeutic activities to my masters in Japan time to time.

- Most people do not believe in jinni or ghosts. They think they are nothing but the figment of our imagination

- I saw paranoia in some people whose minds were prejudiced in favour of Islam.

- I was accused of being a spy, completely contrary to all forms of common sense.

- My thoughts of establishing a Zen centre had to be abandoned

- My insignificant belongings were seized by the Islamic Militia as so-called Warrior trophies.

Chapter 14

Escape from My Motherland and the Shadow of Ignorance Cast by the Islamic Clergy of Iran

"What a terrible era in which idiots govern the blind."
WILLIAM SHAKESPEARE, *JULIUS CAESAR*

Political oppression in Iran was increasing, especially after the war. In the name of the war most parts of the country came under the strict control of the government. The pressure on its opponents was getting more and more intense. One ideology was governing the whole country strictly and that was Islamic fundamentalism. Life became almost unbearable for non-Islamic citizens, especially for those who wished to propagate a new idea or other practice. There was persecution of other people, such as Christians, Jews, Baha'is, Buddhists[69], Dervishes (Sufis), and other activists. There was no freedom of speech because of the dominant position of the Islamists. The right to freedom of speech, either political or religious, is recognised as a human right under an Article of the Universal Declaration of Human Rights and is also recognised in international human rights law in the International Covenant on Civil and Political Rights. This statement says that everyone shall have the right to hold opinions without interference and everyone shall have the right to freedom of expression. This right shall include freedom to seek, receive and impart information and ideas of all kinds, regardless of frontiers, either orally, in writing or in print, in the form of religion, art, or through any other media. But this universal declaration does not (did not) reach the ear of the clergies in Iran, or perhaps they do not want to give any importance to it.

---
69 – My students and I were in trouble since I came back from India

A policy of the government was to exert absolute control over the media. On observing such a problematical situation and encountering so many obstacles in my way, I thought I might at least translate some Buddhist or Zen literature into Persian as a way of carrying out my cultural activities and to distribute them secretly among my faithful devotees. I thought this would be a good way to introduce my people to a new way they could follow which would lead genuinely to their betterment. Because the monolithic government had no knowledge of other cultures, they would certainly regard them as deviant and would fight against them vehemently. Since I came back home to Iran, I have tried my best to establish a small cultural school to introduce some teachings which would certainly help my people to change their monotonous and routine lives, but unfortunately it was all in vain. At the same time I was looking for a means to get out of this perplexing society and thereby not to fall into a world of madness. But unfortunately doors to the outside world were closed with such a thick gum of fanaticism that it was hard to break through. I had to wait for an appropriate time to decide what to do and where to go. This decision did not mean giving up my ambitions, but the times and the circumstances were not appropriate. Although I wanted to spread my ideas independently, I had to postpone my initiative until some other time. Unfortunately the mind of the people was influenced by the media which was under the control of the government fundamentalists, who dominated the destiny of most.

I decided to go back to Japan or to visit other Buddhist countries for more practice, but the political situation in Iran was getting worse and there was no way to obtain a visa without difficulty because of the absurd policies of the Islamic regime. The intellectuals, artists and writers, who were not willing to cooperate with the Islamic regime, started a brain drain by migrating to different countries, especially in the West. After the Iran–Iraq war this migration increased. At present, in terms of brain drain Iran is located at the top of the world; about 4–7 million Iranians are living and working in the service of other countries. It is indeed painful for those with original ideas or creative talents who could not demonstrate or express them in accordance with their own wishes. At the same time these intellectuals did not want their minds to deteriorate, and get spoiled or corrupted by those who wanted to dictate an ideology to them. My position as a teacher in high schools and some liberal universities was satisfactory. I taught some private classes and earned good money, I had a good house and other comfortable facilities.

As a matter of fact, I was among the elite with a satisfactory income and a promising future so long as I was obedient to the system and its ideology. On many occasions, I was directly and indirectly invited to cooperate with them. I was told they would help me if I reached an agreement with them, but I had my own personal opinions based on precious experience which were quite different from the government's ideology. What I had learned could help my people in many different ways, offering practical benefits stemming from their own direct knowledge, whereas the ideology of the clergy relied on a system of forced imposition. Day and night, throughout the media, these so-called religious people who have been selected by God spoke to people using techniques built on false premises and using dishonest methods. I could not cooperate with them because of these two different ways of thinking. My nature was to be genuine, truthful and open. I did not want to be the puppet of others, nor did I want to impose my ideas on others for them to accept merely out of blind faith. The pressure was too much for me. I could not reveal my identity as a caring, responsible Zen monk. I could not even contact my good friends and class students openly. Even as a citizen in my own land, I had no right to do anything. I had none of the basic rights and privileges usually given to a citizen. I could not openly contact my temples and my masters. I was like a man constantly on the move, but never getting anywhere. I needed either to change the environment or to change myself. However, if I were to become part of their Islamic structure and if I cooperated with them in supporting their ideology, then I could get a better post and position in their weird, peculiar structure. I did not want to betray my ideals simply in order to obtain a particular post or position. Gradually, I felt that my mind was getting frozen and my lips were being stitched together. I had no encouragement, no inspiration, no hope, and no sign of improvement. I was trying to march forward, but I found myself tied to one spot, making no progress towards the attainment of my ambitions. This can be indeed painful for anyone. As an ordinary teacher I worked hard both day and night for the government, in villages and towns, in day schools and night schools. I spoke to young and old, nearby and far away, doing the duty entrusted to me by the so-called revolutionary government, which pretended to be with the people and for the people. But the hooligans and the opportunists, who were not at all qualified to do the work they did, were given the best opportunities and the highest wages, hired by the government to suit their own purposes because they were like lambs obedient to their shepherd. As a matter of fact, the government gave them a reward for their blind, uncritical support. In this connection, I remember one of the stories of Sufism narrated by a 'Sheikh' or Dervish as follows:

An Islamic mendicant (Dervish) was watching students playing in an old Iranian school called 'Maktab'. The mendicant sorrowfully narrated this story: A boy from a rich family was eating sweets (halva) and the poor students around him were watching him. Then, one of the poor students, who was looking at the rich boy expectantly and imploringly, told him to give him some sweets. The rich boy says, "I'll give you some sweets if you become my donkey." The poor boy agreed and the rich boy took a ride on his back. The other needy students did the same and the rich boy took rides on their backs on the condition that they would be given some sweets. The mendicant who was narrating this story continued: On observing this painful scene, suddenly tears started flowing from my eyes and I said to myself, "Look! Merely for the sake of some sweets these poor boys are prepared to make themselves the donkeys of the rich boy."

This simple, instructive story reveals a bitter truth that some deprived persons are so attached to the attainment of material goods and position that they are ready to become the donkey of their lords and give them absolute obedience. This is partly because of their ignorance and attachments, and partly because of their inability to stand on their own feet. Although they are being exploited by the higher authorities, they obey the commands of their boss even if this requires the elimination of any competitors. That is why only a few are shepherds and the majority are lambs, and in a tyrannical system of government some minorities overcome the majorities in order to rise to a better position. However, there are also some people who have an eminent position, but they do not succumb to force and become submissive. They do not want to be obedient for the sake preserving their name, fame or position. The intellectuals, who were independent in their thinking and way of life, found themselves in a big jail. This jail is the totalitarian government. It is not possible to stay in it, but it is not possible to find an outlet to escape from it.

In spite of such circumstances I decided to change my method of contacting my people even before leaving the country. I translated one of the books of my master Ven. Harada Shada Roshi, *The Morning Dew Drop of the Mind* into the Persian language. This book was not against Islam or Islamic people. It was the experience of my master about Zen and the way of teaching of the past patriarchs to introduce Zen in a simple way and how to practice it in daily life. The subject of the book had nothing to do with Islam or other religions. There was no reason to call such books deviationist or heterodox. On the contrary my writings could give some good knowledge about mind training based on Indo-Chinese culture. But because it did not support Islamic fundamentalism it was considered subversive by some fanatical members of the clergy. For days and nights I worked on the text and finally I had it ready for publication. Before that, the book needed to be edited and revised by a person who knew about Zen. I went to the late Dr Parviz Farvardin Clinic and talked to the doctor about the book. He was very happy and invited me to his house, promising me to edit it within a few months. I went to Tehran again and Dr Farvardin asked me to contact Behjat Publications in Tehran city who were his friends. I took the book there on the recommendation of the doctor. They said they had first to give it to the Islamic Promotion Organisation for confirmation. The Islamic Promotion is an organisation which decides which books are useful to Islamic society and which are seditious. I waited for more than one year. Finally Behjat Publications apologised and said that my book was not accepted for publication. They gave me some friendly advice not to push any more for its publication or I would face trouble from the prejudiced Islamic groups. I explained the story to my friend Dr Farvardin and he said that he had the same problem with his books and received threats from the Islamic guards after the publication of his book on Zen in 1972 and other books in this field. Dr Farvardin had to reside in his home in Dizin (in the north) as a safe haven until his death in suspicious circumstances in 2000.

The Iran–Iraq war finished in 1988 and many frontiersmen were happily returned to their homes after eight years of being homeless and living like tramps, hoping to rebuild their cities with the help of the government. I also came back to my native place, Abadan, with my family. The Abadan and Khorramshahr cities were destroyed very badly. People preferred to reside in their ruined or half-ruined houses because it was better than being homeless in other cities. The government had promised the inhabitants that it would rebuild their cities even better than before. In the process of time, when most people had gone back to their cities, no proper care was taken by the government and their promises were never kept. In fact, they deceived the people in order to make them settle in their deserted towns and make the government established. Instead of completely rebuilding the cities, they gave some people inducements such as a cooler, a refrigerator or a radio in order to attract them back to their cities to work for the regime. However, after a few months passed even peoples' essential services were cut back. The schools were half destroyed and had no proper chairs or benches to sit on. Some students had to sit on large tin cans usually used for keeping oil. Abadan and Khorramshahr are very near to Basra city. Basra is one of the important border cities of Iraq. During eight years of bombardment by the Iraqis many houses in Abadan and Khorramshahr, including the huge oil refinery, were targeted and badly damaged.[70]

At that time people were thinking about their losses, because at the beginning of the war the people were so shocked that they wanted to escape and to save their lives. They had no time to think about taking their precious belongings with them. They evacuated the cities immediately to other cities after heavy bombardment by Saddam's army. That is why most of them left their city with empty hands. In the lapse of time, people slowly came back to normal life but their minds were hurt and they were still suffering. The people had not only lost their means of livelihood, but they had also lost their nearest and dearest relatives. This was a great tragedy and the cause of deep sorrow in what was a war of ideologies. Ultimately, of course, the government announced that they had won the war against Iraq, a claim which was more a joke than reality, and it was rejected by the world's politicians. Even Saddam Hussain claimed victory over the Iranians after eight years of attritional war. But everybody knew that it was impossible to claim a victory after so many people had been killed and such huge losses sustained for nothing.

I still believed in such a circumstances the 'Teaching' in the form of mind mastery, mind development leading to equilibrium of mind, could help people get rid of their primary miseries, at least to the extent that they had mental problems to address. But I had no motivation and received no encouragement from the government which had prohibited all gatherings in groups, especially in the border cities which the government deemed to be unstable. Any gathering of more than five persons was declared to be against the law and was prosecuted by the Islamic militias especially in border cities. Although I was trying to get things moving, I found myself all alone trying to set up my project. I think, because of two reasons, I was getting discouraged to persevere in my efforts:

---

70 In the Second ᵈWorld War, Hiroshima and Nagasaki were razed to ground by atomic bombing but the cities were rebuild beautifully in about 25 years by the government better than other cities, whereas Abadan, Khorramshahr cities and other border cities are still deficient and incomplete after nearly 40 years of the Iran–Iraq war in 1980.

1. Nobody could cooperate with me in trying to improve standards of mental health because Zen and meditation at that time were neither popular enough nor pervasive enough to attract intellectuals. The fever of revolution, the destruction caused by war and the misery coming after the war did not allow them to think otherwise.
2. The possibility of upsetting the government by my activities, which could place me and my students in a dangerous situation.

Dr Farvardin, who knew about Zen from a theoretical point of view, was in the North and I had no proper access to him. The atmosphere for other thinkers was going from bad to worse and it was risky to continue the process. Therefore in such a situation my plans to spread the Buddha's teachings in the form of Zen failed, not because I became exhausted in my aims, not because of lack of confidence in my task, but because of the pressures and prohibitions imposed by the government. The extent of the government's ignorance will surely be written about in any future history of Iran.

As a long-standing teacher, I was legally appointed and recognised by the Ministry of Education, I had the right to apply for permission to establish a school with special teaching beneficial to one and all. It is not against the law to establish an academy, school or cultural centre for educating people. This kind of institution gives the students the ability to differentiate between what is right and wrong, what is immoral and moral and what is just and unjust, and also a training centre to give them the power to question anything wrong. It helps raise their level of knowledge. According to the constitution, no obstacles should be imposed on the performance of such a sacred task. A school is a cultural environment to help students develop their creativity. Democracy can succeed only when people could express their ideas, to choose and put the chosen ideas before the eyes of others. The real safeguard of democracy, therefore, is education. The fact is, a teacher in an educational institution directs the education of students and might draw on many subjects such as psychology, philosophy, mind training, wholesome relationships and more. In brief, education in a general sense is any act or experience that has a formative effect on the mind, body and character of an individual. In its technical sense, education is the process by which society deliberately transmits its accumulated knowledge, skills, and values from one generation to another.

For this same purpose I focused on establishing an academy in Iran right from the time I graduated from India in 1979, using the knowledge and experiences I had gained. Hence, as a member of the global family of educators, I was expecting to have such an educational centre which was related to my job, my knowledge and my experience. By way of contrast, if I had intended to establish a mosque or an Islamic centre to support the reactionary ideas of the clergies for spying on dissidents, to propagate violence and enmity against western culture, or to show our loyalty in obeying the regime, then the circumstances would have been very different. In such a case, I would have been welcomed by them and given all the necessary facilities to carry out my plans. In order to give the government an assurance regarding my peaceful intentions, I approached them openly and legally, showing that I had nothing to hide from them except my identity as a Buddhist monk. I explained to them the benefits of concentration and the purification of mind especially for the students and scholars, but my reasoning never satisfied the government authorities and they were always reluctant to give up their own views. They expected me to forget my initiative, changing it into an Islamic format, but this was absolutely against my faith and my confidence in the rightness of my own research. I had trained for years to propagate the truth and not falsehood. Truth is something which is known to our consciousness! On the other hand, falsehood is something known to our mind and what our mouth speaks. I wanted to spread the Truth based on my own observations and experience. I wanted to offer my students the opportunity to see the differences.

An application form was given to me by the Ministry of Education for me to fill in. In that form I had to say that I was a Shiite Muslim and was applying to include yoga practice as a subject in my teaching syllabus. As a matter of fact, they forced me, indeed encouraged me, to tell lies because they would not permit to use any foreign name on my application form. In this way, I was hoping that I could teach Zen Buddhism as a form of 'therapy' and as a means to discharge my commitments, a way for spiritual development, and I was absolutely honest in my aim. But granting this simple permission to me was not so easy and I had to go through a hard process. The government laid down certain requirements for the establishment of an educational centre. These conditions related to anyone who is going to set up an organisation, a centre, a school, or any other institute. The conditions, called the 'Seven Khans', were as follows:

To be a Muslim and to obey wholeheartedly the Islamic rules of the clergy.
1. To have served in the frontline of the Iran-Iraq war for a period from six months to two years.
2. To have passed a written and oral test on the treatises of Ayatollah Khomeini, the leader.
3. To know in detail the rules and regulations concerning praying and fasting.
4. To have passed an examination in Islamic ideology, both written and in interview.
5. To have proof of participation in Friday prayers and to answer questions about conduct during the prayers.
6. Not to be dependent on or to have any inclination towards any dissident groups, political parties, or communities who were against the Islamic government.

In our legends we sometimes read stories in which the hero has to undergo many dangerous adventures in order to get married to the daughter of the King, for example, or to gain a valuable treasure, or to reach his ambition. In the Persian language this is called 'Haft Khan-e Rostam' or 'The Seven Adventures of the Rostam' in the *Shahnameh*, written by Hakim Abolqasem Ferdowsi. Similarly, in order to get a piece of paper from the government as a warrant, one has to qualify by passing the above-mentioned Seven Khans. Those who have had the experience of applying for the issue of such confirmation papers in Iran would certainly confirm the truth of what I am saying. In order to reach my goal, I decided to study all the conditions imposed by the Islamic Selection Office. This is usually called the tunnel of Islamic investigation or the 'Tunnel of Horror'. Unfortunately, my mind was not sharp enough to pass all the exams they invented in order to obtain their approval. The exams set by the authorities were harder than the driving test to get a driving license. When I failed a written exam or an interview, they would postpone the process by putting off the next exam for three months or until an unknown date. The Islamic Selection Office used to play this game purposely in order to make the non-Islamic applicant disappointed in trying to obtain such permission. I was so innocent because I did not know their tricks and kept on chasing the matter because I had faith in my 'Way' and commitment to serve my people. I used to go to Ahwaz, the centre of Khuzestan province, and sometimes a long way to the capital Tehran for these tests in order to be granted the warrant. This procedure repeated many times with the hope that to get a piece of paper as a warrant from the government. This shows that that my cultural activities were open to the Islamic authorities. Nothing to hide.

In all, this process took me six years of exertion and nonstop contact with the authorities concerned, but it was in vain. In the end the central education office in Ahwaz sent me their final decision that I was not eligible to have such permission, my application was totally rejected and my file was closed after nearly six years of hoping on my part. Instead, they suggested that I should cooperate with the Islamic Association in the Education Bureau if my experience would be beneficial to Islamic society, but for many reason I rejected their offering. It is indeed hard for anyone unacquainted with the situation in Iran to believe that this is a genuine story, but it is all fact and devoid of any exaggeration and sometimes worse than I have explained. Those who know about the Islamic system in Iran and those who have already gone through this process are quite aware of these facts. There is no need to bring more proof in support of our claims. The story of six years of waiting to issue an ordinary paper to a government teacher and then to give a negative response is like a joke, a humiliation to humanity but such a process can indeed take place in a religious autocracy which looks and sounds like something from the Middle Ages. The abilities and expertise which I had gained through my long and demanding period of study and practice in different countries, is one part of the story. The other part is the cowardly, heartless behaviour of the so-called revolutionary government in their theocracy which was hostile and devoid of any compassion and sympathy for their own people. No one can believe such painful stories unless he has stayed in the Islamic Republic of Iran under the rule of the clergies for at least a few months. This was the curse which the Islamic revolution had bestowed upon me since I came back to my homeland to render service to my people. I was also a part of this revolution and I had a share in this revolution because like other groups I had participated practically as a university student for fundamental change and development. Even the people did not realise that the fruits of the revolution might be stolen from them by the prejudiced Islamic rulers who claimed to be acting in the name of the people. The other parties were soon pushed away by elements in the government because the government did not want the dissidents to accept permanently a particular ideology. The intellectuals wanted to get rid of fanaticism, superstition, hallucination, enmity, revenge, violence and intolerance for which they fought for years in order to achieve a revolution which would benefit the common people. Unfortunately the shadow of superstition and the gift of enmity was cast upon the Iranian people by some fanatical Islamic revolutionaries, who wanted nothing but absolute power to spread their false ideology throughout Iran and overseas.

Having overcome my disappointment about having wasted six years in fruitless endeavour, I decided to adopt another approach. I tried my chances once again, but this time it was with the martial arts masters in Abadan city. I was sure that martial arts formed a good combination with Zen and so this could attract both masters and students. Why is this so? Because there are mutual interactions between Zen and martial arts. Zen and martial arts share a connection between thought and action, which affect each other simultaneously. Both disciplines encourage a person to follow the 'Way' and help create a strong mentality, capable of resolving the inner conflict of the 'Self'. Martial arts without Zen is only a powerful physical training and, while Zen can familiarise us with power and awakening, we must combine it with martial arts. I spoke to the Iranian martial arts masters and I started teaching them Sosakan (deep breathing exercise) as a powerful breathing exercise useful for their practice. I also taught them how to succeed based on the special formula inspired by Napoleon Hill.[71] Most of the martial art students practised it for a few months and they reported excellent results from this experience. All the students and the martial arts masters welcomed the technique and kept on practicing Zazen before and after their physical practice. Unfortunately we had no proper place to practice except the places left ruined during the war. There was a half-ruined mosque known as the Kurdish Mosque not far from the city centre which was quiet and suitable for our practice. For some weeks everything went well and the students were progressing both in concentration and in its correspondence with physical activities, the combination of which could give them extraordinary energy. The students were happy and quite satisfied with the technique and the practice. Gradually, they were able to participate in a friendly championship in Khuzestan province and they obtained good results in their struggles with their rivals in other cities. This was the first sign of their success through the practice of Zen with martial arts. It was a good experience for me too because I found out that Zazen (sitting Zen) and martial art are a good combination

---

71 – This book was changed by me to *Zazen and Creativity*' or *Zazen and Success*, telling how to apply the formula for every success based on true Zazen practice.

not only in sports in general, but also for the sudden realisation of Zen in particular.[72] I first practised my theory on the martial arts students in Iran with good results and this gave me great happiness. Our activities were peaceful, dynamic, creative and promising. This wholesome combination was neither harmful to the government, nor the people. On the contrary, it could help the martial art students to come out of their mechanical training and to gain the spirit of 'Budo'. What is Budo? Budo, in fact, has a deep, uninterrupted connection with morality, religion and philosophy. These qualities encourage the martial artist to welcome the Budo precepts. In the past two decades, martial arts have experienced such rapid growth that they are now considered in Japan and China as a 'temple' or 'school' for the training and development of mind and body. A Zen school is the combination of Zen and martial art, initiated by the first patriarch, Bodhidharma, the founder of Zen and martial art, practiced in the Shaolin[73] temple. Budo is an inseparable part of martial arts. Sports and concentration were brought together for the first time and it was enthusiastically welcomed by the martial arts fans and the masters. Sad to say, most of the martial arts masters and students knew very little about this combination and they practised their art without practising Zen in parallel with it. Martial art can be practised without Zen, but it is not so effective. However, their combination is more powerful and leads to sudden awakening if it is accompanied by the system of meditation (Zazen) passing through the formula for success. We practised it successfully for some time and we were happy that this process would lead to positive results and the students could have better foundation for the development of mind and body.

I was quite happy that I had found another approach in connecting and contacting my students to be with them to teach them and to learn from them.

But after a few months, the kung-fu master and I were summoned separately by the Islamic watchdog Herasat, the Islamic Security Organisation to explain our combined activities. We were summoned many times and questioned by the Islamic investigators differently. We simply told the authorities concerned that we trained our student as how they could concentrate on the movements of their body, how to control their mind. But again, without any reason and in a command way they warned us that our activities were illegal by the government and that we had no right to practice in this way. At that time the

---

72 I have explained this teaching in separate books Zen-*mind*, Arya-*mind*, translated in to Persian as The Dialectic of Zen.
73 Shaolin is a Cha'an Buddhist temple on Mount Song, near Dengfeng, Zhengzhou, Henan province in China. It is led by Abbot Shi Yongxin. Founded in the fifth century, the monastery is long famous for its association with Chinese martial arts and particularly with Shaolin Kung Fu, and it is the best known Mahayana Buddhist monastery in the Western world.

practice of kung-fu was strictly prohibited by the government. In particular, its combination with Zen seemed like a double infraction of Islamic special law. Besides we had to obtain legal permission from the government by showing that our instruction was not only harmless, but also of use to one and all, and that we did not want any confrontation with the government. I could see the clear changes and progress in the youth who earnestly followed the instructions but the authorities were still living in their own hallucination and paranoia. Obviously, I saw some gradual changes as the practice continued. This initiative started in 1988. I was sure that if we could continue the practice together with the martial arts masters, and because of the sharp, retentive minds of the Iranian students, they would certainly make good use of it and register massive progress in the field of martial arts and self-knowing. The young Iranians from Abadan proved this to be true by winning the friendly championships which were held regularly during their training. Because Zen training had been combined with martial arts this gave them the edge over the other contestants who practised martial arts only. There could be no doubt that they could become great masters.

I also remember at the beginning of the Islamic revolution that a kung-fu master named Prof. Ibrahim Mirzai wanted to combine martial art with Zen with the help of the Zen writer Dr Parviz Farvardin. Dr Farvardin and the professor wrote a book together called: *Zen and Martial Art*. Professor Ibrahim Mirzai did not practice Zen but he was inspired by Dr Farvardin's book. At that time the Professor was a candidate in the presidential election in Iran in 1979, but due to the mistaken policies of the regime he had to run away from the country. If he had been in Iran he could have developed and changed martial art along modern lines using his powers of innovation. However, he was forced into exile unnecessarily by the government because he did not want to be made into a blind follower of some prejudiced groups.

In the year 1997 in the general election of Iran the Shiite theologian and reformist politician Mr Mohammad Khatami came to power as the representative of the reformists. He promised change with his beautiful slogans the 'Dialogue of Civilisations'. The majority of Iranians wanted change so they voted for him and he was elected as president of Iran with a mandate to reform. I had already spent six years trying to obtain a warrant from the new government for my educational purposes. I could not afford to wait another six long years. Instead, I was restless to leave the country to receive more training, rather than spending my time in teaching a restricted syllabus and confronted by many obstacles. I had employed every method to advance my cultural task but in vain. This was not an appropriate time for me to establish my teaching in Iran. I had reached deadlock and needed to see my Zen teachers and my Dhamma brothers and sisters in Japan again.

Some points from this chapter

- Kung-fu and the way of Zen were prohibited by the new rulers.

- Our first practice of Zen and martial arts commenced in an old, ruined mosque.

- The story of six years of waiting to issue an ordinary permit is like a joke, but it is true. It is humiliation to humanity.

- Prof. Ibrahim Mirzai, a kung-fu master, came up with the original idea of combining Zen and martial arts.

- A Zen school, the combination of Zen and martial art, was initially set up by Bodhidharma, the first Zen patriarch.

- Martial art without Zen leads only to a powerful body. Zen leads us to awakening.

- The young Iranian students and their masters welcomed the combination of Zen and martial art.

- After six years of exertion, my application to establish a small centre was rejected by the Islamic authorities.

- The conditions for obtaining a warrant from the government were tough and almost impossible to satisfy.

- The constitution gives everyone the legal right to establish a school, but the regime was steadfastly opposed even to some of its own rulings.

Chapter 15

Second Trip to Japan (Inviting the President of Iran to Sogenji)

Having found all the doors in Iran were closed, I made up my mind to try and get a visa for Japan. Things had changed and, given the political situation in Iran, obtaining a visa to visit a foreign country was not so easy. This restriction was imposed by the government. The foreign policy of the Islamic Republic of Iran was so irresponsible and badly handled that other countries would hardly trust or accept Iranian visitors to their country. Visa requirements for Iranian citizens were (are) administrative entry restrictions imposed on citizens of Iran by the authorities of other states. Besides, the government would never provide travel facilities for Iranian visitors to go abroad. This is not because ordinary Iranians are in disgrace or they are nuisance, but because the Islamic regime and their wrong policy has imposed such tough rules over other Iranians. It is the government which is responsible not only for defaming the good name of the Iranian people, but also for the creation of tension all over the world in their attempt to globalise their ideology with violence and terror.

The Ven. K. Noritake-Roshi sent me two different formal invitation letters from Hosenji temple in Kyoto city, but my visa was rejected by the Embassy of Japan in Tehran. The invitation letters were genuine but the credibility of Iranian passports was in question. I tried to go via one of the European countries, but here too there were restrictions for Iranians, except for government officials who could get a visa easily. I decided to go to Malaysia to find a way either to Japan or to a European country. Eventually, I was given a visa to stay for two weeks in Malaysia. I went directly to BMS (Buddhist Missionary Society) in Kuala Lumpur and I met the late Ven. S. K. Dr Dhammananda, the head monk of Malaysia and Singapore. I had regular contacts with the BMS for years, receiving Buddhist literature for myself, and I used to translate their pamphlets into Persian for my loyal students. I also received regular advice from Dr Dhammananda. At his suggestion, I stayed in one of the temples in Malaysia. I explained my situation to the Ven. Dhammananda. He treated me well and ordered that I should be given a good place to stay. I extended my visa for two more weeks in order to apply for a visa for Japan, but once again I faced a disappointment and all was in vain. I was then advised by him to go to Sri Lanka and it might be possible to obtain a visa to Japan from there. The form of Buddhism practised in Sri Lanka is Theravada. In all important matters of doctrine there is complete agreement between the Mahayana and Theravada schools, but there are some differences in the practice. So I went to Sri Lanka, where I stayed for some months, practising the Theravadan techniques with the qualified masters in Sri Lanka, to whom I was introduced by the Ven. Dr Dhammananda. Unfortunately, I still had no success in getting a visa for Japan, but at the same time I made the best use of my time by practicing Dhamma[74] with the qualified teachers. I did not want to lose the opportunities to practice under experienced Dhamma teachers.

From Sri Lanka I went to India. I stayed and practiced in one of the temples in New Delhi for some months. Then I decided to go to Tibet for a long retreat. I went to the Embassy of China in Delhi, the capital. I filled in the visa forms and waited for their response, but because of my Iranian nationality, no positive answer was given to me. Then I stayed in one of the Buddhist temples in the city of Nagpur in Maharashtra State, waiting for a chance to go to Japan.

Suddenly a new idea came into my mind. I decided to try my chance from Nepal. I was sure that Iranians had never applied for a Japanese visa via Nepal. If I succeeded, I would go to Japan and if not, I would stay on in the city of Lumbini in Nepal. So I made my first pilgrimage to Lumbini, the birthplace of the Buddha. Then I stayed in the Swayambhunath or Monkey Temple. This is an ancient Tibetan religious complex atop a hill in the Kathmandu valley, west of the capital. A long staircase, with 365 steps, leads direct to the main platform of the temple. It is called the Monkey Temple because there are many tame and friendly monkeys everywhere. I practised the Tibetan technique and at the same time I established contact with the Sogenji Zen monastery in Japan and my Roshi. The Roshi appreciated my endeavours and this time he sent me a long, strongly-worded official letter of invitation in Kanji characters addressed to the ambassador of Japan in Nepal. I took the letter to the Embassy of Japan in Kathmandu and showed it to the

---

74 Doctrine.

relevant authority, filled in the form and also underwent an interview with the Japanese authorities. Success! Finally, at long las , in 2000 I got a visa to go to Japan. I was very happy that ultimately my efforts were rewarded. I left the Swayambhunath Temple, said goodbye to the monks and flew to Japan.

I was welcomed by the Sogenji's Sangha. Many of the monks and nuns had been there during my previous visit in 1984. They all appreciated my efforts to reach Japan and I was very happy that I found myself among them. First of all, I had a meeting with the Roshi. I explained my situation to him and how I had failed in my activities to spread the Buddha's teachings. I told him all about the incidents which had befallen me. He believed me because he was aware of the political situation of Iran. He showed great concern about my story and encouraged me to restart my Zen practice with him in the group. I undertook the Sogenji training again. I was happy that I had come back to my Roshi, my Dhamma brothers and sisters, and I restarted the training. After 25 years of being away from my temple I saw things had changed a lot. The signs of change could be seen everywhere and Sogenji was totally different from how it was when I first came in 1984. It was remarkable that in a short period and, with the help of the Sogenji's Sangha, the temple had developed a brilliant environment and close attention to the discipline. This was due to the Zen-Buddhism instruction, which is so strong and dynamic that it can develop any situation in an ideal direction. A similar effort was made by the Japanese after World War II when Hiroshima, Nagasaki and Kobe were destroyed by atomic bombs. They rebuilt the ruined cities so quickly that you can find no sign of destruction at all and they may be better than before. I sometimes compared the Japanese government with our Islamist government. The Japanese government, with the help of people who trusted them totally, rebuilt their ruined cities in less than a quarter century much better and more beautiful than before. In the case of Islamic Republic of Iran, however, after the war with Iraq the cities on the country's borders have remained more or less as bad as before, with little or no change and with the same levels of poverty. No fundamental changes can be seen there. Regarding the influence of Zen-Buddhism, Prof. D.T. Suzuki, who was perfectly enlightened in the way of Buddha-Zen and who was also familiar with Japanese culture, explained in his book *Zen and Japanese Culture*, "It is impossible to speak of Japanese culture apart from Buddhism, for in every phase of its development we recognise the presence of Buddhist feeling and strength in one way or another. There are in fact no departments of Japanese culture which have not undergone the baptism of Buddhist influence, so pervasive indeed, that we who are living in its midst are not at all conscious of it. Since its introduction to our country, Buddhism has ever been a most stimulating, formative agent in the cultural history of Japan. We can almost state that the very fact of its introduction was due to the wish, on the part of the ruling classes of the time, to make Buddhism the agency of cultural advancement and political consideration." He admires the effort of his people under the Buddha-Zen and continues, "If we want to see the degree to which Buddhism has entered into the history and life of the Japanese people, let us imagine that all the temples and the treasures sheltered therein were completely destroyed. Then we should feel what a desolated place Japan would be, in spite of all her natural beauty and kindly disposed people."[75]

A glance in to two ideas as a comparison is essential:

1. The Islamic government talks too much and makes promises, but do nothing, focusing only on their own ideology rather than thinking about the welfare of the people, whereas the secular government of Japan (or other democratic countries) works faithfully for their people wholeheartedly based on their social culture.

2. According to my opinion, the Islamic republic of Iran is not a true and caring government because they are not accountable. They are not participatory, transparent, responsive, effective, efficient, equitable either and moreover they are not compassionate to their people whereas we can see all these characteristics positively in democratic countries.

In the Islamic Republic of Iran Islamic ideology has priority to nationalism. No preferences to Iranian ancient civilisation. The history of the Iranians is more than 2500 years. The history of the Arabs begins with their invasion of Persia in about AD 651. The present Islamist are trying to substitute their putrid ideology to our ancient civilisation in order to destroy our pure culture and the civilisation of Persia. Other countries give importance to their own culture and civilisation. This shows that the committed statesmen work sincerely for the benefit of their own nation and country first.

When a Zen master was asked what is his future life would be, he unhesitatingly answered, "Let me be a donkey or a horse and work for the villagers."

---

75 *Zen and Japanese Culture*: Prof. D.T. Suzuki (Chapter: 'Zen and Haiku', page 217–218)

This kind of appreciation by a high, learned Japanese can also be copied by all of us with equal success, providing we do not gaze at the stars, but come down to the earth and understand the needs of the people. They have used Cha'an (Chinese Buddhism) or Zen (Japanese Buddhism).

The Cha'an (Chinese Buddhism) or Zen (Japanese Buddhism) masters not only teach morality to their people but they also show them the ways to develop their own culture and understanding.[76] We can also follow the same procedure with our own pure culture inspired by the sages who appeared centuries ago even before the invasion of Arabs in AD 651.

Prof. Suzuki admitted that their culture based on Zen-Buddhism can flourish the culture of his country, not by observing precepts and depending on supernatural beings but as a pattern or example to bring suitable changes according to the needs of the culture. Such creativity and potentiality is indeed a powerful tool that can transform the snake into a dragon, and the fox into a lion and ultimately a powerful and venerable government. It can awaken the mind to vigilance and bring forth our creativity for use at a conscious level. If the Japanese public officials believed in superstitions, bigotry, self-interest, monopoly and conceit, they would have never reached such a glorious state as they have now.

Everything had changed in Sogenji so beautifully and so quickly that it makes one think about the awesome potential which is able to create such changes in such a creative fashion. Some people may say that Buddhism is nothing but observing some precepts, reciting some Sutras, or at the positive level it is merely sitting and meditating. But in reality Buddhism in the form of Zen goes beyond these simple views. This kind of teaching changes a man from abnormal to normal and from normal to supernormal. It works within the framework of body and mind at the deepest level with a systematic discipline of Zazen, Sanzen, Yaza, Samu, martial arts, etc...[77] Body is not separate from mind. When the mind gets power, it can reflect it onto the body and they move along together smoothly and with perfect results. The old Chinese Buddhist masters believed that physique gives shape to the mind first. The mere sitting in meditation is important but it is not the final goal in Zen-Buddha. The final goal should be directed by genuine meditation and a tool to final destination. We need discipline, proper guidance, suitable environment, these are the bridges between goals and accomplishment.

---

76 Chan was first established in China by the Persian prince and monk An Shigao in AD 148.
77 See *Zen-mind, Arya-mind* by the same author.

This does not mean we should not merely give important to Zazen but to think that we have body as well. Zen trains mind, penetrating in to the body as well.

Hyakajo, the Chinese Zen master, used to demonstrate the importance of the body to his pupils even at the age of 80, by trimming the gardens, cleaning the grounds, and pruning the trees. The pupils felt sorry to see their old teacher working so hard at that age, but they knew he would not listen to their advice to stop, so they hid away his tools. That day the master did not eat. The next day he did not eat, nor the next. "He may be hungry because we have hidden his tools," the pupils surmised. "We had better put them back." The day they did so, the teacher worked and ate the same as before. In the evening he instructed them, "A day of no work is a day of no food. If someone does not work he does not receive food. No work, no food."

I have always wished to carry out positive instructions whether they are given by the Chinese, Japanese or Persian sages. Body moves when the mind commands, and the mind follows according to the movements of the body. The mind and the body are two distinct substances. However, the two interact on conditions. Mental events cause physical events. For example, my beliefs and desires, which are mental states, cause me to act in certain ways. Similarly, what happens to my physical body often has an effect on how I think and feel. This common sense view is called 'Counter Phenomenalism' and holds that mind–body interaction occurs on both directions, from physical to mental and from mental to physical. Physical events give rise to mental events and mental events can affect body. This is the gist of the Cha'an and Zen masters when they emphasised the importance of the mind as well as body, which has been supported by scientific research. I also learned that another kind of concentration could be practised by focusing on the movement of body. The meditation of 'No-thinking' is perfect when mind and body are functioning together simultaneously and spontaneously.

I was welcomed warmly by the Japanese Zen devotees who had known me for the past 25 years. Some of the old monks and nuns were still there. During Takuhatsu (alms giving),[78] the householders would be more generous to the mature monks of long standing. The neighbours who used to participate in the Sogenji's ceremonies recognised me after my absence of 25 years. Sometimes they invited me for food as a tradition. It is customary for Japanese people to invite monks to their house, where the householders will make a small donation.

---

78 Takuhatsu is a traditional form of Dana or alms given to Buddhist monks in Japan. In the practice of Takuhatsu, monks travel to various businesses and residences in order to exchange chanting of sutras in Sino-Japanese (generating merit) for donations of food and money. The main purpose of Takuhatsu is to fight with the refractory 'Self'.

I was invited by some Japanese intellectuals and businessmen to come to Okayama Hotel to express my views about Persian and Japanese culture. The meeting was organised by Sogenji monastery. Mrs. Kimura was my interpreter from English to Japanese. I explained to them the old history of the Iranian kingdom from 500 BCE and the Zoroastrian way of meditation (between 1000 to 600 BCE), and also the Iranian way of approaching theosophy and Sufism.[79] Then I explained the close similarities between Zen and Iranian theosophy. They were attracted by what I had to say and they welcomed it. They asked whether I had a training centre in Iran. They were willing to be invited to visit Iran to have group sittings there and to gain more knowledge about Iranian culture. They had connections with different monks from European countries who had trained in their Zen temples and monasteries. They could not believe the story I had to tell about Iran. They expected to hear about my Zen activities in Iran and even to be told about a Zen temple I might have established during those years (since 1984). It is in fact customary that those who receive training in one of the Zen temples in Japan should have a right to establish a Zen centre in their own countries, if the Roshi confirms the monks. Besides, I was a formal Sogenji monk and there was no obstacle for me to manage a temple in Iran. If I had such a centre in Iran, many monks and nuns all over the world would support and cooperate with me in developing the centre. Then traditionally they would contact with each other as a unified spiritual organisation. And in this way they reinvent the centres no matter how small or big they are. I understood that the Japanese were enthusiastically longing to know about Iran and the possibility of attending my Zen centre in Iran. They were also interested to know more about our customs, our culture and of the good relationship between Iran and Japan. I decided not to go back home to Iran unless permission to establish a Zen school had been granted. Without having such an establishment, neither Zen nor meditation could make a real impact.

Invitation to the president of Iran

Some months later I learnt that the new president of Iran, Mr Mohammad Khatami, and his companions were coming to Japan at the formal invitation of the Japanese government on October 2000. On hearing this and with regard to the failure of my mission in Iran I told my master this news. The

---

79 At that time I knew nothing about the movement of An Shigao or I would reveal the facts about him to the Japanese people.

Ven. Harada Shodo Roshi, the head abbot of Sogenji Zen monastery, was more or less aware of the political situation of Iran and he suggested that the new president, Mr Khatami, and his companions should be invited to Sogenji to show them Japanese culture such as Zen, Kendo, flower arranging, the Japanese tea ceremony, Kabuki (a classical Japanese dance-drama), etc... The policy of the master was to show the Iranian officials, especially the 'Reformists', Japanese culture with a practical demonstration in a Japanese temple. The Roshi wanted to show them some Japanese culture as it is practised. Our master wanted to wipe away the shadow of doubt from the minds of the new Iranian rulers by eliminating any false opinions and convincing them that Zen is not a dogma intended to convert people from one religion to another. I was hoping that Mr Khatami and his companions would accept the invitation, based on his promises before the general election about the 'Dialogue of Civilisations'. Therefore the Abbot of Sogenji invited President Khatami and his companions with official letters sent to both the Embassy of Iran in Japan and the Ministry of Foreign Affairs in Tehran. I was immediately sent by my master to the Iranian embassy in Tokyo with the formal invitation letters before Mr Khatami and his companions arrived. Before going to Tokyo, the master also collected two big and some small, valuable statues of the Buddha and the statues of the Zen patriarchs from his temple Sogenji to be given to the members of the embassy staff one by one.[80]

Unresponsive welcome by the embassy

Among the statues, there were two which were particularly beautiful. One was a sitting statue and the other was a head of the Buddha which Roshi had brought with him from Nara temple in the Japanese city of Nara. This statue was indeed a beautiful and precious example of its kind. It was supposed to be dedicated to the president himself. These were to be presented to the new Iranian rulers as a sign of solidarity and friendship between two civilised nations at the beginning of the reformists' rule. I was happy that I was equipped with peace and friendship to fight against ignorance and doubt. In the busy and crowded city of Tokyo I finally found the Embassy of Iran. There are two separate buildings. One is political and the other is cultural. I went to the first building. As I was wearing a formal Japanese Zen robe, I was greeted and welcomed by the Japanese guards, who guided me with respect to the waiting room and I explained my purpose to

---

80 It is said that, two statues among other statues which were given to the Iranian embassy in Tokyo have been preserved in the presidential museum in Tehran.

the embassy authorities. I was happy that I could explain to them the essence of the invitation and I was intending to give them the beautiful statues offered by the Zen master who had selected them from the Sogenji temple. A few minutes later, one of the Iranian staff saw me in my Zen robe and his suspicions were unnecessarily aroused. He whispered to his colleagues and asked me if I was Iranian and I happily said "Yes" and I started speaking to him in the Persian language. I explained my purpose for coming to the embassy. I was expecting them to appreciate our offering and our kindness as a sign of affection and friendship. But as ignorance is a common characteristic of selfish men, they usually form opinions based on assumptions, not on wise understanding. They started whispering to the Japanese guards in a corner, telling them that they should push me out of the room as if a criminal had entered the embassy. Soon these same men grasped my hands from both sides, pushed me to the exit door and threw me out of the room in such a rude and callous fashion that I was shocked at what had happened in just a few minutes. They threatened me, telling me not to come there again and locked the door behind me. I could easily sue them to the Japanese government. The Government have truly highly respect to their Zen monks especially the Japanese journalists who would publicised such matters not only in their own news but all over the world if their monks are treated badly and the offenders are persecuted or should be accountable. But I did not want the dignity of the Iranians to question although they were uneducated and deserved to be punished.

I had thought the embassy authorities might be more realistic and wise compared to the prejudiced Islamic groups in the Islamic Republic of Iran because they were now living in an advanced and democratic country, and they might have learned how to behave to their fellow human beings. Besides, they were representatives of the reformists who had come to power with promises of change. However, it seemed that these puppets had retained their same nature, whether they were kept chained up by their bosses in Iran or elsewhere. They were in fact mercenaries who were led astray by money and attached to power. This materialism had made them blind. No doubt they were working for money and not for humanity.

Still confused about the hows and whys of their behaviour. It is surely reasonable and polite to enquire first about things and then decide what action to take. However, of one thing I was certain: although they spoke Persian, it seemed they were not originally Iranians or any sympathy to their compatriots, but had been brought up in a foreign culture (probably one of the Persian Gulf countries). They were opposed to Iran and the Iranians in every respect, in tradition, culture, art, relationships and creativity. In other words, they had put spokes in the wheel of Iranian progress [They put spokes in the wheels of Iranian progress means; to make it difficult for someone to achieve something they had planned to do, or deliberately do something which spoils their plans(or, their progress)- a bar or stave instead of sopke]. This can decelerate the motive forces of Iranian genius, knowingly or unknowingly. One thing has taken priority over other things in the Islamic Republic of Iran, and that is their homemade brand of Islam, which is what they preach and propagate in order to universalise their own beliefs.

Outside the building, there was an Iranian who saw the incident and wanted to help me. He understood me and guided me to another building nearby. Although I felt humiliated by the political authorities, I wanted somehow to convey to them the message I had brought from the temple. The staff in the second building seemed to be kinder, perhaps because it was the cultural section. They listened to me and they received the formal invitation letters. They also promised they would distribute the precious statues among the staffs, and they promised they would give the big statue of the Buddha directly to Mr Mohammad Khatami, the president. They said they would arrange a day for Mr Khatami and his companions to visit the Zen monastery in Okayama city. I had to trust them, but I did not know about their sincerity.

I submitted all the official invitation letters to the embassy authorities and got a receipt for them. At the end I asked them to provide me a place for at least one night to get back to my temple the next morning as I'm not so familiar with Tokyo city, in order to find a bus or a train to go back to my temple, but in response they said that embassy was not travel agency and they guided me to the exit door and left me alone. That night I suffered a lot wandering the whole night in Tokyo until the next day to find bus station in big Tokyo. I preferred not to tell this incident to the Roshi as it humiliated to the Iranians and Iran.

Welcome by the Roshi

I went back to Okayama and handed the receipt to the Roshi. Roshi was happy about this mutual understanding and cultural exchange, and the way the Iranian reformists spoke politely. The Zen master provided the necessary requirements for his guests in advance of their arrival. He informed some Zen masters in the cities of Kyoto and Nara. He obtained the necessary requirements for performing Zen, a Kabuki play, the art of archery, flower arrangement, the art of tea ceremony, etc. Knowledge of these traditions can only be gained directly and genuinely from Zen temples in the presence of experienced Zen masters. In addition, it would be a good opportunity for me to tell the new Iranian leaders about Zen and the desirability of establishing such a centre in Iran.

The embassy's disloyalty

Everything was arranged to welcome and entertain the Iranian guests. However, a few days later when everything was ready to welcome the guests, Sogenji received two official letters from the Embassy of Iran in Tokyo. One was sent to the Roshi, and another to me. They made the excuse that they had no security coverage for the president's trip to Okayama. Honestly speaking, we did not expect such a late rejection of the invitation. They could have told us beforehand. Their excuse was neither reasonable nor in line with common sense. Visitors from all over the world with different ranks and positions usually participate in such ceremonies for at least half a day and no security coverage is needed. Whether the invitation letters were given to the president or not, I have no idea. I was sure that Mr Khatami and his companions would welcome this invitation if they had been informed by the embassy's authorities beforehand. Besides, the embassy could have told us earlier if the Iranian authorities did not want to come. There was also the possibility that the statues were not distributed among the intended recipients because we received no appreciative response either from the president or his companions. If the embassy authorities realised the value of this invitation, they would certainly appreciate this chance to open a new gate in the relationship between Iran and the rest of the world in the field of spiritual growth.

Being an Iranian citizen, I felt shame for such an unwise decision taken by my embassy. When the embassy accepted the invitation letters and when I was given a receipt, the temple and I were assured that the president and his party would certainly come. I think the embassy had either misunderstood the temple's invitation, or maybe were suspicious that it could be some kind of plot to lure them into danger. This led them to believe they could simply say "No" to an invitation that could have opened their eyes to a new world of spirituality. I personally could not see any difference between the people I encountered in Iran and the people I encountered in the embassy. Both had the same narrow mind and prejudiced attitude towards other thinkers.

They were all part of one system, known as the Islamic system, and their agents were all over the world. Because of their narrow-minded ideology, it was wishful thinking to expect more from their limited way of thinking.

It was shameful for Sogenji that such a big and honourable ceremony should have been ignored by the Iranian authorities, after everything had been prepared for the president and his companions at a historic juncture in the Iran–Japan relationship. The opportunity was lost. The Roshi was disappointed and said, "A frog in the well can see the world at the size of the mouth of the well." He meant that, if the frog comes out of its well, it can see the true world, in full and without restrictions. Not knowing about other cultures and yet commenting on them blindly is nothing but ignorance. I tried not to think about the matter anymore, but simply took it as a valuable experience. Instead I concentrated on my practice. After a month or so, the shock caused by the embassy officials having changed their mind started to subside, but both Sogenji and I will never forget it.

Believe or not – an unknown saviour

The schedule at Sogenji was going on systematically with the usual three courses every month. A one-week course is usually tough with about yen hours Zazen (sitting meditation) per day. After one week's O-sesshin an event happened to me which is really worth knowing about.

But before I tell you my next astonishing story, let me tell you something. Some people believe in guardians, and some believe in spiritual beings etc… As I said in previous pages, I myself do not believe in such things and I could remove this kind of hallucination from my mind by observing the reality. However, after this story you may change your mind because of this very unusual experience, although I would still say I do not believe in ghosts. Instead of ghost or jinni, the Buddhists believe in Bodhisattva because Buddhists do not believe in ghosts.[81] For me this event seemed to be just a coincidence which could easily happen to anyone in a proper time. Perhaps I was wrong, but I thought there was nothing very special or significant about my experience and for years I gave it very little thought. However, when I told other people about it, they were truly amazed and that was when I realised that this was indeed another lesson in Zen Buddhism which lead me experience what I did. The story I am about to tell is a true story, even though

---

81 In Buddhism Bodhisattva is a 'Savior', a compassionate being . He/she appears among the people and they are with them. Bodhisattvas are often called 'Buddhas of Compassion', as love in action guided by wisdom is their aim.

it may seem very strange and difficult to believe. This event happened to me during my training at Sogenji. I now realise that it was very peculiar and I think it is important to recount it in detail, exactly as I experienced it. It is possible that many of us have had similar experiences, but sometimes we do not attach much significance to them and pay little heed to their importance. I shall recount this story in full detail, exactly as it happened and without any embellishments on my part. I have no intention to try and convince anyone to believe such a story. I myself attach no significance to stories which appear to be figments of the imagination. I place credence only on facts, direct experience and personal observation. However, sometimes events take place to teach us something and to give us a lesson that we are meant to learn. Being a practical man, I was never influenced by chance, miracles, fate or superstition. However, when I feel and observe something personally or when I experience things with my open eyes, then the matter is different and it arouses my curiosity. Events are happening around us all the time. Sometimes we are fully aware of them and become curious, and sometimes we drop them into the rubbish bin of our memory.

The following incident happened to me and brought me a big surprise because at that time I had nothing to do but concentrate on the matter.

The Roshi and his assistants had gone to the US in order to conduct a one-week retreat (O-sesshin). They usually go to One Drop centres in the U.S. and European countries to teach Zen. During their absence from Sogenji we usually have light work and enough time for individual Zazen (Zen meditation), sports, study and other activities within the framework of the monastery and under the supervision of the head monks. After a one-week retreat (O-sesshin) in the temple, we usually have one day off. On this occasion some members decided to spend their free time playing football in a place far away from the immediate location of Sogenji. The Sogenji Temple is located not very far from the city, in a very calm and quiet place on top of Okayama's hills. There are many thickets of bamboo and green trees all around. This jungle ranges right up to the west side of the city and even beyond. Because it is situated in the hills it is remote and undisturbed. Sogenji Temple is deep within these woods. The football ground was a bit far from the temple, in fact it was almost outside the Sogenji area. We had to walk through clumps of bamboo and on into a new area. All along the path, there were beautiful, tall, strong trees. There was nothing manmade around that area, no houses, no factories, nothing, just plain woodland and green fields. It was a perfect place to meditate and relax. It was very quiet and calm and we could hear the birds singing. It was impossible to see the sky but the summer breeze indicated that it was a beautiful, sunny day. It was about 2 pm, a suitable time for all of us to anticipate having a good time. We went through woods thickly populated with bamboos. We walked a very long way, but finally we came out of the woods onto the site of a new habitation which was very far from the temple. The football ground was still further to go and I felt little enthusiasm to continue with them. I said that if they would be going for a long time, I would prefer to go back to the Sogenji Temple because I was tired and not as young as them. They thought I knew the way back to the temple and it appeared to be a simple matter to get back safely. At least, that was how I felt. To me it seemed easy and was just a question of retracing my steps along the same path and going back from where I had come. However, while entering the forest I lost my way and instead of taking the right path I took the left. I totally lost my sense of direction. At first, I did not think I could possibly have taken the wrong path and I kept walking in the hope of seeing the temple very soon. I had no map, no food, no torch and nothing to help me find the way if I got lost. The more I walked, the more I seemed to be travelling away from the monastery. Sometimes I went up a hill and sometimes down. I became tired by the walking since I had travelled a long distance. Eventually I felt I needed to stop for a moment, as I did not seem to be on the right path. At that moment I felt that I was lost in a jungle which did not seem to have an end. Everything looked the same so there were no signs to guide me back to where I had come from. It seemed that everything had closed in on me. The woods were dark and there was no way out. I was getting tired and disappointed, and I felt that I was completely lost. I had never had such a horrible experience in my life. There was no sign of any village or people or even evidence of human habitation. There were just the bare, dark woods with no end in sight. The sounds of the birds coming from deep in the forest were not familiar. It was getting darker and darker, and I was walking around in a confused state without knowing where to go. I suddenly heard a noise among the bushes. What can it be? Is it a wild animal? Should I hide or run? A person? I dared not go close so I shouted: Is anyone there? Help me please. I am lost. No sound came but suddenly a rabbit came out of the bushes and disappeared. It gave me a shock. I was looking for a spark of hope to get me out of these dark, gloomy woods. What if I don't find a way out? What happens if no one finds me? All these confusing thoughts came into my mind, but I had to stay calm and not give up. I had to be at Sogenji before 9 pm in time for recital of the night Sutra, otherwise everyone in temple might get worried and start looking for me. I thought I might stay in the woods but there was no hut or other place to spend the night. I decided I could climb a tree and sleep in safety until the next day when I could find a proper solution. But bamboo trees are hard to climb. It is not possible to stay on bamboo trees since their branches are high above and are not suitable for sleeping on. Even the small trees were not safe enough for the whole night. I continued wandering in the forest and eventually I saw a faint light in the distance. I went towards it quickly and I felt happy that I might find an exit which could be near the temple. When I reached the light, I saw a middle-aged man. I was surprised to see him in such a remote part of the jungle where there was nothing around except trees and bushes. I said konichiwa (hello) to him and asked him for help. He nodded his head. He did not utter a word. He was an ordinary man, just like myself. He knew no English and I tried to explain my situation to him in broken Japanese. He looked at me and paused for a while, then he disappeared into the woods in the direction from whence I had come. I followed him into the woods but he disappeared among the trees. I didn't know where he went. He completely disappeared. How could that happen? Was I dreaming? Was he real? Why didn't he help me? Where did he go? I found myself back in a more open environment which I liked better than the dark forest. However, it was getting darker and darker. By this time it was almost completely dark. It was still a remote place with no signs of habitation in the vicinity. It struck me as very unusual that I should have encountered a person in such a place. Who was he? What was he doing there? When I came out of the woods I saw an old, ruined temple among some trees. It was located up a little hill. I was happy because I could spend the whole night there till the next day. At least I would stay safe till morning. The door of the main temple appeared to be locked. I pushed against the door, but there seemed to be some wooden statues inside leaning against the door, which prevented me from opening it. However, I knew I could manage to stay in the grounds outside the temple. While I was looking for a place to rest, I heard the sound of a van or a car. I asked myself: Am I dreaming or am I really hearing the sound of a car? I rushed out quickly and I saw something very strange. A man was collecting some dry tree branches and was putting them in his car. But to my surprise there was no proper, asphalt road running to where we were. I asked myself: How could this man come up such a rough road? As a matter of fact, there was no smooth track into the forest. How did this van come up to this place? It seemed I was very far away from Sogenji temple. The place where I came down was very far from the city and the main road too. I asked myself: How could I get back to the temple? I dared to ask the man about the Sogenji Temple and how could he guide me there. He looked like the same man whom I saw first at the entrance to the forest. Initially, I did not notice this because to me all Japanese look more or less alike. I asked him about Sogenji Temple. I was in a monk's robe and he looked at me compassionately. He nodded his head and said nothing. I did not hear a word from him which I found very surprising. Disappointed with him, I left the man and went back to the old ruined temple on top of the hill in order to spend the night there. After a while the man drove up near the temple. He left on the lights of the car just in front of the temple and myself, because the area around the temple was dark. I thought it was a sign of help from this strange man. I went to him again and told him my story in broken Japanese. He finally sat in the car and with a gesture told me to sit beside him. I did not know where I was going with that strange man, but my heart was telling me that he was reliable and helpful. On a gravel road lined with bushes he drove down to the main road. I slowly saw the flickering lights of the city in the distance and I felt happy I was coming out of the frightful, dark place where I had spent so many hours roaming around. It is surprising to say that it took nearly one hour to drop me exactly at gate of Sogenji temple. On the way to Sogenji I sometimes spoke to him in Japanese and sometimes in English, but I never got a word out of him. When he finally dropped me safely at the gate of Sogenji Temple, I thanked him very much. I kissed his shoulder and paid deep respect to him. I immediately showed my arrival at Sogenji and went to Yaza (night meditation) which goes on from 10 pm until late at night. Later when I recounted my story before some of the head monks (among them Bodhi-san, the Indian monk), they simply said that the man was a Bodhisattva. The Bodhisattva Ideal in Mahayana Buddhism contrasts with the Arhant of the Theravada school of Buddhism. The Mahayanists believe that a Bodhisattva is the personification of a savour or guardian angel who may appear in the form of a compassionate human being. I do not know whether to believe this or whether to deny it. I saw the reality for myself. Everything was strange and abnormal to me during the period of my entanglement and this getting entangled or meeting the Bodhisattva cannot have happened at random. The man with the same features appearing on two occasions in a deserted place where no one was living. No asphalt road for the car's going back and forth, the presence of a man in such circumstances. Also, I was saved unexpectedly and, according to the believers, this unexpected event can only be explained as the help given by a Bodhisattva. Incredible as it may seem, I cannot doubt the reality of my experience. Many of us who encounter such things are too busy and do not pay much attention to them. Some people call this fate and some call it luck. I call it a Bodhisattva. Previously I had been disinclined to believe in such beings, but now I had to acknowledge that they are among us and help us when we need help. Miracles happen every day but people do not look into them very much. I felt lucky and fortunate being saved by that man. Zen teaches us lessons in the strangest of ways. That is why it continues to fascinate me.

A plot or a kind invitation?

After a few weeks I received a letter from the Iranian Embassy inviting me to Iran to talk to the persons concerned in the president's office regarding my project of building a Dhamma centre. At first I did not believe them and I did not want to make a quick decision about their offer, but this was a positive development that I had to think about and I took it as a good omen. I never thought about any negative aspect because my intention was sane and human. When I consulted the Sogenji Sangha, they welcomed it and advised me to talk to the Roshi. The Roshi was not sure with this invitation to travel to Iran because of the breaking of their promises for the invitation made by Sogenji, suspecting it might be a trap but did not tell me directly. He did not want to disappoint me by telling me directly not to go. He told me to be careful about the whole situation that I was facing.

At the beginning of Mr Khatami's administration many people were hopeful that things would change for the better and that there would be real progress under a more enlightened government. In the beginning, there were changes in the fields of art, newspapers, reporting, and writing, giving a measure of hope to the people for more improvements. We could see some changes, but we did not know if in the long term these promises would turn out to be mere tricks. Being a monk I never encountered the dirty face of politics. Besides, I found nothing wrong in my aim. There was no bad intention behind it. I found no reason as to why my demand should be rejected or considered to be at odds with government policy. I was quite sure about the transparency of the path I had stepped on. It is like a benevolent person who is enthusiastic and willing to give charity to the society. If he/she is invited to distribute their charity they would do it with open heart. The new government had the power to help because it had taken full control, but it did not want to do so. I was also happy in the hope that at long last I would be permitted to establish a training centre with the help of some wise person or persons in the new, reformist cabinet. I still had a spark of hope in my heart that I would at last be permitted to pursue my humanitarian goals for my people.

My friends and my old students encouraged me to come back home to Iran to make a centre with those who were more or less familiar with the culture of Zen. However, the nightmares of the past were still fresh in my mind, but the new government according to my close friends and old students was different. My old students and my good friends said they would speak to the new government on my behalf in order to give me some assistance. I was in a dilemma, uncertain whether I should go or not, so I wrote a letter to my old friend, Dr Parviz Farvardin.

Sad to say, I received a letter from his family saying that he had passed away in his residence in Dizin in 2000 when I was in Japan. This was very painful news to me. I wrote to another friend of mine, Mr Nami Potgar, the great painter. He also encouraged me to come back and he promised he would arrange a calm and quiet place in Nowshahr, a city in the north where he was living. Among others, he also trusted the reformists who had recently come to power and believed in their policies. He said he and his friends would help me to make a training centre with the support of the new government. I thought I might lose this special opportunity, so I decided to restart the same process of application, but this time with the new reformist government which seemed more democratic than the previous rulers. Again I spoke to my Roshi, but he advised me not to be so optimistic about sudden change in Iran. I was also reminded that the new government (the reformists) were part of the Islamic system with the same ideology which had little tolerance of other thinkers unless they resist against the rules of previous government, but I had to be optimistic rather than pessimistic. I was not a politician but trusted on the advice of my good friends and my students. Even world statesmen believed that change might be seen in the new government. Because Mr Khatami had been elected by the majority of Iranian people (nearly 22 million voted for him), I imagined there must be some hope that things would improve as time passed. I trusted in the votes cast by my people. The fact is the Iranian people had given their votes for democracy, freedom of speech, human rights and so on. Mr Khatami seemed to be the representative of all these policies. The people were waiting patiently for the promises to be kept by the reformists.

I left Sogenji for Iran and I was very happy I was going back to my motherland to revive my plans to build a Dhamma centre, expecting the help of a democratic president, although my Zen master was not so optimistic. But a Mahayana devotee is always hopeful about conveying the message of enlightenment and peace to the ears of the people. I was hoping that something would happen, and was confident in my expectation that it would come true. This also needed a certain amount of perseverance, believing that something would be possible even when there was some evidence to the contrary. Hope may be directed toward something minor or towards something extremely significant. 'False hope' is hoping for something that is extremely unlikely or unrealistic. I was hopeful for the change, but this did not mean I had faith in it. The difference between hope and faith is that faith has the confidence factor. Hope has an element of the unknown or according to Albert Einstein; "Learn from yesterday, live for today, hope for tomorrow. The important thing is not to stop questioning."

Being a practical monk I never stopped losing my hope and kept on persisting on my aspiration.

Some points from this chapter

- Although travel restrictions had been imposed by the Iranian government, I felt I had no option but to leave my country.

- I went through different countries to reach Japan.

- I was welcomed by the Roshi, the Sogenji's Sangha after 25 years of being away.

- I used to report my masters about my cultural activities.

- The meditation of 'No-thinking' is perfect when mind and body are functioning together simultaneously and spontaneously.

- Mr Mohammad Khatami (the president of Iran), and his companions were officially invited to Sogenji by the Roshi and the Sogenji Sangha.

- As a sign of friendship (solidarity), some small, valuable statues of the Buddha and the statues of the Zen patriarchs were offered to Mr Khatami and some members of the embassy in Tokyo by the Roshi.

- I received brutal treatment from the political section of the Islamic republic of Iran's Embassy in Tokyo.

- I could sue the Iranian officials in the embassy in Tokyo for their inhuman behaviour, but I condoned it.

- The Sogeni's invitation to Mr Mohammad Khatami was first confirmed by the Iranian Embassy in Tokyo.

- Some examples of Japanese culture and some Zen activities were painstakingly arranged for the president and his companions.

- Unexpectedly and surprisingly the invitation was rejected by the Iranian authorities.

- I was lost in the bamboos and saved miraculously.

- I believe in Bodhisattvas. They are ordinary persons among us full of love and compassion.

- I was invited to Iran, apparently by the 'Reformists'.

- My friends and my old students encouraged me to come back home to Iran to make a cultural centre with those who were more or less familiar with the culture of Zen.

- I was trapped in a plot which I had not foreseen.

Chapter 16

The Inefficiency of the Reformists – My Final Decision

> *"The Ministry of Peace concerns itself with war, the Ministry of Truth with lies, the Ministry of Love with torture and the Ministry of Plenty with starvation. These contradictions are not accidental, nor do they result from ordinary hypocrisy they are deliberate exercises in doublethink."*
> GEORGE ORWELL, *1984*

Enticing invitation – 'Dialogue of Civilisations' as an absurd motto

In the year 2002 I came back home to get the backing from the new government to support my activities. One may wonder why I decided to go back when there was a possibility of having to face the same nightmare situations which had already caused me so much suffering. But for the following reasons I felt encouraged to go back home to renew my efforts:

1. The majority of people had voted for a reformist policy of change based on their persuasive policies and attractive promises.
2. I was formally invited to Iran by some reformist politicians.
3. Many of my friends advised me not to miss this opportunity.
4. My old Zen students in Iran told me that they were hopeful of change.
5. At the beginning of the Reformist Administration some changes were obvious, but no one knew a reasonable way to forecast the future.
6. Even the world's politicians who were observing the political situation of Iran were hopeful regarding the new government.

7. The motto and the promise of the new president Mr Mohammad Khatami was 'Dialogue of Civilisations'.

Mohammed Khatami attracted global attention during his first election to the presidency when he captured almost 70% of the vote. Khatami had run on a platform of liberalisation and reform. He promised to advocate freedom of expression, tolerance and civil society, together with constructive diplomatic relations with other states including those in Asia and the European Union. Khatami is known for his proposal of the Dialogue of Civilisations which attracted many to this beautiful motto. Later, the United Nations proclaimed the year 2001 as the United Nations' Year of Dialogue Among Civilisations, on Khatami's suggestion. These characteristics were enough to encourage others to support his policy. I was also encouraged to go to Iran full of hopes for change for the better. I felt that no better place in the world than my motherland living among my fellow countrymen.

For a period, I was a contract teacher, the new government allowed me to continue my job as a formal teacher in high schools and Open Universities after three years of being homeless and jobless. This new appointment boosted my hopes of further cooperation from the new government. It was at the beginning of the new president's administration and I was hopeful that things might develop in my favour. Later I met my good friends who would cooperate with me in this endeavour. I got together with them and my old Zen students and I started arranging programmes for the future. They were happy that I had not forgotten them and my commitment to them. I was cautious not to let anyone in the ranks of the reformists know about my ordination as a Zen monk.

At the beginning, the reformists' new constitution seemed wholesome and the general atmosphere was positive, so I felt happy and optimistic for the future. I was thinking about my ideals and my persistence in following them. I had been away from Iran for more than two years and I felt it would be prudent to work inconspicuously. I contacted my friends in this matter. They too were full of hope and they supported my plans. At the same time I contacted my Zen temples at Hosenji and Sogenji giving them reports about my activities. They also advised me to move slowly and cautiously, and not to tell anyone about my wish to introduce the teachings of the Buddha into Iran.

My first appearance in front of my people - a trap

A few months later I was invited to one of the higher schools of education where students get prepared to go to university a year later. I was asked to speak to the students about my experiences in Japan. This invitation was sent to me by the principal of the university. I took it as a good omen, a fruit of the struggle of my people for freedom of speech. Now I could speak freely about other cultures and my precious experiences. The principal had already arranged everything for my talk and many people gathered in the hall. It was an appropriate opportunity to talk about my experiences in India, Japan, Korea, Sri Lanka, Nepal and some other places I had visited. It took nearly three hours to give an outline of my trips to different countries, their culture, their behaviours, universities, the way of thinking and so on. First, I talked about the Japanese culture and what I learned there. I reiterated the quotations of professor D.T. Suzuki about the influence of Zen-Buddhism penetrated in to their culture and a new way of life since Zen entered the country. A concept which brought about a system of thought which helped people in the field of education, culture, beauty, discipline, morality respect and other achievements. I said that Prof. D.T.Suzuki, who was an enlightened person was familiar with Japanese culture, admitted that the present Japanese culture was indebted to their religion. The audience was listening very carefully and I was inspired by their curiosity.

Japanese culture merged with Zen, and this combination consolidated their faith in what they achieved. I also spoke about other places I visited. All the students appreciated the talk and I was happy that some of my experiences were conveyed to my people. at the end I wished that the new government to get inspired by this talk and to provide the facilities to have a small cultural centre.

I was hoping that by giving talks on a regular basis, some reformist authorities might be influenced to cooperate with me and my friends in establishing a cultural centre or an academic centre for a cultural relationship of mutual benefit between Iran and other countries based on the 'Dialogue of Civilisations'. The improvement in Iran's relationship with other countries had always been a declared policy of the 'Reformists', especially the president, Mr Mohammad Khatami. Apparently everything went well and I was happy that things were in my favour. Although I was free to talk and to express my ideas, I was cautious not to go to extremes and not to reveal my real intentions for propagating Zen- Buddhism.[82] My first appearance among my people went well and I was indeed happy about it.

---

82 Propagating Zen, Buddhism, Christianity, Bahaiis, Jews and other religions have become a nightmare for the regime who proclaims they are the most powerful country in the regions.

On another occasion I was asked to give an interview to some reporters from the city's newspapers. I genuinely believed myself to be in the pure land of Iran and I was taken in by people's strong professions of interest and enthusiasm. I felt proud to be an Iranian citizen. Now Iran had put its foot into the house of the democratic countries and with the support of the people could be one of the most brilliant countries not only in the regions but also in the world. I answered some of the reporters' questions and they asked for any photos I had taken during my research in other countries. I was too gullible to realise that this was only pretence. Because of my innocence or naiveté, I gave them some of the photos I had taken during my researches in various places. Among them there was a photograph I had taken with my Zen master at Sogenji Zen temple in which I was wearing robes and had a shaven head, a symbol of a Zen-Buddhist monk. They took some of the photos and promised they would return them to me soon. I never had any negative thoughts or doubts about the reporters and considered them as pro-reformists, whereas they were not. On the contrary I was thankful to them that they are disseminating the idea through media.

The reporters seemed to be friendly and I was careful to answer their questions wisely and intelligently. I did not suspect that they could have taken away the photo for some hidden purpose, and I did not know why. I was happy that the circumstances had changed and Iran was opening the gate of democracy to the world, giving the reporters freedom to reveal facts to the people, concerning subjects which had previously been closed to them. However, my happiness did not last long and my dream did not come to reality. After a few months, I felt that I had to undergo another bitter experience, similar to what I faced before leaving Iran. In reality, the prejudiced Islamic groups were still the most powerful elements in the government, still under the influence of their so-called religious leader who was the only decision-maker for all Iranian people. Although the power appeared to be in the hands of the reformists, the Islamic hardliners were the true decision makers. As a matter of fact, even though the president had been elected by the people, it was a ceremonial office and the decisions of the president and his team had to be approved by the religious leaders, especially the top religious leader, Ayatollah Khamenei. We had the same issue with Dr Abolhassan Banisadr, who was elected as president by the votes of 11 million people in 1980, but was sacked in one day by the proclamation (Islamic Fatwa) of the supreme religious leader, Ayatollah Khomeini. In other words, the president was elected by the majority of people but he was sacked by the hierocracy. Ayatollah Khomeini made a speech, in which he said if 36 million people (the whole population of the country at that time) say "Yes", I can say "No." The groups who interfered in the decisions of the people are called 'fundamentalists' or hardliners. They can be seen everywhere to interfere in every field of people's lives.

Again, in the trap of fundamentalists

Then came a shattering blow. Those men who had interviewed me claiming to be reporters had manipulated my interview and had published a distorted version in the daily newspaper, but I did not know the reason. It was a shock for me and my friends to see such a false report. I read the newspaper and I found it quite contradictory to the facts I had given to them. A few weeks later I was summoned by the intelligence headquarters known as 'Setad Khabari' (a branch of the Islamic intelligence Service) under the supervisor of the Islamic zealots in Ahwaz city, the centre of Khuzestan province. I did not know why I had been summoned. I had to give them an explanation concerning the article in the newspaper and the photo of me in a monk's robe. First, I told them that the article about me in the newspaper was not correct and I had not expressed any opinions which could be interpreted as anti-religion or against any other institutions, but they did not want to believe me. I emphasised that I was not speaking against a religion or any other ideology. I explained to them that I had to wear a robe because everyone in the training centre had to wear uniform as a sign of unity in the centre. I did not want to tell lies but sometimes telling lies is useful for both parties. I could not say that I was a monk because things would become more complicated for the investigators and for me. I tried to make them understand that my researches were not harmful, but of practical benefit. For the whole day, I was investigated for no good reason, only because they feared that I might represent a danger to the government and to Islam. They feared that I might slowly attract the youth from the mosques with the purpose of corrupting them with my own ideas. I was a teacher in Abadan city but Setad Khabari, where I was investigated, was in Ahwaz 70 km from Abadan. Every Monday from 10 am to 2 pm I had to attend the investigation. Sometimes I was questioned and sometimes not, but I had to be in their detention centre for four hours. Sometimes I was put in a dark, damp room seven metres long by two metres wide, which was a special place for investigation. This kind of torture gradually caused pains to develop in my neck and it spread down my right arm. In the process of time this torture made me disabled. Aches started in my neck and my right hand

and I did not know why I had to suffer because of a misunderstanding by the so-called Islamic religious groups. There were of course some opposition groups who intended to overthrow the government. For example, Marxist groups with a variety of names and other armed groups were trying to take over power from the government by violent means. Therefore the government had to defend itself with force. However, my case was quite different to theirs. My case had neither political nor material goals. Nobody could find any evidence of violent intentions on my part. We did not strive for political power but we trained to learn about harnessing the power of mind. Hence, there was no justification for opposing me by using persecution or torture. But a cowardly government which does not have the people's support may be afraid of anything. They were afraid of other people's thoughts which might be in conflict with their thoughts. They were even scared of their own shadows. On many occasions they claimed that they had found pigeons being used to spy against them. Sometimes they thought squirrels and dolphins were also spies, and they officially claimed that they had arrested them as the subversive animals. However, they had no right to accuse people on account of sins they had not yet committed. Nevertheless, because power was in the hands of a minority of the people and because these people had no limit to their aggression, they thought they had the right to do whatever they wanted, even to assume absolute domination over the minds of others.

In 2003 I was taken to hospital for scanning. Scans from my neck and my right arm showed that my cervical vertebra had been damaged badly during the time of my torture and I needed an operation.[83] At the same time the Islamic investigators warned me not to tell other people about their investigations. This warning was because they wanted to pretend that at the time of new president things have become better and freedom has been bestowed upon the Iranian people. They ordered me to present myself for more investigations in the same place whenever I was asked. My interrogation was held in a long hall. There was a distance of nearly seven metres between the questioner and myself. The place where he was sitting was dark, humid and horrific but over my own head a strong lamp was burning. Sometimes he made me repeat the sentences loudly. After asking me some initial questions, he then asked me why I travelled to different countries.

- "I'm a government teacher, Sir, and because my subject is philosophy, I have to research to gain more knowledge."

---

[83] Later in 2009 I had neck operation in the Charing Cross Hospital, London.

- "What is your research?"
- "Human science."
- "Do you pray?"
- "Yes, Sir, I pray." Again, I had to tell a lie because indirectly he forced me to tell a lie.
- "How many times in a day?"
- "Many times in a day."
- "No. I mean how many units are there in the prayers?" He wanted to know if I knew about the 'units'.
- "Seventeen units, Sir."
- "Do you read Quran?"
- "I read religious books."
- "I mean, the Holy Quran."
- "Yes, Sir, I read Quran every day."
- "Which sutras (verses) did you read?" He in fact wanted to know whether I read Quran.
- "Sir, I read it in Arabic version and unfortunately I do not know Arabic."
- "Why not in both Arabic and Farsi translation?"
- "I was told by my parents to read Quran in its original text. They said God would accept it better."
- "Didn't you find out about the mind of human beings in Quran?" Then he advised me that I could find everything in Quran. And the next question was:
- "What do you do in temples and ashrams or training centres?"
- "I practice concentration," I said. "I learn the traditions, customs, and the way of thinking of other people." He immediately translated an Arabic sutra (verse) to convince me that there is concentration in Quran too. His speech lasted more than one hour in order to convince me of the truth he believed. And again he asked:
- "What were you doing in Sri Lanka? Did you meet Tamil Tigers?"

Honestly, I did not understand what he meant. I thought he was talking about the tigers in Sri Lanka's forests. Tigers, leopards and wild cats are famous in Sri Lanka.

"I saw no dangerous animals in our place, Sir, it was a calm and quiet place for concentration."

- "Do you make fun of me, lizard," he said angrily as if I was making fun of him.
- "No Sir, I did not understand you."

- "Were there Americans, Israelis, or British in the camps (temples) where you were practicing?"

- "Sir, there were different nationalities. I don't know whether they were Americans or British. I did not check them."

- And suddenly he asked, "Who is the leader?"

I was surprised by hearing this accusation but I did not react to it as though I did not hear him. I did not know what he meant. But usually this is the trick of investigators to see the reaction of the oppositions to the accusation and I calmly said, "Leader of what, Sir?" He paused and said, "I'm sure you are not the leader."

- "No I'm not, I'm the leader of myself."

Leaders or the heads of a group have always been nightmares for the Islamic regime. For the same reason they threatened the dissidents whether they belong to any organisations or movements, or leading those organisations.

During six months of investigation by the Setad Khabari, they asked me many pointless and irrelevant questions. They were taping my answers on a tape recorder to add new information to my file.

- "There is no need to put you in detention," he said. "You are a government teacher and we can call you anytime we want," he emphasised. Again he repeated his warning that I should not tell anybody about this investigation.

It was ridiculous to be investigated, tortured, abused and threatened on account of an innocent matter which the authorities interpreted as terrifying and dangerous to them or something they do not know about. Only psychotics and ill-minded persons can have such a paranoid state of mind. Since I was not allowed a solicitor or other defender to help prove my innocence, such biased investigations cannot be just or civilised. Rather, this was the work of a religious tyranny which wanted to impose its ideology with the help of force and threats. They thought this kind of policy could bring about stability and consolidate their power. The events which had happened to me and many others like me were more like a nightmare than reality. Unfortunately, these proceedings were all too genuine. This story is true and my file can be seen up to now in the Ahwaz educational archives, if they have saved their records.

On another occasion I was called by the head of the Islamic guards to the Education Bureau in the centre of Khuzestan Province. The investigator had a bundle of white papers. He asked me a series of questions and each one had to be answered on a separate sheet of A4 paper. For example, he asked my name and I had to write my name, all by itself, on one piece of paper. This did not mean that they were generous in spending money on paper. There was some purpose behind it which was unknown to me. Each and every question had to be answered on a separate sheet of white paper. The investigator tried to force me to sign at the bottom of each paper, advising me that it would help my case, but I refused to do so and told him that I had not committed any sin and had nothing to confess. He nodded and said, "It will cost you." I still do not know the reason for using such an amount of paper in this investigation. For exactly three hours nonstop I had to use almost 200 hundred sheets of A4 paper, that is one sheet per minute. He was questioning me in such a way as if they had arrested a serial killer or a famous terrorist. I did not know that any non-Islamic teaching could be seen as so horrific or dangerous. Maybe it was because I did not cooperate with them in their activities, or perhaps because of my activities in Japan and the arrangements for inviting Mr Khatami and the reformists, or they might have been told that I'm the Buddhist leader in Iran supporting by the foreigners. It was strange to me. Besides, Buddhists are (were) considered as apostates of Islam. In contradiction to Christianity, Judaism or Zoroastrianism, which apparently have holy books, the Buddhists are not allowed to follow their religion, because they lack any books[84] and are a threat to Islam. According to the Mullahs, Buddhism is an idolatrous sect and divergent religion which should be fought against with determination. They are constantly subjugated to persecution and oppression.

But one thing was obvious: Why do these Islamic groups think otherwise? They were very attached to their ideology but they were so full of doubts and uncertainties that they thought even pigeons, squirrels and dolphins could be spies and represent a danger to the Islamic Republic of Iran. This was (is) not a joke or an exaggeration, but an honest exposition of the truth that has been repeatedly announced by senior government officials and can also be confirmed by those who are more or less familiar with the totalitarian government. Even recently, the Islamic Intelligent Service announced that they had succeeded in arresting some pigeon spies in some parts of the country connected with foreigners. This had been broadcast through media as well.

I did not know that the harmless culture of Zen horrified them so much. From time to time I appeared before some uneducated enquirers for their baseless accusation coming from their own distorted imaginations. I did not know that I might be considered as very important or dangerous to them. I did not know that although I was in the right, I had to suffer a lot in the

---

84 It is said that more than 18,000 books have already been written about Buddhism, apart from the main religious texts.

Islamic Republic of Iran. But I knew that I had the power of truth. I knew that I could attract a mass of students to the right path, although I was their Buddhist leader. To be a nonbeliever in Islam was not so important to the lunatic Islamists, but to propagate fresh ideas or to direct people to new and different goals was dangerous and risky for anyone who was a truth-seeker. So, for a variety of possible reasons they had investigated my activities seriously and placed various bans on me. I guess these may have been the reasons:

1. Maybe because I had not cooperated with them in their activities since the time I was first employed by the Ministry of Education.
2. Maybe because I had some martial arts followers who showed a sincere interest in combining Zen and martial arts. Almost all of the martial arts students were attracted to this new approach.
3. Maybe because of my activities in Japan and the arrangements for inviting Mr Khatami and the reformists to give their support.
4. Maybe because of my past involvement with the Marxist activists in India before the revolution in Iran. I had a record in the Consulate of Iran in Hyderabad city.
5. Maybe because of my interest in the fields of psychology, philosophy and meditation which were opposed to reactionary ways of their thinking.
6. And finally, the fear of being a Buddhist leader who may create trouble for them in the long term.

The ways of their investigation were mysterious and I could not clearly understand the main reason for their suspicions. It was readily apparent that Buddhism or Zen was not at all harmful to them but the fundamental idea of Zen or Buddhism was quite different with their ideology. So I was at a loss to understand their thinking. However, one thing was very clear: I never cooperated with them in accepting or propagating their ideology. I was in fact at odds with their idea. I attended none of their activities. Perhaps in their eyes I had not established a good record in supporting their religious ideologies and, at the same time, I had been seen to be actively supporting a weird foreign practice. Besides, as a researcher I used to travel to different countries meeting different masters.

At that time, I did not want to blame or to criticise the policy of the reformists because to some extent they were supported by the people. When they first came to power, there is no doubt that they planned to establish a huge training centre for us. Although they had in their hands all the necessary power, they delayed to use their power to benefit the majority of the people. In some way or the other, they had fallen under the influence of some fanatical Islamic groups. This meant they had to be careful how they implemented their policies for fear of upsetting these Islamists. I found out that the kind of people now ruling and dominating the country was worse than during the previous regime. In the history of Iran no such a reactionary, tyrannical government has ever ruled. We had elected a democratic, reformist president but he was not independent. He was not efficient in carrying out his tasks. He (the president) was not brave enough to support the demands of the people who had trusted him and had voted for him. He was trying to introduce some changes in the same old system, but this was not possible. His delay in reforming the country created a tragedy for the majority of people. The story of Hamlet, written by Shakespeare, tells us about the hesitation and procrastination of Hamlet on hearing a true story from his father; he still delays and postpones a decision until some time in the future. The procrastination of Hamlet created a tragedy for which it was impossible to compensate. Similarly, the changes which the new president promised the people were hidden under the dark cloud of the totalitarianism. The coercion and suppression which marked the rule of past rulers remained as it had been and there were no detectable changes.

I met some of my martial art students, but I could not contact them openly. Some of them had escaped to the Persian Gulf countries to avoid prosecution. One of our faithful disciples committed suicide when he found the Islamic police were chasing him in Jahrom city in Fars Province. Those who were serious about ordaining as monks wanted to go to Sri Lanka and India. So I gave them certificates of conversion which would help them to stay for a long time in these countries. I came to realise that there was no hope of improvement in the government of the so-called 'Reformists' and I became totally disappointed.

The majority of the people were still hopeful of changes in line with the reformists' promises which they had made before they came to power. By nature, Iranians are mostly optimistic and not negative. They place trust in the rulers whom they have elected and expect them to keep their promises. The people have a peaceful culture and rarely use violence in support of their rights. However, their patience is limited. If they know that their rights have been violated and if their demands have been neglected, nothing can prevent them from asserting their rights.

After eight years of futile war, the country needed a period of reconstruction to rebuild all the destruction, especially in the border cities. I was also a part of these people. I also had to share in this reconstruction. Reconstruction does not mean only to rebuild houses. Everyone, according to their individual ability and creative powers, has to help their people to build a perfect, sane society. During the war, whilst I was a teacher, I participated in building small towns where people affected by the war could settle down and live in places protected from bombardment by the enemy. More than that, I also wanted to help my people in the cultural field, to give them energy, self-confidence, creativity, happiness, unity, mental stability and self-belief. However, I had no chance to show my ability or to cultivate people's creativity, especially among the youth. There was no inspiration or encouragement from any government source. Instead, they were trying to find something blameworthy in me by bringing false charges unacceptable to any human mind. I never wanted to introduce my ideas in order to gain fame, name, power, or to spread harmful ideas or to gain material achievements. I was thinking about the benefit to my people who were sharp enough to grasp and even develop any good idea. I believe in the potential and talents of my own people. I know that Iranians especially the youth are sharp enough to take the best advantage of a new idea or new way of thinking and to channel it in a creative way if their minds are not tied with the chain of the Islamic reactionaries. Their culture is against violence and superstition. They are ready to make contact with the rest of the world and live in peace and harmony. They can learn about different cultures and useful ideas, and even surpass them. For example, a master may transmit his ideas to his students in the course of his teaching work, but there are intelligent students who take the idea, work on it and they can surpass what their master has introduced. They do it with perfect ability and efficiency. Nevertheless, I was not fortunate to exploit this potential due to prohibitions and obstacles placed in my path. The doors were closed to me, not for one day or two days, not for one month or two months, but for years. I can say for more than 25 years.

The pressure on me was heavier than before. In spite of all these hindrances, I could not resist giving a taste of Dhamma, in disguise, to those who were seeking it. I remember the whisper of the Roshi was still resounding in my ear that, "A Mahayana devotee has to carry forward the light of the Buddha's teaching everywhere to everyone, to wake up sleeping minds, to correct false ideas, and to help people to have the right viewpoint."

Dotetsu

There were many students who wanted to know about Zen and the practice of Zazen. Sometimes you show your students a way to climb some part of a mountain, but you see in some of them the ability to conquer peaks which are beyond your own imagination. Goethe, the German philosopher, said, "Treat a man as he is and he will remain as he is. Treat a man as he can and should be, and he will become as he can and should be." But the the Islamic culture is intended to bring back the mind of people to the past (since the 6th century A.D.) rather than an ideal future. There is a difference between what we really are and what we think we are. What we think we are may be based on assumptions, projections, desires and preconceptions. Our task is to see through this veil of conditioning in order to see clearly into our true nature.

On different occasions and in different ways, I had already spoken many times about mind development and the formulas of success in my classes. I had already spread booklets, pamphlets and notes on Zazen practice among the 'seekers'. However, mere reading the theories was not sufficient for them. The curious students were asking for something more than theory. They were seeking inner truth. They needed something practical. For example, if one were talking repeatedly about swimming, one would certainly ask for a swimming pool in which to practise. Unfortunately, I did not have a place for practise, nor was the government wise or compassionate enough to care for its people by establishing an environment that could change the entire course of their lives. It would have been easy for the Islamic intellectuals to acquire a basic knowledge of Eastern culture so that they could judge things rationally and wisely. If they could have done so, we would have had no problem in establishing an academy for cultural exchange, sports, therapy, and other wholesome activities. The people would develop greater confidence in their rulers.

In one of the junior high schools, when I announced that I could teach students some of the techniques of mind-training in spite of the prohibitions and hindrances, almost all of them coming from different classes, as many as 90 students, showed their interest, and consented enthusiastically to find a quiet place for group sitting Zazen. Before starting, they showed the place to me to see whether it was suitable for a casual sitting. The place chosen by the students was far from the city in an isolated place. The place of meditation was bare and simple (a wasteland), with no shelters, no rooms, not even basic requirements for our short group sitting, only a starting place for beginners to show them the alphabets of mind mastery. We visited the place one day before we began and I confirmed the place would be suitable for a half-day sitting and that we would start the next day. Buses and minibuses were arranged by the students to take them to the place. We were supposed to start at 2 pm and to end the practice at 8 pm. It could have been a lovely experience that for the first time in Iran nearly 90 devotees could begin the practice of Zen which could bring about an immediate and profound change in their lives. In the morning of the day of practice I went to buy a small bell, some candles and incense to start our practice with a simple ceremony. When I came home I had a message from Herasat or Islamic Security, which was an office in the heart of the education bureau. I had to go to the office on what they said was a confidential matter and which should not be mentioned to anyone else. The boss of Herasat asked me questions impertinently:

"We are told that you are going to take students out for a picnic, are you?" he said. I was surprised how they came to know about this programme so quickly. However, they have always some zealots in classes and in the community to act as spies. I said, "Yes, it is true."

"When?" he asked.

"Today at 2 pm."

"Where?"

"A place near Chobdeh, 20 km from the Abadan city," I said.

"Have you obtained permission from Herasat?" he asked.

"I don't think we need permission for a simple picnic," I answered, "because it is only a few hours of recreation and not far from the city."

"I do not want to argue with you because I think you are a headstrong and bull-headed teacher," he said. "Cancel the picnic now." He was giving a command exactly like an army commander, as if he was unaware that he had an educational role in the Ministry of Education, not that of an officer in the army. Besides he was not so educated to speak to the teachers respectfully. Moreover, he did not have even a high school degree for his position. The post was given to him was for his absolute obedience to the system.

"Sir, I've promised them and I have to take them to the picnic. There is nothing to worry about. You can also participate in our picnic if you want," I said firmly. "Everything has been prepared and we are about to go. There is nothing to worry you, I told him again in a kindly fashion." This kind of forthright answer made him angry. In order to show his power he said, "I warn you of one thing, teacher. You are taking some students out with you without permission and without any clear acceptance of responsibility by your organisation." He continued, "If, for example, some students get involved in a fight and if one student hurts another or kills him, who will be responsible for that?"

On hearing this threat, I felt the chill down my spine. I was sure there would not be any such conflict between my students. I had been with them for many years and I had never seen even a small quarrel between them. Killing one another was unimaginable and not plausible, but I immediately perceived the danger of his threat. I knew exactly what he meant and he wanted to make me understand indirectly that he could arrange some criminal activity that would put me in trouble forever. These are the tricks and threads the regimes always use against their oppositions. I immediately agreed with his instruction, not to protect myself but to remove the danger that might seriously harm my students. This had been done many times by the fanatics to show their power and to make the dissidents keep silent. Many writers, artists, journalist and other oppositions were killed by the same dirty policy in order to create fear in the dissidents. I immediately went to the house of the head students who had organised the picnic. I told them personally and in confidence to cancel the meeting immediately. They were surprised but I preferred not to tell other students about the dispute between me and the chief Islamic guard. I realised that, from then on, I would have to be more cautious about my activities in and out of the classes. The story of Mr Mohammad Khatami's invitation put me in deeper trouble. I realised now that these groups of prejuduced Muslims, whether radical or reformists were more dangerous than I had thought. Not only did things fail to improve, in fact, they became worse. I understood that my return to Iran was a trap set by these Islamic groups and I had made a great mistake, but with a precious experience. However, because I loved my people and felt compassion for them, as their counsellor, their friend, I was prepared to try to help them, even when there was only a small chance of success. The people had given their vote in favour of the reformists to bring in change and I respected their decision. Of course, I could have simply stayed in Japan for as long as I wanted, but I did not want to keep my experiences of calming the mind for my own selfish benefit and not share them with others. I belong to the Mahayana tradition of Buddhism and I have responsibility towards all human beings. I wanted to share it with my people in a healthy atmosphere to develop relaxation, realisation, concentration, treatment, friendship and compassion. For these entirely humanistic aims, I was being persecuted and prosecuted. I was tortured. I was abused, humiliated, threatened, sacked from my job, and made into a homeless wanderer because they took back the house given to me by the Ministry of Education. I had to endure all this only because I was a researcher with an independent mind in order to show my people something different. They accused me of heresy against Islam in a cunning and underhand way. Their false accusations might even be used as grounds to deprive me of my citizenship.

Someone may think that these pessimistic remarks about the Islamic rulers are nothing but an exaggeration, but an understanding person would soon realise the awful situation of other religious minorities in Iran which was even worse and more dangerous than my own position. For example, religious minorities who are following their own simple precepts and observing their religious ceremonies are not safe in their own land of Iran. To the authorities, Buddhists are atheists, Baha'is are enemies, Marxists are infidels, Dervishes, who are part of Shiite Islam, are regarded as having deviated from the Quran, Christianity is a plot of the West, Jews are untouchable, Sunnis are not pure Muslims and so on. They called all these people nonbelievers and proclaimed that those who propagated these religions or ideas had no rights in the Islamic Republic of Iran. The religious minorities (or we better call them Iranian ethnics) and also other thinkers had to be obedient to the structures laid down by the so-called Islamic clergies who call themselves the representatives of God and pure Islam. According to the rules of these prejudiced Islamists, a Buddhist is harmless as long as he believes in the Buddha just by himself/herself. Buddhists are dangerous, as are atheists, if they propagate Buddhism in order to carry out conversions, that is, changing a Muslim into a Buddhist.

As a matter of fact, I certified four old students to be monks in order to help them find a place for their Dhamma practice outside Iran. I did this at their own request, but neither their family nor the regime knew about their conversion. The last person was converted to be a monk in 1994. I used to issue certificates for the monks to go abroad for retreats and free practice. The certificates were approved by Sogenji and Hosenji Zen temples. As many as 400 youths were converted into lay Buddhists, but without the issue of certificates. It was obvious that if the regime came to know about these kinds of activity, I would inevitably suffer severe punishment. The fundamentalists are in fact swimming against the tide. They cannot bring themselves to cooperate with other religions. They cannot be compassionate to other thinkers on account of their fanaticism; they will ultimately plunge into the marsh of ignorance and be dropped into the bin of history. The teaching is intended to be introduced in order that my society and my people could be cultured and civilised and live in peace and harmony. All of life's most difficult problems can be better understood if we but try to learn and practice from the wise and sages. The teaching approaches to the problems and suffering of mankind and nothing to do with the 'must', or 'must not' of religion. The technique illuminates the Way of mankind to cross from a world of darkness, hatred, revenge, superstations enmity, to a new world of light, love, forgiveness intellectuality and pure unconditional friendship and brotherhood. No bad label can be put on it. However, this idea had no place in a totalitarian government. We have learnt that monopolistic government or authoritarian ways of thinking are a kind of political system where the government, usually under the power of a single political person, faction, or class, recognises no limits or restrictions to its authority and strives to regulate every aspect of public and private life wherever feasible. It is indeed hard to come into conformity with such a system. There are three ways to choose:

1. To accept the system and to cooperate with it to the end.
2. To rebel against it violently.
3. To keep away and awaken people to their rights until an appropriate time comes for further teaching.

For me to leave the country for good or my life would be in even more danger. As a teacher, I was unable to teach my favourite subject after spending years in researches and studies at university, academies, temples and different meetings. I was not welcomed by the education office, nor was I even a little bit appreciated by them. As a matter of fact, I was of no value to the new Islamic regime because I wanted to be an independent teacher in order to reveal my own experience after years of hardship and perseverance. As a monk, I could not reveal my identity openly and I could not propagate my ideas. I could not even have a simple little 'hut' of my own to call a temple or a Dhamma place for my prayers and practice. As an Iranian, I could not have my own rights and privileges as a true citizen. Besides, I was not a person to cooperate with prejudiced Islamic groups. Therefore, I was an unwanted and useless person for them. Since I was not cooperating with them, I had become an outcast from their society. There was only one way left, to emigrate. I had no place to live with my family. The house which was given to me and to my family to live in was taken back by the education bureau and we had to rent a house although my salary was low.

I had another chance to get out of my entanglement. My sister and my nieces were British subjects living in the UK. They knew something about my Buddhist activities. One of my nieces had helped me to hold meditation classes in her house when she was in Iran. We had maintained contact with each other, from time to time, especially when I was at Sogenji temple. They became concerned about my predicament and my hard circumstances. My sister finally offered to send me an invitation letter to come to England to visit her. I was also longing to go to Japan via the UK. In Iran I was living like a tramp, my mind full of fear and being chased around by the authorities. I preferred to go to England to get out of my all-pervasive difficulties, to make my mind calm down and to decide what to do and where to go. I received an invitation letter in 2004 to go to the United Kingdom to see my sister after nine years of separation. Although my first application for a visa was rejected, another application was made with my sister's steadfast encouragement. This time I obtained a visa having declared (untruthfully) that I was still a teacher. I had obtained help from a friend in the education office who provided me with a letter of confirmation. Not only my life but also the lives of many of my Zen students were in danger and I had to provide a fake paper to save our lives.

My sister knew about my situation in Iran very well. She suggested to me that I should think about coming to the UK as a safe place and also as place for my Zen activities. I consulted my good friends, my students and finally decided to do so. It was hard for me to leave my own country, my relatives, my good friends and my faithful Buddhist students, but I felt that I had no choice but to emigrate.

I started preparing the necessary papers for getting a visa, but it was not so easy to go through all the formalities. My situation was going from bad to worse. I had already translated a pamphlet *God Idea* from the Buddhists' point of view and it had already been distributed among my students and others. This put both myself and those who read it in some danger and at risk of persecution. In general, the contents of the booklet had no controversial points. It was not offensive to the feelings of religious people, but it could be used as a pretext by some Islamic groups to make something out of nothing in order to create trouble for me. Because of this ongoing danger, it was not wise to stay in Iran anymore. The situation was getting risky.

Ultimately in the year 2005 in spite of my inner feelings, I decided to leave my country for good.

Some points from this chapter

- I decided to go back home as it seemed there would be changes in the new government.

- The Islamic agent started collecting some documents against me during my recent journey.

- The same prosecution and persecution were conducted in the time of the reformists.

- Apparently the power was in the hands of the reformists, but they were controlled by the supreme religious leader.

- Mr Khatami was elected by some majority of people, but the final decision was in the hands of one person, Ayatollah Ali Khamenei.

- Collecting false papers and documents by the Islamic prejudiced groups put me in trouble, facing torture and horrific investigation.

- The regime still did not know about my formal conversion to Buddhism.

- After coming back home from Japan, life became more miserable for me than before.

- My case was neither material nor political, which confused the Islamic authority and made it difficult for them to find any evidence or documents against me.

- The government was weak enough to be afraid of such an uncertain situation.

- One might be surprised to learn that the regime claimed that the pigeons, dolphins and squirrels are spies of Israel and Western countries.

- In 2003 I practically became disabled by their tortures.

- Almost all of my investigators lived in a world of either fantasy or paranoia.

- In the time of the reformists I was welcomed by torture and inhuman investigation.

- My story is true even though it looks unbelievable.

- I was persecuted and prosecuted for no reason except non-cooperation with the regime.

- Some of my devotees escaped to countries in the Persian Gulf.

- There are differences between what we really are and what we think we are. What we think we are may be based on assumptions, projections, desires and preconceptions.

- Our task is to see through this veil of conditioning in order to see properly our true nature.

- Most students were attracted by the new way of thinking.

- My return to Iran was a trap set by these Islamic groups and I had made a great mistake.

- In order to save the life my students and I had to reduce my activities in classes.

- Totalitarianism is usually characterised by the coincidence of authoritarianism.

- - It is indeed hard to come into conformity with a system with a way of thinking that goes back to the Middle Ages behaviour

- It was hard for me to leave my own country, my relatives, my good friends and my faithful Buddhist students, but I felt that I had no choice but to emigrate.

- In Iran I was still hiding my identity as a Zen-Buddhist monk.

- In order to preserve my practice, I had regular contacts with Sogenji in Okayama and Hosenji in Kyoto.

- I was deceived in an interview with some journalists who were dedicated supporters of the regime.

- The votes of millions of people could be easily ignored or even cancelled by the religious leader.

- I was always surprised for being tortured, abuses and humiliated at the hands of the Setad Khabari (Intelligence Service) for no valid reason.

- My investigators were illiterate and their investigation showed no respect for me as a government teacher.

- Nearly 22 million people voted for Mr Khatami, the reformer, to bring change, but they were deceived.

- The character of Mr Khatami, the so-called reformist, showed an irreparable weakness which resembled that of Hamlet in the Shakespeare play.

- I was always supported wholeheartedly by my students, even though I was humiliated by the regime.

- In the Islamic Republic of Iran, group sitting in meditation was regarded as a plot supported by foreign countries as their sworn enemy.

- I was sternly threatened not to approach my students on anything except strict matters of education.

- In the Islamic Republic of Iran, the Buddhists, Jews, Christians, Baha'is, Marxists, Dervishes are nonbelievers. In fact anyone who does not adhere to the government's narrow interpretation of Islam, are seen as the friends of their enemies.

Chapter 17

In the UK – Moving to a Safer Place

> *"The perfect dictatorship would have the appearance of a democracy, but would basically be a prison without walls in which the prisoners would not even dream of escaping. It would essentially be a system of slavery where, through consumption and entertainment, the slaves would love their servitude."*
> ALDOUS HUXLEY

Why emigrate?

It is indeed hard and painful for those who face separation from their beloved people and their home country, their relatives and friends. They have to leave behind so many places and people who are the source of so many sweet, unforgettable memories from the past. In the past three decades most of the Iranians who emigrated to different countries did so not because of poverty or in search of a better environment, but merely due to the unendurable circumstances in their homeland which they could no longer accept. This was totally intolerable and this provided the impetus for the so-called 'flight of capital' or 'brain drain'. This simply drives the mass emigration of technically skilled people from one country to another country. This kind of escape can have many causes, such as political instability, lack of opportunity, government's insufficiency in answering the people's demands, or other oppressive factors, only demonstrating the regime's paranoia to justify their persecution and prosecution, increasing conflicts between the government and the inhabitants, especially putting pressure on intellectuals, artists, scientists, journalists, men of skills and other elite groups. These reactionary circumstances become associated with pressure, threats, insecurity, and lack of creativity, a passive state of mind and lack of freedom for opposing political parties. During the years I was living in Iran until the time of my departure in 2005, I personally experienced all these kinds of problems, even though I was not involved in politics. I found myself handcuffed by the restrictions placed upon me. I could not help my people as I wished to do, and moreover I encountered prohibitions which I did not deserve. This was not because of my own shortcomings or lack of ability, but because I wished to follow a harmless path, on which outside agents imposed restrictions. Iran is a rich, beautiful country with a variety of races and cultural groups, each with their own principles and traditions. Therefore in a compassionate, democratic country each of them should have their own rights and privileges to enable them to work for the glory of their country. If they feel that their beliefs and their rights are being violated, they naturally emigrate to safer places. In order to avoid dangerous confrontations, they have to keep their mouths shut, calm down their minds, and obey the rules and regulations which have been imposed on them.

I was not at all happy to leave my country after being in it for 57 years. However, in order to save my life and also to save the lives of my faithful disciples and school students, all of whom had a deep connection with me, I had to escape from my home to a foreign country. I did not want to take any more risks. In this way I could also maintain or revive my faith in human nature, and not to be deluded or contaminated by the political tricks of the Islamic regime. I did not want to become their puppet and be used for their wicked purposes. I did not wish to be corrupted by their misleading incentives that were usually offered to dissidents in order to tame and silence them.

Before I left Iran for the UK on 20th March 2005, I visited my fourth converted disciple, Mr Mostafa, at his home. When I talk about conversion, I mean those who voluntarily asked to be ordained as Buddhist monks. Here I should like to explain the ways of conversion of my disciples during my mission in Iran. First of all I must make it clear that there is no force used to make converts to Zen or any school of Buddhism. Buddhists are not required to seek out potential converts and persuade them to abandon their original faith and embrace a new one. Zen initially is a treatment or healing, and does not involve the adoption of a religion in the sense of worshipping or being obedient to a supernatural power. There is no requirement to worship or placate the Buddha as a messenger of God. Moreover, the acceptance of Zen depends entirely upon the mental background or karmic state of the devotee. There is no advertising. No argument, logic or plausible reasoning is used to convince the devotee to support the doctrine. The teaching of the Buddha has always been described as 'come and see' and not 'come and believe'. This means inviting people to come to experience the truth for themselves with their own eyes and ears. They should rely on their own observations and not use the eyes and the minds of others. They should not be influenced by legends or stories. These characteristics encourage followers not to fall into doctrines of duality, with inflexible distinctions between good and bad, and rigid commandments telling you to do this and not to do that. You are not won over by false assurances of some imaginary paradise, as described and promised by some agent or authority. Therefore, conversion in Zen does not mean to add more people to the army of the religious leaders or patriarchs. To Buddhism in general and Zen in particular, quality matters most.

Risk to my life

Mostafa and three others were ordained by me as Buddhist monks with the permission and confirmation of Sogenji Monastery and Hosenji Temple. This was done at their own request in order to travel to Buddhist countries for long retreats. Those who did not want to become monks remained as lay Buddhists without the issue of certificates or the wearing of robes. They would in fact observe the five Buddhist precepts as part of their practice.[85] The numbers of this kind of disciple are too many to name, both those living in Iran and those who have fled the country. Mostafa had just returned from Sri Lanka after his long retreat in Dhamma Kuta Vipassana Meditation Centre, Sumatipala Na Himi and also Kanduboda Vipassana Meditation Centre where I practiced Vipassana under the supervision of top monks in 1999. Before going to Sri Lanka again I advised him not to contact me or his family during his training there. Once there, he had some photos taken with some monks from the temple, showing him dressed in the orange robe of a Buddhist monk. Having the certificate of ordination and the photos, he came to my house in Karaj city, where I was living, with one of his friends, Mr Amin. Carrying such photos was dangerous for both him and me. I took some of the photos from him and advised him to keep the rest in a safe place or to tear them up.

---

85 Granting ordination to my students was not as systematic as other Buddhist temples, but the certificates were approved by Sogenji and Hosenji temples in order to allow the Iranian monks to go abroad and stay in temples for as long as they wanted to practice without charge.

The night before I left Iran, Mostafa's friend Amin came to visit me to say that he could not come at the airport to see me off the next day. Amir showed Mostafa's photos in his monk's robe to me and asked if Mostafa had converted from Islam to Buddhism. His behaviour and the tone of his voice struck me as rather strange and abnormal. This aroused my suspicions, so I corrected Amin by saying that Mostafa wore Buddhist robes in Sri Lanka in order to stay in the temples free of charge during his practice. Later Amin showed the pictures of Mostafa to Mostafa's family and poisoned their minds with a story of the Mostafa's conversion. This caused a great shock and commotion in the family. Mostafa's family was prejudiced against this event. They were furious that their only son had forsaken the path of Islam in order to follow another religion. They felt they were disgraced in the eyes of the Islamic community in which they had lived for years. The family wished to send Mostafa to Qom, which is a religious city 40 km north of Tehran, the capital. Hawzeye Elmieh Goam 'Seminary' was established there for Islamic ordination as a Mullah and the propagation of Islam. This place provides Islamic training for anyone who wishes to become a member of the Islamic clergy – a Mullah. This theology centre is meant to promote Islamic thought in the way required by the Mullahs. Mostafa had been nominated for this position by the Mullahs at the request of Mostafa's family and he was about to travel to the city of Qom. His family members could not believe that their son had become converted to a path which ran contrary to their old, traditional beliefs. It seemed that they had educated their son in the ways of Islam right from the time of his childhood in order to maintain the old traditions, and now some very different teaching had taken its place. On the other hand, the new doctrine which Mostafa had chosen for himself could save Mostafa from falling into the marsh of the clergy's ideology and help him to develop his personality according to his own endeavours. The new path could open a fresh horizon in his normally routine life, and bring about a great change in accordance with his increasing understanding of the Dhamma. Moreover, this different path had been chosen by him voluntarily and not by force. I became suspicious of Amin even though he had been a close friend of Mostafa for years. I suspected that he might be an informer working for the regime. I was seen off by my son at Tehran Airport and I asked my son to find Mostafa and to tell him about Amir. It was unbelievable to see such treachery from someone whom we regarded as an old and close friend of Mostafa. Mostafa had always been kind and helpful to him and his family.

As soon as I arrived in the UK, I wrote to my son asking him to give me some news about Mostafa. He said that the family had reported to the Ministry of Islamic Culture and Islamic Guidance about the conversion of their son and Mostafa had to go to Sri Lanka again. My son said that I was fortunate to escape from the country in good time or I would have been punished by the Islamic regime who would have showed me no mercy. It was 11 days after my arrival in the UK, that is on 31st March 2005, that I received an unexpected telephone call from my wife to say that our home had been raided, my small daughter was beaten, my son was taken for long interrogation, and that the material showing that my conversion to Zen Buddhism had been taken. They also removed the copy of my ordination certificate, the ordination certificate I had given to Mustafa, and a copy of the book *God Idea* which I had translated into Persian. My computer's case was also taken by them and some translation papers concerning *God Idea* and other materials in order to accuse me of being an atheist. I was happy that Mostafa was not in Iran or he would have been in serious trouble.

I immediately wrote to Sogenji and Hosenj temples, explaining to them in detail about my past and present situation. I was hoping to find a way to get to Japan for more training, but I had to wait. My sister helped me a lot to come back to a normal situation. At the same time I did not want to be an inactive person in the UK. In London I came to know about a Buddhist temple in Turnham Green, the 'London Buddhist Vihara', near my house. It was a good place for relaxation after the miseries I had experienced in Iran. I used to go to the temple to revive my practice. The Ven. Bogoda Seelawimala, the head monk of was indeed helpful to me in many fields. There I gave a lecture about the Buddha Zen and my missionary in Iran. I was happy to have come to the UK with its possibilities of learning and spreading the Dhamma which I was not successful in my own country.

Inspiration from Zoroaster

Later I came to know about a Zoroastrian centre not far from where I was living. I used to attend their sessions and I found new Iranian friends there. I attended their centre and I was happy I could talk to them freely about different matters. Sometimes I gave a talk about my experiences and at the same time I received knowledge from them about Zoroaster's doctrine which was interesting and new to me. It was a mutually enriching experience and I was happy to find myself among Iranians abroad maintaining the old

Iranian traditions and beliefs. In my own personal researches I learnt that the orthodox Zoroastrians practised meditation as means of healing even before the time when the Upanishads and Bhagavad Gita were written. Daily meditation and indeed concentration during all five watches of the day were seen in their practice as being both preventative and curative.[86] This was all in accordance with the doctrines of Zoroaster. I was told by these Iranian Zoroastrians in the centre that research by Westerners had confirmed the authenticity of these practices, including meditation. They also told me that five times a day they spent time praying, sitting in one place to recite some of their Sutras, followed by a period of relaxation. This was an opportunity for them to take a periodic break from the pressures of the day to develop a quiet, calm mind by sitting in meditation and reciting a mantra. According to the reliable tradition of the Zoroastrians, this ancient practice of healing and mind development goes back to circa 600 BCE[87] which is even before Hinduism came into existence. This information surprised me as I did not know that meditation is so old that it goes back to such a distant era, and was practised by the Persian Zoroastrians. This knowledge persuaded me to make an offer to the Zoroastrian intellectuals that we should cooperate with each other in establishing a centre for group sitting meditation and also researching into the teachings of Zoroaster as an ancient doctrine. Some of the learned men and women in the Zoroastrian centre welcomed my suggestion, but ultimately they preferred to limit their activities to some ceremonies, reciting mantras and observing their own precepts. I understood that Zoroaster's pure teaching can be outlined as follows:

1. Concentration and meditation – 'Moraghebeh'.
2. Healing through meditation.
3. Reciting mantra for mental relaxation.
4. Retreats for long meditation.
5. Group sittings for inspiration.

These activities are widespread in many traditions of meditation in general and Zen meditation in particular. However, I could detect no sign that these Zoroastrian devotees used Zoroaster's techniques of meditation as a means to

---

86 Later I translated The book, *Zoroastrian Meditation*, by Dr.Jose Luis Abreu in to Persian language, Satrap Publishing and translation, London.

87 The modern estimate of Zoroaster's date is approximately from 1000 to 1500 BCE.

promote healing the mind. Because they were not familiar with meditation in general, they might have missed the essence of the subject as taught by the master. According to my research and experience, meditation at the time of Zoroaster was not as systematic as it is practised in Zen Buddhism and other schools of meditation today. To them, sitting and doing nothing was a basis for orthodox Zoroastrian practice. No one knows what kind of meditation techniques the Zoroastrians used in those days, but one thing was obvious: the content of the meditation was more or less the same as it was practised in the era of the Upanishads[88] but with some small differences. Nevertheless, the form of the meditation in terms of systematic and profound training was only preliminary. The word for meditation in the Persian language is Moraghebeh which means self-introspection, self-analysis, self-scrutinising or, to put it simply, inward journey. In the famous book *Mouse and Cat* (*Moosh-O-Gorbeh*), written by the famous 14th century Persian poet and writer Obayd-e Zakani 4, we find the word Moraghebeh. Obayd illustrates how cats maintain concentration on the hole used by a mouse for hours without any movement. Therefore, we can clearly realise that there are similarities in both Zoroastrian meditation and the meditation presented by the Indian and the Chinese sages. If we look at the matter from an unbiased point of view and if we are fair in our judgment, we find that the practice of meditation as healing goes back at least more than 600 BCE by the Persian sage Zoroaster. There were no special forms, but the content was beneficial.

Is believe that the ideas of the Persian sages were original and entirely their own. Their technique was to allow the mind to flow freely like a stream without interference. We can acknowledge that this technique of mind purification is similar to the teaching of the sixth Zen patriarch Hui-Neng (AD 638–713).[89] To let the mind go in its own stream without any obstacles was the basic teaching of this Chinese Zen master. Hui-Neng played a special role in the history of the evolution of Zen. He was against the method of concentration on a particular subject. On the contrary, he emphasised letting the mind run freely and allowing it to become settled by itself. The master believed that the true mind is 'No-Mind' which is to say that it is not to be regarded as an object of thought or action, as if it were a thing to be grasped and controlled. Hui-Neng said, "To attempt to work on one's own mind is a vicious circle. To

---

88 Upanishads, the concluding portion of the Vedas, the early religious writings of the Hindus; also called Vedanta, the end of Vedas.
89 Hui Neng, the famous Sixth patriarch of Chinese Zen Buddhism; the virtual founder of 'Sudden' school, distinct from the 'Gradual' school of his disciple Shen-hsiun.

try to purify it is to be contaminated with purity." Thoughts come and go by themselves and the mind should let them go. Free association was emphasised by the Austrian psychologist Sigmund Freud in his theory of psychoanalysis as a way of clinical treatment. From the above-mentioned experience we find that the Persian sages and philosophers had the same viewpoint in their meditation practice of simply sitting.

Tibetan Buddhism also has a tradition of the short path, which is considered as a swift and steep ascent to the awakening of the Buddha for those who have the necessary courage. However, a Tibetan doctrine more suggestive of Zen, emphasising immediacy and naturalness, is found in the sixth precept of Tilopa as "No thought, no reflection, no analysis, no cultivation, and no intention. Let it settle by itself."[90]

Sudden understanding as taught by the Rinzai Zen masters without any special contrivance or intention can also be traced back to Zoroaster's ancient teaching concerning the 'easy' or 'natural' state of the liberated sage. These experiences are exactly what the Persian sages taught in 600 BCE or maybe earlier.[91]

Frankly speaking, I am not in a position to compare the teaching of the Persians with the later technical training of Zen Buddhists, but these instances show that the tradition of a direct path existed in India and China, had some original sources in old Persia long before the time of the Upanishads. At some time in the past, the followers of Zoroaster may have reduced their doctrine to some mantras and precepts only. In this way, they may have lost the true teaching of Zoroaster because they were perhaps not so curious to understand analytically the subject matter of their great sage. Unfortunately, I could not convince my Zoroastrian friends that they should investigate facts unknown to them. I was eager to have mutual cooperation with them on the path of mind-training which was emphasised both by the Zen masters and Zoroaster going back to more than 600 BCE and also the holy meditation teachers who came after him. However, I had to proceed on my own way, although we maintained friendly contacts with each other for a period of time.

I had almost finished my first book on Zen in English in 2006 whilst I was in London.[92] I was looking for a way of editing and publishing it. The Iranian

---

90 – Tilopa, in Sankirit Tilopada (AD 988–1069), was a Tantric practitioner, a kind of practice intended to accelerate the process of attaining Buddhahood.

91 – Dr Jose Luis Abreu writes that " Zarathushtra was born on March 26, 1767 BCE, bringing with him, for the first time, the first original school of meditation which can be found in the Gathas of Zarathushtra." *Zoroastrian Meditation* has been translated in to Persian by the same author. Satrap publisher, London.

92 *Zen -mind, Arya-mind.*

Association, which was established to help Iranians in London, guided me on how to publish the book. When they came to know about the subject matter of the book, and also the way of my teaching, they were attracted to it and encouraged me to teach the technique to the Iranians living in London and the suburbs. It was a good suggestion and I agreed eagerly to cooperate with them, as this was another way of helping my own people. I started with a few people and gradually many came to participate in the meetings which were held first in the Iranian Association Building. The place was not ideal for the practice of Zen and Zazen, but it was necessary for all of us to start sitting as a preliminary to learning about the basic self-realisation teaching. The Iranians who had come from Iran knew little about Zen and Zazen. So I arranged things as best I could. Our sessions were divided into two parts. 1. The theoretical part of our practice, and 2. The practice itself. I was happy that for the first time I was teaching Zen without the fear of being persecuted or prosecuted. There was no interference from the government or other authorities; there were no obstacles to block our path, and no interference from biased or prejudiced people. On the contrary, the UK government was always helpful and ready to provide the necessary facilities for our activities because our activities were welcomed by the majority of people.[93] For the same reason the government was giving their nonstop support to various associations or organisations to assist citizens in the fields of culture, art, social and therapeutic services, sports, etc. The government has a responsibility to build a sane society and to help their citizens to be happy in every respect. This was exactly the ideal atmosphere which I had always wished to have in my own country for my people in order to build a sane society there. Centres of this kind are welcomed in democratic countries as they render an important service to the people and they receive wholehearted support. For example, in the process of Zen training at Sogenji monastery or other temples in Japan, the trainees usually get trained for six months or one year in order to qualify them to convey the teaching to people in their own countries. Then the trainees can set out for their countries and take a pride in establishing a training centre to train others and form a mutually beneficial cultural relationship with people from these various countries and foster an international brotherhood of practitioners. On many occasions when I visited Sogenji, I was told by my co-religionists that their government encouraged them in their sacred task

---

93 At present more than 1000 Zen and Buddhist centres are free to follow their practice all over the UK, knowing that they bring benefits to their supporters. Some centres get charity from the government too.

and would take responsibility for building academies for them in their own countries. The governments did this because their leaders were educated and wise enough to realise the importance of opening their doors to people from other cultures for their mutual benefit and improvement. Unfortunately, in my own case, the reverse was true. I was not such a fortunate trainee that I received similar support and assistance from my government in flourishing the culture of my people, although I had spent three years being trained in temples with the same training centre. If we forget the Arabian countries in the Persian Gulf and consider Iran alone, in over 3000 long years of civilisation it is sad to say that there has never been even a small temple or mind-training centre established in Iran[94]. As a matter of fact, I wish I had had the opportunity to establish cultural and religious ties with some of the more democratic countries. On the contrary, the Islamic government of Iran, where I was a true citizen, did not recognise my own rights to express my ideas, but they did their best in establishing mosques all over the world based on extending their own ideology all over the world.

These differences between democratic countries and some medieval reactionaries make the former advanced and the latter handicapped. This raises the question of why some rulers are clever and wise in helping their people wholeheartedly and supporting their endeavours to advance their country and some others are stupid and ignorant, ruling over their people with force giving important to their false ideology rather than the benefit of people. These differences had a powerful effect on my subconscious mind as why the Islamic regime are so undeveloped and backward due to their veils to the reality of the world. The memory of the past I had in Iran was indeed painful to me and has not been eradicated even now. At present I am happy to find myself in an environment where I can express my ideas freely and at the same time to give benefit to my people who are indeed in need of it.

In order to continue my activities on the path of Zen Buddhism, the Iranian Association authorities advised me to get genuine permission from the local police to proceed with my activities legally. At first, I was disappointed with this suggestion because I remembered the difficulty I had in Iran struggling in vain for nearly six years to get such a certificate. I thought I would have to follow the same procedure in the UK and that this would involve a long

---

94 Before Islam invaded Persia there are authentic evidence that Iranians came to know Buddhism even at the time of the Buddha Sakyamuni Himself. They built the first temple in Balkh (one of the major cities of Khorasan). And again in AD 148 Dhamma was propagated by the Persian Prince An Shigao. More details in a book *An Shigao, Bodhisattva* by the same author.

process of applying and waiting. The horrible shadow of the past prevented me to do so at first. I remembered the many days when I suffered a lot, struggling to obtain a warrant for my cultural activities from the government in Iran. It took me six years and finally the Islamic authorities rejected my application. Anyhow, I found that I had no alternative but to apply for permission to teach in the UK. I went to the nearest local police station and put matters before them. The officer-in-charge was not present at that time and the receptionist said he would come back within an hour or so. However, she gave me an application form to fill in and charged me a fee of £10 for the stamp. I filled in the form, paid the money and waited for the chief to come. After about an hour the officer in charge returned. He checked my application and my other documents, asked me a few questions and finally to my surprise he issued a certificate or warrant to carry out my Zen activities. I could not believe I could get such a certificate in less than one hour. To be assured that the process had been fully completed, I asked the officer whether the permission has been granted and he simply said, "Yes." I asked myself: How is it possible to obtain permission in a foreign country for me to carry out my Zen activities, whereas I had to try for six years in my home country and then receive a negative response? I could not resist telling the officer about the procedure in Iran for the same kind of case. Speaking with a heart full of kindness I asked the officer,

- "Do you know how long I spent trying to get such a certificate in the Islamic Republic of Iran?"
- "No," said the officer, "how long?"
- "Six years," I said to the officer.

The officer could not believe what I was saying and in order to correct me he said, "Six hours, you mean, don't you?"

- "No sir, six years, I spoke correctly."

Again, to correct my English language the police officer says, "Six days… six days! Oh of course, it is a long time." And he continued, "Some countries have special restrictions and it may take even six days," he corrected me.

I did not want to argue with him about the reality of Islamic rule in my country and it was useless to persist with what I was trying to say because a logical mind could simply not accept the facts which have always been and will always be the way of Iran's Islamic rulers. I thanked him very much and invited him to a session of group sitting as soon as our centre had been established.

Obstacles and prohibitions are to be expected in a society dominated by self-centred religious extremists, who will even resort to violence as a means of attaining their objectives. I was happy that I could propagate my ideas out of the sight of those fanatics whose ominous shadow had hung over my head for years. I was happy I could sit with my people and to discuss different matters freely, finding myself in a foreign country where I was a stranger. I do not want to go too far in praising a foreign country and humiliating my own country by showing it in a bad light. The fact is, my country is controlled by a small number of prejudiced people who follow their own, narrow ideology inherited from their ancestors, and who will not let other thinkers express their ideas, even though their noble teaching will work as a medicine for the people who are suffering. Xenophobia and paranoia were the main reasons the government wanted to prevent other thinkers from expressing their ideas. These small Islamic groups, who exercise governance over the majority of people, do not think about people's feelings. Instead they prefer to establish themselves in absolute power to an extent not even seen in the Middle Ages.

The place where I started teaching Zen in London was given financial support by the British government to help Iranians living in London to solve their problems. I gave my services there on a voluntary basis for nearly one and a half years to a group of Iranians who were attracted to my teaching. From the time that my fellow countrymen learned about my techniques from the Iranian Association, they derived some excellent benefits. Although they were greatly helped, the place was not ideal for systematic Zen training. I was looking for a better place to create spontaneity in both mind and body. In the long run these practices are the core of Zen teaching. After about one and a half years, we moved to another Iranian centre which was in a calm and quiet suburban area in West London which was suitable for daily Zen practice. We also established a small library for those who were interested to explore and investigate our practice more deeply. This library could help us to strengthen our ambition to expand our teaching in an improved environment. Then I distributed pamphlets both in English and Persian among the Iranians in London to encourage them to visit our cultural centre. People started participating in our sessions and it seemed they were happy about the regular practice, although the duration of sitting in meditation was not so long. The present place was better than the first, but even so it was not ideal for a long retreat. A retreat for long meditation (one week, two weeks, etc.) needs a larger place with facilities to invite many people and where they can stay comfortably and practice sincerely. It was my ambition to establish genuine long-term Zen practice. However, for temporary practice and in order to get familiar with Zen and Zazen, this was a good start and I was sure this healthy gathering would help to develop a better atmosphere. It was indeed fruitful to have this success during the beginning of my Zen teaching in the UK after so many disappointments and difficulties for many years in Iran. Beginners can confirm that their experience of Zen meditation practice is often more effective than some other techniques.

I indeed happy that my emigration could give some benefit to my fellow countrymen out of Iran. I wish I could have the same opportunity in my own country for the majority of people. The fact is, some people emigrate by choice, e.g. someone who moves to another country to enhance their career opportunities. Some people are forced to migrate, e.g. someone who moves due to war or famine. Some go in search of a financially secure future, a high standard of living, education, for political reasons, a soul mate, etc. However, mine was none of these, but merely for scholastic reasons and my commitment is (was) to transmit the spirit of Enlightenment to them.

A wide range of political and religious reasons is covered by the term 'emigration'. Some people migrate to spread their ideas among various countries all over the world. Moreover, few people think that they will not enjoy ample political and religious freedom, so they immigrate to other countries in search of the same. Some change their citizenship to gain a new identity, some to get religious rights in order to fulfil their religious duties freely.

Conclusion

I'm neither a politician nor interested in politics but sometimes we indirectly get involved in politics by the government or their prejudiced supporters even though we stay away of politics. In fact, politics will be imposed to us.

I personally never interested in politics because my way of thinking and the idea I've chosen in my life is nothing to do with politics, but in a government that telling lies has been well organised among their statesmen, and lying has become a political and social convention, the easiest way for everyone is to tell the truth and to reveal the facts by any means in his hand in a peaceful and democratic way. An ordinary citizen needs not to advocate any groups, parties, or to be a sympathetic to any political organisation. He/she should not be indifferent to the affairs related to the people. On the contrary, they must have responsibility for it and a strong commitment to tell the truth to awaken the people to the facts unknown to them. In this way, he/she has done the most political matter although he or she is not a politician. All of us are responsible to revive the truth not to be diluted by the dust of disinformation. The Persian land which has been occupied by the Arabs invaders in nearly AD 633 has now been encircled with lies in a format in which the Islamic Republic of Iran call themselves the 'holy' and the only appointed messengers by the God almighty, whereas they are not. A true Iranian, a patriot, is the one who is bound to criticise, to write, to speak against these kinds of indoctrinations and also to participate in any activities arranged by the people and to be with them against lies, oppression, servitudes, coercion, bullying etc... Those who fight for their freedom and against these inequalities are not the enemy of Iran but true friends of the country.

Therefore, the prerequisite of democracy or a secular government in Iran needs a common commitment of the people and revealing the truth under any circumstances. It is indeed betrayal (treachery) to oneself and the people to either be indifferent to the events or hiding the truth.

My true story is based on my awakening after years of persistence and perseverance and to convey the message to my people in writing to suggest them to taste it. If it is beneficial to them then they can take it as a lamp on the way of wisdom and enlightenment.

For this I intended tried hard to establish a small centre in my own country exactly after coming back home in 1978. This was my dream since the beginning of the so-called Islamic Revolution, but unfortunately I failed as some of my story has been reiterated in this book. My purpose was (is) to bring back the pure idea for the Persians, their true culture, the way of their thinking which is peace, friendship, solidarity, peaceful relationship with world, goes back to Persian religion and tradition even many centuries before the Arabs' invasion in AD 633.[95]

Graham Bell invented telephone, and millions people benefited by his invention without knowing even his name or his nationality. Louis Pasteur, microbiologist, discovered the principles of vaccination and many people were (are) cured by his discovery without trying to attach to his name. Thomas Alva Edison (was an American inventor) who is the greatest inventor for discovering electric power generation, and many other things served peoples unconditionally.

So also, the Buddha discovered a tool, a technique by which one can get rid of their suffering and pain to live happily and to have harmonious life. He sat under a tree and got His Enlightenment and invited people to see the reality

---

95 See the book *An Shigao, Bodhisttva* by the same author.

with their third eye to obtain their awakening without expecting to worship Him or to attach to the precepts. Many discoverers and inventors served people without expecting to be obedient to them blindly. Like many other researchers I also followed the path of the wise and I was awakened by their true teaching trying to convey this humanitarian message compassionately to my people first without expecting to get anything in return. In fact I call myself a transferor between the teaching of the sages and the people with my own initiative (in Pali 'Upaya', Japanese 'Hoben'[96]) without expecting a name, fame, or mundane benefits, and according to the Persian proverb, "The green leaf is the gift of Darvish"[97] I've tasted something and wholeheartedly willing to offer it to my people first and to let other people know about it and get benefitted if they desire it so.

But unfortunately this achievement not only did not welcome by Islamist authorities but also they responded my years of research and investigation by torture, humiliation, homelessness and restrictions which persuaded me to emigration in order to save my life and the lives of many. The message of this book has some points worth mentioning:

1. To make my people know about the differences between their two cultures, of two periods, the past and present (what we had and what we are now).
2. My enthusiastic desire in establishing a small cultural-therapeutic centre for the benefit of one and all since the beginning of the Islamic rebellion (or so-called revolution).
3. To familiarise my readers about Islamic government who revived the primitive Islam of AD 633 with the same precepts we are following now.
4. About my experiences of two schools of Buddhism.
5. Satori (or, a flash of intuitive awareness) which happened to me spontaneously and can happen to everyone here and now.
6. Emotional link between myself and my people.
7. Success in spite of many different obstacles.

I'm sure the present situation of Iran will not last long. There are millions of Iranian people in and out of Iran who are enthusiastically willing to rebuild

---

96 Upaya is a Pali word (Jap. Hoben), meaning 'skilful means', a creative method used to know the better understanding of a subject or technique.

97 This idiom is a term used to be given to a person when giving a gift(s), or in response to the appreciation of the persons who found the gift. 'Green leaf' is an indication of a gift that does not make any donation to its grantor.

Iran conjointly after years of been occupied by invaders. When the situation gets changed Iran will certainly come back to her glorious civilisation where the Zoroastrians and An Shigao and many sages were reinvented Persia. Being an ordinary Iranian citizen, I also ready to participate as an ordinary citizen in building a sane society if I'm eligible to cooperate.

Mat all sentient beings reach perfect enlightenment
May all beings be happy

"May all beings realise Truth."
K.D. HAIDARI (DOTETSU) 1.01.2019

Some points from this chapter

- The mass emigration or 'brain drain' increased after the Islamic Republic of Iran had come to power.

- Iranian emigration was caused by the government's inefficiency and inability to meet the demands of its people.

- The conflict between the government and Iran's intellectuals and elites also caused emigration.

- I was not happy to leave my country at the age of 57.

- Sometimes 'escape' means saving others rather than himself alone.

- My fourth converted disciple was put into serious trouble.

- There are two kinds of disciple: 1. converted disciples 2. lay students.

- Conversion in Zen Buddhism takes place at the request of the disciple.

- I finally decided to leave my country for good.

- Our teaching is based on 'come and see' and not 'come and believe'.

- The government used its skills to play tricks on the dissidents and in order to tame and silence them.

- I was informed that my house in Iran was raided by groups of prejudiced Islamists.

- To choose an ideology or a new religion may mean to be labelled as an atheist or be accused of heresy, which would result in the loss of one's legal rights.

- I joined in the activities of the Zoroastrian centre in London.

- Meditation and concentration were practiced in more than 600 BCE.

- The Zoroastrian system of mind training and their way of mental development existed even before Hinduism, the Bhagavad Gita and the Upanishads.

- My work started flourishing only when I found myself in an open environment outside my country where everything was in my favour.

- I regained my previous position as a teacher out of Iran

- I did not leave the country at pleasure, but I was forced to leave.

- My time was wasted after 34 years of nonstop exertion in the Islamic Republic of Iran.

- The word for meditation in the Persian language is Moraghebeh.

Additional References:

1. The path of purification By: Bhdantacariya Buddhaghosa, translated by Bhikkhu Nanamoli
2. Animal Farm by: George Orwell
3. A Popular Dictionary of Buddhism: Christmas Humphreys
4. The way of Zen: Alan Watts
5. A manual of Abhidamma: Narada Maha Thera
6. Think and grow rich: Napolian Hill
7. 101 Zen Stories : Nyogen Senshai
8. Morning Dew Drop of the Mind : Shodo Harada Roshi
9. How to practice Zazen: Mumon Yamada Roshi
10. Zen and Japanese culture; Prof, D.T.Suzuki
11. How the Steel was tempered: Nikolai Ostrosky[Persian Translation]
12. Iron Heel: Jack London[Persian Translation]
13. Gad Fly: Ethel Lillian Voynich [Persian Translation]
14. The basic Principles of Marxist Philosophy : George Politzer[Persian Translation]
15. The seeker's Glossary of Buddhism
16. Zoroastrian meditation: Dr. Jose Luis Abreau

www.ingramcontent.com/pod-product-compliance
Lightning Source LLC
Chambersburg PA
CBHW022100090426
42743CB00008B/665